Thinking Through Badgers:

Researching the Controversy
Over Bovine Tuberculosis
and the Culling of Badgers

Stephan Price

University of Exeter

Vernon Series in Communication

VERNON PRESS

www.vernonpress.com

In the Americas:
Vernon Press
1000 N West Street,
Suite 1200, Wilmington,
Delaware 19801
United States

In the rest of the world:
Vernon Press
C/Sancti Espiritu 17,
Malaga, 29006
Spain

Vernon Series in Communication

Library of Congress Control Number: 2016958914

ISBN: 978-1-62273-188-6

Table of Contents

List of tables

List of figures

Acknowledgements

This book relies on the commitment, courage and goodwill of those who shared their views and participated, even though it was a stressful situation. Strenuous efforts have been made in the text to maintain their anonymity, but for their contribution, I am very grateful. The research reported in this book was envisaged and designed by Clare Saunders, Robbie McDonald and Steve Hinchliffe at the University of Exeter, and I am grateful to them for their leadership, openness, and collaboration. We worked closely with the argument by design, Dialogue Matters, and Marketing Means on important parts of the project, and greatly appreciate their professional help. The research was partially funded by the UK Economic and Social Research Council (Grant no. ES/L008106/1). I owe a huge debt to Clare for her continued support, and I am grateful to Professor Gail Davies, Professor Henry Buller, Dr. Kezia Barker, and Dr. Daniel Keith for their interest and engagement at various times, and Dr. Isobel Tomlinson, whose idea this was, for her comments on the text, and patience.

Foreword

Clare Saunders

As this book goes to press, the culling of badgers as a strategy for managing bovine TB (bTB) is once again prominent in the news. In late August 2016, badger culling was extended beyond the initial trial culling areas of Gloucestershire and Somerset into Hereford, Cornwall and Devon. The debate is as controversial as ever. Those who are staunchly for or against badger culling appear, on the face of it, to have increasingly entrenched views. The Independent Expert Panel that reported on the outcomes of the trial culls could easily be characterised as being doubtful of the humaneness and effectiveness of shooting badgers. Yet different sides of the debate continue to interpret the evidence in different ways. Those in favour of culling might question the doubts raised about effectiveness by quite rightly pointing out the impossibility of knowing the percentage of badgers that were culled. They might, alternatively or additionally, blame protesters for getting in the way of effective culling. In contrast, those against culling might more easily come to the conclusion that the culling was not humane, and that the target to remove 70% of badgers was, in any case, arbitrary. In my role as a social scientist, I have never seen it as my job to prove which 'side' of the debate is right or wrong. Instead, I see it as important to understand how people come to hold different 'knowledges' and what might be done to resolve the conflicts that result.

Badger culling caught my professional interest for two key reasons. First, it resonates significantly with my long-standing interest in protest politics and political participation. The Badger Trust and the League Against Cruel Sports mounted strong anti-cull campaigns. Hunt saboteurs joined with other more conservative wildlife lovers to disrupt the cull in peaceful and less peaceable ways. A petition against the cull, supported by musician Brian May, received the then largest known number of signatories ever for a parliamentary poll, reaching 300,000 by the Autumn of 2013.

Second, the issue reveals interesting tensions in the generation and use of evidence-based policy making. The National Farmers Union, the Department of Environment Food and Rural Affairs and the government have a pro-culling view that can be juxtaposed against the anti-culling stance of many countryside groups, the Badger Trust, the Wildlife Trusts and The League Against Cruel

Sports. The nature of the polarisation is interesting in itself, even if exaggerated in the media. But what might be seen as more interesting still is the way in which different sides of the debate tend to mistrust science that does not fit their preconceived ideas about the topic. This makes it difficult to trace any semblance of a straightforward line from objective science to individuals' positions or to government policy. In the recent past, the same scientific evidence was used to support different policy options for bTB management across England (badger culling), Northern Ireland (badger vaccination) and Wales (selective vaccination or removal). Similarly, the same evidence, or different snippets of the same scientific paper, can be used simultaneously by those for or against culling.

The badger culling debate seems to exemplify a hybrid of post-truth politics and post-normal science. Post-truth politics is a term that characterises political decisions that are seen to sideline experts and are considered to be based on lies. Post-normal science is an approach to science that recognises tensions of knowledge across disciplines and among actors. It seeks to democratically bring them together to find solutions to difficult problems. Anti-cull campaigners would argue that DEFRA has engaged in post-truth rhetoric: sometimes apparently contravening advice from policy-makers. Pro-cullers might bring their knowledge to bear to support (or contrast with) that of so-called experts, stressing the need for moving beyond a narrowly defined set of experts. Both sides and the policy-makers who need to act as intermediaries will, I hope, come to realise that the post-normal approach has the highest potential for a non-conflictual means for managing bTB.

The Economic and Social Research Council (ESRC) funded research project on which this book is based took place during the last issue attention cycle on badger culling (2012-13). At that point, the Conservative-Liberal Democrat coalition government had given the go-ahead for trial culling of badgers as part of a package of management tools for controlling bovine TB (bTB) in Gloucestershire and Somerset. In the run-up to the trial culls, I joined the Environment and Sustainability Institute, University of Exeter, Penryn Campus as a Senior Lecturer. It was there that I met the bioscientist Professor Robbie McDonald who has extensive experience of researching human and wildlife interactions, including the management of bTB. He encouraged me to think about research on badgers and protest and introduced me to Professor Stephen Hinchliffe, whose work I had read as an undergraduate. Together we were awarded an ESRC Rapid Response Mechanism Grant. These are grants available to generate data at relatively short notice on urgent social, economic or political matters. I had previously worked with Stephan Price (the author of this book) on topics as diverse as climate policy networks (www.compon.org), street demonstrations (www. protestsurvey.eu) and community-based initiatives for saving energy (www.southampton.ac.uk /engineering /research/projects/community_based_inititatives_in_energy_s.page) and was delighted when he agreed to help us out.

Our project, entitled Doing TB Differently (ESRC grant reference: ES/L008106/1) had two key aims: (1) to investigate the way in which knowledge is articulated and enacted in a critical environmental policy arena during an acute episode; and (2) to explore the extent to which it is possible to bring together a range of knowledges in dialogue to intervene in and even provide solutions or avenues for progress for seemingly intractable policy problems.

A range of research methods was deployed in order to achieve these aims. I will only briefly introduce them because Stephan does an excellent job of talking the non-novice through them in subsequent chapters. Stephan's first task as our post-doctoral research fellow (or 'dog's body', in more or less his own words) was to interview a range of people who were pro- and anti- cull in and around Gloucestershire and Somerset. These interviews were used as the basis of a 'concourse' (a set of statements) that were used in a Q-set. A Q-set is a set of statements to which individuals can agree or disagree to varying degrees. Q-methodology was used to map the different viewpoints of a range of publics. We mapped the viewpoints of groups of individuals before and after an online deliberation. Finally, we ran a face-to-face forum of Devon-based TB stakeholders using a conflict resolution expert to help participants begin to tease out areas of common ground and potential ways forward for the debate. We surprised ourselves and our participants by reaching a degree of consensus that participants would like to share information with one another (after realising that they were sometimes reading the same sources differently, but on most occasions reading different sources entirely). We plan to follow this work up with future attempts to facilitate such co-operation.

In this book, Stephan takes the reader on a journey with him through the minefields of researching the social science of bTB. It is a fascinating journey of personal discovery in his role as our 'dog's body'. At universities, we usually present our work in a somewhat sterile fashion, largely devoid of our own thoughts and feelings. We are encouraged to strip out the subjectivities. True to the notion of post-normal science, Stephan not only reveals what it is like to work on a social science project as a post-doctoral research fellow, but he also lets the interviewees speak for themselves. The interview excerpts are only lightly edited and some of them are lengthy. This allows us to read in some depth contrasting points of view. This, too, is an unusual outcome from an academic project. However, it is one that I welcome given the need for policy to incorporate multiple viewpoints. Stephan masterfully describes how he traced the range of interviewees with whom he had conversations: badger protectors, farmers, vaccinators, vets, a shooter and even police officers. Never openly taking sides, he is able to adjust his questioning to suit the research participants. He cleverly adapts the questioning to new lines of inquiry as they emerge. His interviewees clearly show that this is not a straightforward debate with only two sides.

Stephan claims that he is not an ethnographer, but this is as close to an ethnographic account of the research process as I have ever seen, replete with discussions of awkward moments through the pure joy of discovery. His very personal encounters with social theory are discussed as openly as his encounters with research participants, making for an usually detailed foray into the research process. It is all-too-rare for an academic to step back and be honest about things that s/he struggles to understand. We often wrongly present ourselves as know-it-alls, when the history of science itself confirms that we can always ever only know a part of every story.

Stephan's portrayal of the career minded academic as someone who does little but work and sleep appears to be not far from my personal experience. Stephan reminds academics that there is more to life than working, and, moreover, that there is more to writing that being a research machine. Let's not forget that all researchers have their own subjectivities. To see Stephan's subjectivities revealed so openly and honestly is fresh and novel. It also makes for a blisteringly good read. The outcome is not an academic book in the strict sense. Indeed, some academics may struggle with its frankness. But it is an interesting story that has appeal for multiple audiences. The audiences include post-docs struggling with a high level of responsibility in temporary research positions, anyone interested in the philosophy of social science, and all those people across the country who are dedicating – in many different ways and from multiple points of view – time and effort to the eradication of bTB. It is important to take note that the approach taken by Stephan in this book means that this book is not only for those seeking to eradicate bTB, but is also, in a sense, written by them. The whole research team is exceedingly grateful to everyone who participated in our research: the interviewees, the online forum participants and the deliberative forum participants.

Tenured academics rely heavily on post-doctoral researchers to aid them and the quality of projects often depends heavily on their competence. We were glad to have Stephan on the team, but in the book he expresses a tension about working in academia that other post-doctoral researchers share. We are lucky that Stephan has persisted despite academia not feeling like a natural home. He is one of many promising researchers who feel alienated or side-lined by the competitive nature of academia. I know several inspiring and intelligent individuals who have not made it so far as secure tenure and have consequently left before they reach their full potential to develop or communicate interesting ideas. In addition to telling interesting stories about badgers, bTB and Stephan's personal research journey, I hope that this book will also be a step towards encouraging universities to create more nurturing environments in academia for researchers to work with important ideas and subjectivities within a critical post-normal approach to the (social) sciences.

Clare Saunders

Penryn

September 2016.

Introduction

The one thing that hits me as I put down the phone is his pride. The whole atmosphere around the badger culls has been one of resentment and at times even ridicule. In 2011, shortly after coming to power, the Conservative Secretary of State for the Department for Environment, Food, and Rural Affairs (DEFRA), Owen Paterson, announced pilots for the culling of badgers in the south and west of England. Bovine tuberculosis (bovine TB or just 'bTB') is a variant of tuberculosis, a tough bacterial infection that usually affects the lungs, nasal passages and immune system. Although the 'bovine' name refers to cattle, it's a zoonosis, which means it can affect humans. Pasteurization prevents cross-infection to humans through milk, but in the 1930s in Britain as many as 2,000 people a year died of bovine TB transmitted through milk. Although farmers, vets and dairy workers can still be at risk, it's mostly animals that now suffer in the UK: cows, sheep, pigs, llamas, alpacas, cats, dogs, deer and badgers. Over the last ten years in particular, bovine TB has been a growing problem for cattle farmers, especially in the south and west of England and Wales. Herds of cattle are tested for bovine TB, one or more cows show a positive response to the test, they're slaughtered, and the farm is 'shut down', unable to move cattle until it has passed two tests without a positive or 'inconclusive' result, at intervals of sixty days. Some farms, once shut down, stay shut down, destroying farmers and their livelihoods. The incidence of the disease in cattle has been rising since the mid-1980s, but the problem has become much larger in the last fifteen years (Godfray et al. 2013). Since 2003 the number of cows showing a positive reaction to the test has increased by around 50%, from just under 21,000 animals to just under 32,000 in 2014 (Baker 2015) or around 95 cases for every 10,000 cattle in the national herd (DEFRA 2015)[1]. For a while, even the rate of spread of the disease seemed to be increasing, as were the costs to government: £90 million in 2009. To put that into context, back in 1964, we thought we'd got on top of the

---

[1] Total cattle herd on 1st December 2014, 3.4 million. 3.4m/10000=340
32,000/340=94.1

disease: cases of bovine TB were down to 6 in every 10,000 cows in the national herd. Then it came back.

What's needed, the man on the phone believed, was a cull of badgers. He didn't just believe it. He'd been going out, at night, with a rifle, doing the job. He was proud to have been doing something for his community that was difficult, dangerous, and desperately needed to be done. He wasn't going to brag about it. In fact, he wasn't even going to tell me his name, so concerned was he about the risks of being attacked by animal rights activists. Since 1971 we've known that badgers in Britain – especially the south and West of England and Wales – are infected with bovine TB. In the areas where the disease seems to have got out of control, anywhere between 2% and 40% of badgers are infected (although some think it may be more in some places) (Godfray et al. 2013). Cattle give bovine TB to badgers, and badgers give it to cattle, though it's not fully clear, and it's very difficult to pin down, exactly how (Godfray et al. 2013, although see Woodroffe et al. 2016). The culling of badgers goes back to the 1970s, but the most recent attempt to answer the question of whether it had a positive impact on reducing the incidence of bovine TB in herds of cattle, the Randomised Badger Culling Trials (RBCT), has become grounds for dispute among scientists, farmers, government, and animal welfare and wildlife campaigners. Culling may or may not improve the situation with bovine TB. Meanwhile, determined campaigners work to oppose the culling, and some of them have got such a scary reputation that meetings about the prospect of culling happened under police guard, and anyone involved is kept anonymous. Or is supposed to be.

It's a raw contrast; the rage at the situation farmers are in and the pride at being able to help them, the rage at the scapegoating of badgers, and the pride in standing up for them. Delayed a year by the need for proper estimates of the badger population in the target areas, the pilot culls finally began in August 2013 in West Somerset and West Gloucestershire. The National Farmers Union (NFU) and the companies organising the culling took out a court injunction against several named individuals and groups, trying to prevent them from disrupting the operations and harassing people. Problem was, there was also a popular and entirely legal campaign led by the Queen rock-star and animal rights campaigner, Brian May. There were members of the public, exercising their legal right to walk public rights of way, out at night, on patrol, looking for wounded badgers, getting in places my anonymous source didn't want them to be. The cull contractors were given six weeks to kill 70% of the badger populations in those areas. They failed, in part due to the level of disruption caused by civic resistance the law couldn't or wouldn't do anything about, while Owen Paterson claimed that the population of badgers was not as high as expected, issued revised targets and extended the culls. More precisely, he said 'the badgers moved the goalposts'. The derision could be heard underground.

But there was to be no backing down. Compared to other countries in the EU, the UK – or to be precise, England and Wales, as Scotland is 'Officially Tuberculosis Free' – looks like a bad place to be a cow. In 2012, double the proportion of its national herd tested positive for the disease, 10%, compared to the next worst EU member-state, the Republic of Ireland (EFSA 2014). The five member states with the highest levels of the disease in their herds, the UK, Ireland, Spain, Italy, and Portugal (in that order, as of 2012), receive money from the EU to tackle it. Of these five, only the UK's stats were deteriorating. The message coming from EU commissioners to the government was clear: do something about the disease in wildlife (DEFRA 2013a). The subtext was '- or lose the money and have your exports banned (again!)' (*The Times 2013*). While Spain, Italy and Portugal had some problems with bovine TB in wildlife and big game such as deer and wild boar, Britain and Ireland are the true homelands of a much smaller, much tougher animal whose whole ecology has become intricately interwoven with the cows that are an important part of the agricultural industries of those two countries. While the rest were reducing bovine TB in their herds by testing the cattle and removing the cows showing a positive result, Ireland was culling its badgers. Now Britain would too.

Culling is a routine way of dealing with unwanted animals. Within herds of livestock and flocks of poultry, it's not just used to control disease, but also to get rid of unproductive or infertile females or economically useless males. Though lots of us feel uncomfortable about this, many carry on eating animal products as long as they don't think about it too much. It's when it comes to culling wildlife that the big controversies occur – and yet, even then, the rule is inconsistency. Deer have been culled in the UK at a rate of three thousand per year since the 1980s as a way to keep a lid on population numbers in the absence of any other predators. Recently, calls have been made to lift this cap, as the population of deer in Britain has exploded anyway and is doing serious damage to crops and woodlands (*Countryfile* 2015). Response?

Nothing much. Increasingly, people are saying that instead of culling we should reintroduce the natural predators of certain animals where there's a population problem (for example, Monbiot 2013). Others point out that Britain is a very different place to what it was when wolves last roamed the land, and there's not the economic and ecological space for them (*Farmers Guardian* 2015). Even in France, more space hasn't stopped wolves being culled as a result of a series of clashes with farmers and rural inhabitants (*Independent* 2015).

Economics, disease, population, conservation and landscape management and conflict with human inhabitants or interests are all reasons animals are culled. In Britain, deer, wild boar, cormorants, grey squirrels, foxes, and seagulls have recently been, or are being discussed as, the subject of culling. The animal rights lobby never agree with any of it, but threaten badgers and enter a storm. In 2013 a record 300,000 people signed a Downing Street petition against the culling of badgers (Team Badger, 2013). For some it was bad policy; for others, badgers are special. For a few, badgers stand for them all.

This book isn't a work of popular science. We'll discuss science research about bovine TB when it's necessary, but there is no pedestal for scientists here. The research that this book is based on – UK research council-funded work carried out at the University of Exeter – starts from the premise that science can't on its own give us all the answers about what should be done, can't on its own help to resolve the social conflict that has emerged around the issue, and so can't on its own help create a viable long-term policy that delivers, as the NFU's strapline goes, 'healthy cattle, healthy badgers'.

It isn't nature-writing either – or at least, it's not the kind that we've got used to, publicizing at length the enchantments of the countryside, wildlife or the wilderness, trying to stir up, maybe, a bit of concern or action, or stimulate a sense of nostalgia, or, at least, envy in the reader of the author's green-gilded existence. This book comes from a place of disenchantment, looking for the intellectual and practical means to find a way through. The psychologies of wonder and bitterness are only relevant insofar as they get in the way.

Whether it's natural history, bovine immunology or badger ecology, knowledge is political. How do we engage with the debate about the issue and the conflict around it, without engaging *in* partisan debate and conflict? How do we find a way through this and get to a more desirable place, with less social conflict and less biological dis-ease? These are, themselves, political questions, reflecting specific choices, the choice to ignore neither the social side of a science problem nor the material side of a social problem. No short-cuts, no convenient blind-spots, except the ones I haven't seen. What follows does not just inevitably reflect my own perspectives and biases about people, politics and nature, but aims to show as clearly as possible the process by which that perspective develops. For reasons that will become clear, that process is deliberately exploratory and reflective, and the outcome is my own perspective, it should not be confused with the views of those I record in the text or with those of the other members of the academic team involved.

It is, then, a book about doing social science, looking for a different register to both the turgidity and privilege of the strictly academic literature and the over-easy, comforting, and de-politicized/overly-ideological styles of popular writing. It is upfront about three things: the process of research (messy), the academic context (problematic), and the engagement with ideas (difficult). I am simply assuming that you are intelligent but that you might not have had much opportunity to find relevant information or become familiar with the issues and ideas in this book. I hope it gets you thinking about research and the sanitised stuff called 'evidence' we're always hearing about in the media. I hope it gets you thinking about the institutions within which knowledge of different kinds is produced and consumed, not least the university. I hope it gets you thinking about some of the most challenging ideas available to western philosophy. And I hope it gets you thinking about the people whose voices we hear throughout the book. Farmers, protestors and patrollers, vets, police. I've let them speak, through their interview transcripts, at length – for more than I can bring under some neat control myself. Too often, for spurious reasons of length, interview material is cut down to the smallest symbolic paragraph, limiting what the real experts (the people there) have to say to what the academic experts have to say about them. Not here – perhaps that means you find the most interesting thing here simply isn't dealt with; in that way too, this is a partial account.

Chapter 1

First time out

The 'Stop the cull' posters are green and red, and look like every animal liberation poster you've ever seen – except they have a badger on them. They appear along the cycle path that runs past my house. The path goes through some of the poorest neighbourhoods in the country and some of the cheapest housing, places that have always attracted activists with big ideas and no money. It's frequently decorated with chalk, spray paint, and posters against Tesco's, or advertising edgy films and protests against cuts.

As I ride past, I think several things. Animal rights activists: I don't want to get involved with them. I know, vaguely, about the violent tactics that had been used against people connected with animal testing. The thought of being associated with them is off-putting. The cull must already be happening, somewhere, but it seems far away. I have a vague idea that badger culling has gone on before. And I have a claustrophobic reaction to what seems like a very localised and politically isolated issue. The animal rights movement doesn't really have links with the larger environmental movement. On the face of it, culling badgers doesn't seem right, but this is not for me.

So when Clare Saunders asks if she can put my name down as a researcher on a bid for a project about the badger cull she needs to submit in a hurry, I don't sound very enthusiastic. It isn't just that. Looking at the research jobs I've done so far, and at what I would have to go through to have a chance of a career as an academic, I feel crushed. There doesn't seem to be any room for my own values and thought, or indeed for a life outside. Faced with a choice between financial insecurity in work that is stressful, isolating, and leaves me feeling like I'll never be good enough, and the same insecurity in work that's enjoyable and where there is space for my own social and intellectual life, I start toying with alternatives. However, none of them seems realistic, not with a child and a mortgage to think of. There doesn't seem to be any choice at all. We wrangle a bit about start dates. Could I start on October 1st? No, I would be spending time with my daughter, it was already booked. Over the year I'll need all the leave I can get to keep my family diaspora to-gether. OK, I could start on October 21st, the last week of the cull.

Exeter is one of those institutions where everything has a name. You don't go to the library, but The Forum. You are not directed to Geography, but to Avery, so unless you know the library is in the Forum, and the geography department is in Avery, you're lost. I check my diary. *Go to Amory – Politics.* I look at the map. Amory, Avery. My parents are quite excited that I'm working here. "It's a beautiful campus", they told me. I tried to say something like 'it might have changed since you were there', but I didn't push it; happy memories, I hope. I'm not too surprised when Avery turns out to be a low-rise, brick-and-render belvedere from the universi-ty's expansion years.

By half-past nine, I'm outside Steve Hinchliffe's office. *Professor Stephen Hinchliffe.* I've met professors before, but from what I'm told this one's actually human. Immediately, he invites me for a coffee. This has more or less the same meaning as it does for dating, just the professional, academic version. I'm letting you in. So far so good. He's met my wife and we're chatting about her on the way down to the business school, part of the latest expansion, all pale stone, steel, glass and blocks of colour. I mention my parents and he tells me, no, it's basically a neo-liberal university now. We sit in curvy white plastic chairs in the smooth open-plan café and talk about the project. Steve's interested in developing digital research methods, and he starts telling me about Twitter and Scraperwiki. I have no idea what he's talking about. And then he asks me about my career plans. After a pause, admitting that I don't intend to carry on as an academic feels good. I decided while I was with my daugh-ter. That felt good too; I was happy about my life-career plan again. So you're probably more interested in the methods and techniques side of things, Steve concludes, as if no intellectual project could possibly survive outside a university. I agree, picturing myself using sophisticated online techniques for my own projects, thinking about how I could avoid the self-imposed nightmare of the last time I tried to do 'digital research'.

So I'm happy that this project, at least, will involve talking to some real people. I cling onto that through our first team meeting as the conversation turns to how we are going to apply Q methodology in the later stages of the project. Jargon like 'Q-sort' and 'concourse' flies over my head (they were being used incorrectly, but I don't know that yet). Some letters become part of a zeitgeist, don't they?

They get tacked onto all kinds of words to signal cool. A few years ago it was 'e-'. Right now 'i-'. Will 'Q-' become the next zeitgeistig letter? Probably not. Back at work, we talk about the questions I would ask in interviews, and I promise to sketch out a draft list. The idea is that I gather interviews from a range of different people connected with the culls, for, against, and otherwise. This interview material will feed into a long list of statements that characterise the issues and views people talked about (*this* is the 'concourse'), and these will form the basis of a Q methodological study. The point of 'Q methods' is that it helps to summarise the views of a larger number of people, a bit like a survey, without losing the integrity of the respondents as people, unlike a survey (more on this in chapter 10). Reducing information in this way could be powerful as it might allow us to say something reflective of the bigger picture, the way people's views are arranged around the issues on a larger scale. Seems like it might be a good idea, but it also seems like a bit of a waste. Interviews and the richness of the detail and expression that comes with them can also offer a means to say something which could be powerful too. What none of us have quite realised, though, is that just trying to arrange some interviews is going to involve a rapid immersion in different worlds.[2]

I'm itching to get into the field – but if there's a reason to hurry, it isn't just personal. It's October 21st. The cull in West Somerset finished on Monday 7th October, but they've been granted an extension until November 1st. The culling operatives in Gloucestershire have applied for an extension, but we don't know how long that is, or even whether it will be granted. If the cull is stopped, the resistance in Gloucestershire will end and I'll never get hold of anyone who took part. The Wounded Badger Patrollers have vowed to continue beyond the end of the cull, but how many of them will keep going? Even so, at least there is an organisation to turn to. Down in Somerset, a lot of attention has been attracted by Camp Badger, a focal point for more direct-action minded activists who come as individuals. I have ten days to reach them before the cull in West Somerset ends and the activists disperse. I need a hire car to get out

---

[2] For introductions to interviewing for research, see Berg and Lune (2014), Galletta (2013) and Longhurst (2010).

to these locations and back home in the middle of the night, but none of the finance and administration systems for the project at the university have been set up.

On Thursday 24th, I hire a car on my credit card and drive to Newent. I'm off to join a Wounded Badger Patrol. This is what I know about the WBP. Groups of citizens meet in Newent and Longhope in Gloucestershire every night and walk the footpaths around the area wearing high-vis vests, keeping a look out for badgers that may have been wounded as a result of the cull. If they happen to come across a marksman, or come close, the marksman has to stop. They all sign a protocol promising to obey the law and be safe. Tonight, they're meeting in Lewall car park, behind the Co-op in Newent. And so are the local biker boys. It was still light when I arrived, and this spot, at the back of the car park, looked as safe as any, but as it empties and the street lights reveal their absence, this turns out not to have been such a great place to park. I've been in the car since about six-fifteen, listening to my favourite radio station and making sure I've had enough food to eat before spending the night doing – I don't know what.

I have a backup plan. Wandering up and down the high street of Newent in the hours after I arrived I'd spotted a notice taped up on the door of a second-hand shop opposite the George. *Police and Crime Commissioner question and answer session, Sheppard House, Newent.* If this Wounded Badger Patrol is a ghost walk, or unwelcoming, I'm going there. I walk up and down looking for Sheppard House, but I don't find it. That's OK, I can always ask in the Co-op if I need to. I sit in the George for half an hour to warm up, turning the pages of my newspaper. *The Guardian* is reporting that Sir David Attenborough is against the eight-week extension that has just been granted to the cull in Gloucestershire. What a coup for the opposition. The God of Nature has been criticised in the past for failing to make political statements, even when it was safe to do so. The government are ignoring the results, says God. Owen Paterson, the NFU, the DEFRA chief vet and scientific advisor support the extension. But the head of the National Trust, the top scientific advisor to Natural England, The Badger Trust, a scientist involved in a previous round of culling (the Randomised Badger Culling Trial or RBCT), and God, are against it. The article also suggests that the incidence of illegal shooting of badgers has risen in the last fifteen months, although it's hard to see how that is related to the subject of the story. It provides context, maybe. It's no surprise that *The*

Guardian is sceptical about the cull, or that *The Telegraph* covered the same story on the same day with a mere seventy words. But the story leaves me buoyed. Since my first team meeting I've visited a lot of websites and social network sites about the cull. I've found the arguments about science, the 'small people' passion against the cull and their commitment, compelling. If a cull would only be marginally effective, why do it?

On my way back to the car I continue to look in the shop windows for notices or posters about the cull. Newent is the kind of small town in which all the shops have signs, notices and adverts up in the window. But I can't see anything. As I walk up the street, my feeling about the cull and the protest begins to change. It is as if there are two worlds, the top-side, day-time world of everyday community life, made up of yoga classes and second-hand furniture for sale, and an underside that goes on at night, unnoticed or not talked about, expunged from normal consciousness. Clandestine. The sensation is reinforced when I do finally find a sign, on a battered and smeary community notice-board down a narrow alley along the side of a youth centre.

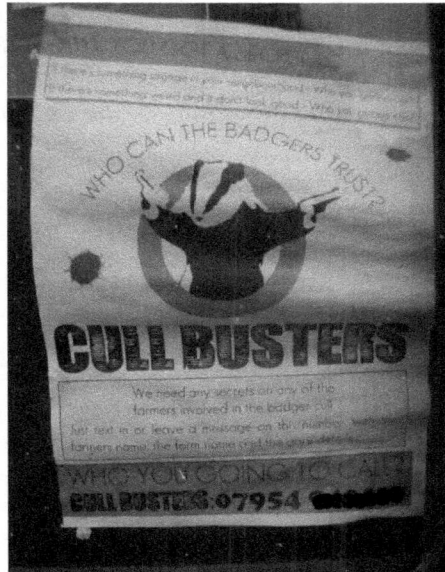

Figure 1.1. An anti-cull campaign poster.

I sit and watch the only lit part of the car park, the only place where cars come and go now, and try to ignore the bikers buzzing motors and pulling wheelies over in the darkest corner to my left. Every time a car or a 4x4 pulls in, I stare and try to make out if this is just a shopper or if they stop and talk in a group, or start pulling wellies and waterproofs out of the boot. I have my kit, and a change of clothes, in the back. At 6.45 I decide I'd rather not leave the car here, move it to a space in the main car park. I continue looking through the windscreen of the car. Every time someone parks and gets out my heart is pumping, but no, they move off, innocent.

At five to seven things start picking up. A couple of cars pull in, their drivers get out, approach each other, and stand, talking. There's something else as well. A black pick-up pulls through the car park, slowing down on the way out, as if to allow the driver to get a good look at the people standing there. Now every car doing the loop looks like it's watching the group. There are five people standing together now. Imagining all the *other* reasons these people could have for being there, I get out of the car, trying not to listen to my doubts.

It's them. I introduce myself, mentioning straight away that I'm a researcher. 'That's good', someone says. 'I think it's important to be transparent'. I'm afraid that someone is going to be concerned about me being there and I'm going to have to field a barrage of aggressive questions. But that doesn't happen. Instead, the group are immediately pre-occupied with the cars that are passing them in succession now, going slowly. Someone is writing down number plates. Variously, they suggest to each other that this one, or the other, is the police. In a few more moments, there are eight of us. We look -

Normal. There are five men and three women. They're dressed in jeans, coats, wellies. Some are tall, some are short. Some are jolly and chat with each other, some are quieter, but nonetheless, easy to talk to. I talk to the couple next to me about my research and resist the urge to ask too many questions about them. I stick to their participation in the walks. I'm probably the youngest person there, although there's another man in his mid- to late-thirties who seems local and is prepared to go off on his own. There's an older man who seems to be taking charge, a sort of grizzly Attenborough. He writes down our names in a little notebook and draws a couple of others over to the bonnet of his car, where they lean over maps for twenty minutes discussing how to divide up the walkers, and where they should go.

Meanwhile, the rest of us chat, trying to ignore the buzz of surveillance. A properly decorated police car hoves into view, slows down, and drives off. And then a little later on, a van with what's obviously a camera mounted on top. Carrying on from their talk about surveillance, they start talking about other conflicts with the police. There's a feeling that the police are working with the culling contractors, gathering information about the walkers to pass on to shooters (that's the word they use, instead of 'marksmen'), and ignoring or playing down incidents. They talk about being followed by police, or by an unmarked pickup at close range with its headlights off. They talk about the injunction and the extension – about badgers and goalposts. 'When I heard that the extension was for eight weeks, I decided I had to come out'. Still, there are only eight of us, and one of them is me.

The news is that even though the extension has been granted and a legal challenge by The Badger Trust thrown out, there's not going to be any culling tonight. But then a battered estate car pulls up, and a man leans out of the window. 'Are you with the Wounded Badger-?' He says he's been hearing shots all day. 'Do they sound like loud bangs or as if they are muffled?' 'Muffled'. Someone says that means it probably was culling. They give him a telephone number to use in the future, and share some more information, and then he drives off. It doesn't make any difference. Even if the newspapers had run front-page headlines saying 'Night's rest for badger shooters' the patrollers would still be here. Especially if the newspapers had run those headlines. They're taking no chances, and they've stopped believing anything the authorities say. And that includes the newspapers. Even so. I'm used to activists' scepticism about authority and mainstream media. I feel I've seen this preoccupation with the police overriding the issue before, but I'm surprised. These aren't really activists, they're just normal people. They're older, friendlier, less egotistical. But they're talking like radicals.

We split into two groups. There's that odd moment where people seem to allow themselves to be moved by some invisible magnetic force so it doesn't look like they're making an obvious expression of their preferences. Two of the women are friends; they and a partner move to join the leader as if nothing could be more natural. They seem to know each other. I'm going with the remaining two, a man and a woman who appear not to have met before, at least, not properly. It looks like we're going to be sharing cars. I ask about it though, and our driver, a man in his sixties, says: 'the police prefer us to share', instead of going in convoy. Given what I've just heard, I'm relieved.

My companions for the night are about as far from 'the usual crowd' as it is possible to get. Anthony (I have changed his name) is a retired senior executive, now much involved with his local community. Elizabeth is an experienced professional. Before we leave the car park, Elizabeth solves the first challenge, clicking on her torch. 'I'm good at reading maps'. And she is, guiding us up country lanes and footpaths even when the signs have been removed. Even though Anthony and Elizabeth keep up a constant level of conversation, the mood doesn't lighten for a while.

Anthony, in particular, seems preoccupied with a series of incidents involving the police and shooters. With good reason.

He's had a firecracker thrown at him. Not only that, but the police were there, and failed to stop his assailant. In his view, they more than failed to stop it, They let it happen. He's also been followed. So by the time we arrive at our first stop, pulling in at a lay-by a little way along from a house, I'm pretty tense. We find our path using the map. The footpath sign has been removed. As we cross a field, we hear a car approaching along the lane. It slows as it reach's Anthony's car. We try to crane over the hedge to see who it is, but the angle is too oblique. It might be the police. Or it might not. 'They might be letting my tyres down. Too late now. Might as well carry on'.

We're going to visit my first sett, a few holes that emerge on the path, a few metres into a field. As we climb the hill, passing jumps for a horse, Anthony turns his attention – and his tension – to me. He asks me a series of 'You know about … don't you?' questions, giving me a feel for what it might have been like to work with him as a junior member of staff. That's ok. Being patronised comes with being a researcher. If people feel like they're the expert, they're more likely to tell you what they think. There's a limit, of course, but Anthony is a long way off that.

Anthony talks about his sense of connection to the countryside, how it goes back to his parents, but also how things have changed, how people used to just accept authority. Anthony isn't making the same mistake. "You know what the purpose of this cull is, don't you?" I parry with something about the government wanting to reduce the number of badgers because they think they are responsible for passing bovine TB to cattle. "Well, that's part of the disinformation that's gone out about the cull, because they're claiming all they're doing is trying to test the methodology..." There's no need for me to reply. Anthony and Elizabeth agree that public opinion was turning against the cull, especially with the extension, which made it obvious it had failed. The problem, though, was the news blackout. Again, Anthony and Elizabeth were unanimous, the BBC were rubbish, they didn't seem to be covering the cull at all. They had a bit online, but nothing on the TV news. Sky, Channel 4 and ITV were better. Why did they think that was? Anthony said he felt the Savile Inquiry[3] had allowed the government to gain control of the BBC. Elizabeth said there was footage on YouTube of various confrontations with the police. Anthony is sceptical, "Yes, but who's going to look at it and how do you find it?"

Elizabeth says she's found a bit via 'Wearethechange Gloucestershire', but Anthony hadn't heard of them.

Whatever I think of the specific arguments Anthony and Elizabeth were making, one thing is clear: this is about much more than how to deal with a disease that affects cattle and badgers. They have a strong sense of wider institutional and government corruption that stays just short of conspiracy theory. But they return to the same themes: what the countryside is for, who it is for, and how it should be run. They mention fox hunting. There appears to be evidence of links between the cull going on in Gloucestershire and the Ledbury Hunt, a reputedly bullish and nasty bunch of riders, they tell me. Why are they involved, and what do they get out of it? But the conversation moves on. They mention free schools, bought by property developers and asset-stripped of their grounds. And they are critical of farmers: the way they arrange their tax affairs so they always look poor, how they get preferential treatment on inheritance tax, how their farms are often over-capitalised with too much expensive new, underused heavy machinery -

---

[3] He's referring to a series of inquiries and reports by different organisations into numerous allegations of sexual misconduct by the BBC television presenter Jimmy Savile which were carried out and published after his death in 2011.

The sett. Two or three quite large oval holes, wider than they are tall, with dug earth trampled down around them. Anthony, a naturalist, tells us what we're looking for. A stick across the entrance would reveal that someone was monitoring them for activity. We shine our torches into the edge of the wood. There's no sign of a cage. It's dark, and there's not much to see. We head back to the car. It's fine. On the way to our next stop we pass a police car and a police van pulled up on the grass near a gateway to a field. Just beyond them, a couple of people are standing around in high-vis vests. One of them is smoking. We don't stop, but we're back onto policing again. How they were more aggressive at the beginning – maybe not the Gloucestershire police, but maybe the West Mercia lot. One night, Elizabeth had finished patrolling with another woman and returned to her car. She was taking her boots off when a riot van pulled up, disgorged about eight police officers who surrounded her, shining torches in her eyes, and aggressively demanded her name and ID. She found it irritating, she was acting completely legally, there was no need to treat her like that.

Tramping through a field to our next point, we move on to shooters. Anthony recalls the sabs – the saboteurs, day job: hunt saboteurs – bivouacking at a sett to protect it, waking to find a laser sight scanning over them, as if they were about to be shot. We reach a gate. Anthony's not going any further, the police we saw are just across the field, over the hedge. I think he doesn't want to meet them. Elizabeth and I carry on. Somewhere on our right, there are the remains of a motte and bailey castle. Not the first time this area has seen tensions between the citizenry and the current authorities, then. The sett is somewhere on our left, but we're heading over to the road, a little way down from where we saw the police. There are a couple of footpath signs there where someone had posted copies of the NFU injunction. Illegally. Speaking of breaking the law, Elizabeth's telling me about the sabs. She was wary of them at first, and hadn't been keen to accept a lift from one of them when offered. But now, after six weeks of this conflict, she's come to learn how they're really good people, and how amazingly calm they are when they're confronted with the police. The signs have been taken down – Elizabeth had reported them to the council – and we head back. I'm still amazed by what Anthony has told me. Aiming at people? Who are these thugs? Anthony has a good idea where they're staying. They come in at about seven o'clock and talk about their kills over breakfast, he says. He doesn't say, and I don't ask, but I'm wondering where it is. I want to know, because I'm supposed to interview them. But I also want to know.

The next stop is the first time I know where I am, not because I've been there before, but because we park in a village by a place called Tibberton Court. There's a path running along the side of a drive, and then we're heading down the hill towards a sett. There's someone down there, a flash of a torch. "It's alright", says Anthony, "they're friends."

They are two women in their late twenties, with backpacks. They weren't there at the original meet-up in Newent. I don't understand if they're wounded badger patrollers assigned to babysit this particular sett, if they're freelance, or sabs, but they're here and they're part of the opposition. The conversation, inevitably, circles around intimidation, police, shooters, the injunction and the extension. Over their shoulders, two torchlights appear and start wobbling towards us. "Cops. We met them earlier."

A man and a woman, both in their thirties stroll up to us. For a while the conversation moves backwards and forwards. They're asking a few questions, and the patrollers are finding out a bit about them. They're not Gloucestershire Police. One's from Devon and Cornwall, the other from South Wales. They see the cull as a chance to learn about policing protest events. Especially as Devon and Cornwall will also have a cull, if it is rolled out next year - "There a lot of people with a strange way of life down there. It might be quite difficult to police", Elizabeth comments. But why are they here? Well, Gloucestershire only has a small police force, so they're here as part of what they call, without irony, 'mutual aid'. The patrollers like the idea that Gloucestershire has had to draw help in from other forces. "What are you going to do if it's extended to the wider area – it'll be unpoliceable!" The officers talk about how hard it must have been for the patrollers too, especially in bad weather. Elizabeth replies, "I'm used to it now, going to work, coming out in the evenings, and back to work the next day. I can do it." Later she tells me she'd said that deliberately, wanting them to understand her determination.

So far the talk is fairly relaxed, even jokey. Liaison officers are picked for their social skills, obviously. They even go as far as to say that the blame for all this lies with the politicians, but they stop at giving an opinion: they're not going there. We get onto the injunction, and the patrollers complain about the elision of civil and criminal law. "Well, it's quite complicated..." the Devon officer begins.

This is a mistake, slipping into a patronising register. Anthony isn't having any of it, interrupting, "It isn't complicated at all, it's perfectly straightforward..." You can hear his controlled anger.

They try asking a few more questions, but Anthony has lost patience, and interrupts again, deliberately turning the direction of questioning onto them. What time did their shift finish? Where was their car? What was that large police van doing over there? And, then as the other two patrollers take their opportunity to move away, he starts challenging them about some of the incidents and problems he'd heard of. Were officers leaving shooters unaccompanied? Were they 'spotting' for shooters, telling them where patrollers are? What were they doing about farmers intimidating protestors by driving up and down next to footpaths? (This gets a convoluted response, which amounts to 'he's not breaking the law'). What about the shooters following people at close range with their headlights off? What about the landowners blocking roads and footpaths? The crow-scarer comes up. Anthony insists that it had been shot from a gun towards a patroller. The police believe otherwise, or at least, what they've been told. The officers' response to all of Anthony's concerns is the same, either 'No, we don't do that,', or 'You should report it', or 'Were you there? Don't believe stories you hear third-hand.' I think their response seems strange. Surely they know that every incident from every night is already collected up and reported via a liaison committee with senior officers? Surely even a third-hand report of assault with a firearm would elicit some investigation in any other situation – it's undeniable, you shouldn't believe rumours, but in this situation, isn't a bit simplistic to dismiss them? It seems like they reckon they know of the incident Anthony is talking about, and believe they've got the true account. It feels like they're not here to 'liaise', but keep a lid on things, even to push the process of these citizens' relationship with the police here back to square one. As if they hadn't already been followed, intimidated, and threatened.

The officers head back to their car for a break, and in a few minutes we head back to ours. Elizabeth and Anthony confer over the map for a while. Elizabeth's proposing we go and check on a sett she's only visited once before. As we tramp along a path with wide grassy borders, Elizabeth comments that 'this farmer is one of the good ones – they do exist!' – because he's withdrawn from the cull. Reaching the sett we use our torches to see if any bait has been put out, which would signal that shooters have found this sett and want to shoot there. Nothing. The weather's starting to turn. We go back to the car, and head for the car park. As I'm putting my wellies back in the car, the two police officers drive up in their unmarked Mondeo. They dangle a friendly question out of the window, but I'm not biting. As a researcher, I have freedom of movement. I could go up to them and explain about the project, ask them for an interview. But I don't feel like it, and it's a long drive.

Chapter 2

Camp Badger, Somerset

Clare gives me directions. She visited the camp the week before I started. We look it up on an internet map. Ash Priors, that's it, then first right, first left. It's down there. The university's still not come up with a system for administrating the project, and – well, I was so tired after my trip to Gloucestershire I left my wallet in the car hire depot – I don't have a credit card anymore. I take the train and the bus to Bishop's Lydeard. Things come in threes, I've also no watch and no phone. I make a note of the bus times from the village, and start walking, counting my paces. If one pace is a metre then it'll take me fifteen minutes to cover one thousand. I'll need to leave at least that to catch my bus back.

At around six hundred I reach the common at Ash Priors, and stop for lunch. I don't know when I might get the chance to eat again today, and it's a good idea to be well fed before starting. In truth, I'm stalling, nervous. I play my nerves off against my knowing, post-activist-ish identity and it helps for a bit, but then I set off again, down the lane where I'm supposed to find the camp and I'm tight. Wounded Badger Patrols are easy, this is the real thing, whatever that is. An action camp. I'm fully expecting touchy, strictly auto-nomous people with dim views about university researchers.

That's if I find it. As I carry on down the lane, seven hundred and fifty or so, I begin to have doubts. The only sign of life I've seen is a white van parked in a passing place opposite a gate. Of course, the camp, if it's there, won't be beside the road, will it? Is that some-thing behind those trees? Can't tell. I carry on and there's no further sign. I come to a track that doubles back up the hill behind the road. Well, if nothing else I can get to some higher ground. Maybe have a look behind those trees. I'm not hopeful. So when I come to a pud-dle the size of Loch Lomond blocking the path I think, that's it, I'm going back. If I go back, sod's law has it that the camp will have been just beyond the puddle, around the bend in the track. If I cross it, it won't be there. Now I've had the thought, I have to cross, even just to prevent it from having been there. Question is, how? No logs or stones. Wading is not an option, my boots are not *that* waterproof. The track does have a mohican of grass running down the middle. Shallower there. I tip-toe.

Around the corner there's a gate. Nothing. Another. There it is, just where it shouldn't now be. It's exactly where I had thought I'd seen something behind the trees. I'm so surprised I have to go and sit down and prepare to do all the things I had now thought I wouldn't have to. I stand up and lean on the gate, preparing a face. Maybe no-one's there. It looks abandoned. There's another van and three cars 'parked' near the gate at the top of the field, something like a shed halfway down, and a marquee and about ten tents at the bottom. I look to my right. Under the hedge there's a pile of high-vis jackets and vuvuzelas. I'm in the right place then. And that's not a shed; it's a compost toilet. Still no movement. It's abandoned, the appalling weather has driven everyone to leave the site. Don't blame them; it is the last week of the extension.

I go down to have a look anyway. As I'm walking down the hill I hear a voice calling '*Hello!*' I look round. There's no-one. Then I see half a face over the top of the half-door across the loos. '*Go down to the main tent. Make yourself at home!*' The inside of the marquee looks like it's been hit by a storm. That's because it has. The night before, high winds and heavy rain had struck the South West. The ground in front of the entrance to the tent is poached and, where it's not covered, on the inside too. It looks like people have been sleeping here, possibly after abandoning their own waterlogged tents, and there are sleeping bags and clothes trodden into the mud. There's a pile of non-descript kit in front of me, a table with maps, books, and pens at the back, notices taped to the plastic walls above it, a few camping chairs in a sort-of circle, sinking into the mud, and over to the right a trestle table overflowing with pots of herbs, tins of tea, cartons of milk (fake, obviously), used mugs, used plates, cutlery (to be honest, these appear all around the tent), cooking gear, a gas stove, kettle, and just inside the entrance, something that looks like a shrine, or that would look like a shrine if it didn't have the remains of someone's dinner on it. A typical action camp, then.

"Cuppa?" The voice, first heard from the compost loos, is Fran. Fran has become the camp matron, keeping the other activists fed and watered, and cleaning up after them. There's sometimes an aura that comes off radical activists. A certain aloofness, a reflex suspicion of strangers, a certain self-conscious sense of something. Sometimes it's '*I'm so cool*', at others, '*I'm so right*', or some variation. Fran is not that. She is down to earth, matter of fact, direct – I was going to say normal, but she's not like the patrollers I met either; the twists and turns with which most people achieve the status 'normal', the duty to social convention – Fran doesn't have that. She's unapologetic. She's normal minus apologies for thinking what I think and being who I am. I'm telling her about the research, and she's telling me about the camp, what she's been doing, what she thinks about the cull.

Benjamin and Charlie turn up, with a dog. They're both, maybe, forty-something. The conversation turns practical. We're sent up to the top of the field to collect the cans of water that have been left there. And then, in a few minutes, we're up there again, trying to push Charlie's van out of the mud. He wants to go home tonight, a five-hour drive. I'm pushing, head down, hoping Charlie's spinning, smoking back tyre is not going to catch a bit of loose turf and fling it over yours truly. It's not going anywhere. Charlie's still smiling, he doesn't seem to mind much. He and Benjamin stand at the top of the hill for a bit, chatting about burnout – not tyres: activists. Charlie says he has ME, and hasn't been able to go out at night as much as he wanted. Benjamin reckons ten or twelve days is about as much as anyone could last. He came for a weekend, and then returned. He's been here the last ten days. Beneath the inevitable dirt, he looks sallow.

We get onto the cull. The top of the hill is the only place with any signal, so Benjamin's checking his messages while picking apart the government case for the cull. He says he doesn't know why the government is talking about New Zealand, the example of the possum is a complete red herring, because you can't compare a native species to what is an alien species over there. Again, I'm learning that this is not just a conflict between people who think it's ok to kill badgers, and people who just think it isn't. There are many more sides, much more detail. Possums were introduced to New Zealand from Australia, where they have several different predators, in the nineteenth century (DOC 2016). They are associated with a number of problems, including transmitting bovine TB to livestock. The New Zealanders cull them, using poison, dropped from the air. Does he have a point, or is the 'native' - 'alien' distinction irrelevant – a red herring in itself?

Back in the tent, things multiply. Fran, Benjamin, and Charlie are angrier and more forthright than the wounded badger patrollers, but like Anthony and Elizabeth, their issues are wider than the cull

itself. They are also looking for hidden motives. It's not about badgers because badgers aren't the problem. What else could it be?

For Fran, the cull isn't even about cattle. It can't be; there were
hardly any cattle in the cull area. Instead, it was probably about
pheasant shooting. She had heard shots the day before. Badgers,
Fran reasons, eat pheasant feed and would eat a pheasant if they
could get hold of one. She's angry and eloquent:

> *It's about sanitising the land for the pheasant shoots so that there
> are no predators because it's not just badgers, it's foxes, it's corvids
> and it's raptors now as well, they're taking them all, they just want
> these foreign birds that they're ridiculously stupid and they release
> them in their thousands to be shot for entertainment, for rich
> people and that's wrong, it's not illegal but it should be, killing
> things for pleasure is not civilised.*

(Yes, I am cheating. This long section comes out of the recorded
interview I conducted with Fran later; I would never be able to remember this much of what she said, word for word. In fact, as I
have a particularly bad memory for spoken words, any quote from
someone that I have not put in its own italicized paragraph is based
on my notes, hurriedly made later on, so I can't promise they're
accurate. Sometimes I'm more confident, so "they have speech
marks around them" because they resonated easily – although I've
avoided this up to now, or sometimes I might use indirect speech.
Sections that are italicised and indented from both edges of the
page are direct quotes from recorded interviews.)

It's not just pheasant shooting; it's also fox hunting. The purpose
of 'exterminating' the badgers is to create a justification for the
repeal of the hunting act. No badgers, no competition for foxes,
foxes fill the niche left behind. Look, haven't fox numbers exploded
since the hunting ban! That's why we need to bring it back, legitimate role, controlling numbers. Fran is convinced of the hunting
community's determination. As an example, she mentions the Isle
of Wight, how foxes were introduced just so there could be a hunt.
It's also deer. Deer are also victims and carriers of bovine TB, but,
Fran and Benjamin tell me, they are not targeted because it would
cause the value of venison to plummet if attention was drawn to the
fact that they are also infected.

We veer away from cattle and badgers. Someone had offered a
workshop on hunting with beagles at Eton College. Naughty. Sheep
in the area around the Camp. Some obviously healthy, some ob-

viously not. We steer a little closer to the cull. The Conservatives must be shedding support because of this. This on one side, UKIP on the other. The Liberal Democrats aren't going to get more than 10 seats at the next election (an accurate prediction, as it turns out). To my surprise, Benjamin seems prepared to imagine supporting Labour, but he wishes they were more socialist. And then he says, apropos of a conversation that's moving on fast: "I wouldn't mind if there was a button you press and just wipe out humanity, or if there was a system like a lottery where, if your number's come up, you get killed, for the common good". He says, if my number came up, I would go, so people can't claim I wouldn't. Mm, I say.

But while we're on a thoroughly misanthropic line of thinking, let's talk about shooters, police, and the NFU. More claims about crow-scarers and firecrackers, a new one about a shooter knifing a dog. Police facilitating the cull. Turning up four times more slowly in response to calls from protestors than to cull operators. The NFU, only representing 13% of farmers. Linked with the Countryside Alliance.

We tack back to cattle and badgers. Fran's got another good line: "You can't monetize badgers, but you can monetize pheasants" - and other animals. You can lower EU standards to allow live animal transports to China, or you can allow meat from diseased carcases to enter the food chain, as meat from TB infected carcases indeed does, sold cheap into the catering industry -

My head is spinning, and I'm struggling to remember everything that's been said and compute new ideas at the same time. Which way does that last point argue? Is the fact meat from TB infected carcases is entering the human food chain a scandal, or is Benjamin commenting on the sort of culture which would consider that scandalous, or at least stomach-turning, a culture that wants to eat meat but cannot accept the reality of meat production, that animals catch diseases?

Luckily, Benjamin, Charlie and Fran are also quite interested in themselves – they're not egotists, they just like telling stories about us, the Camp. These stories have characters, so they're easier to remember. One theme crops up a lot: commitment. In fact, there's even a t-shirt. Only those who had done something *on the ground* could have one, keyboard warriors might want one, but they haven't done anything. Brian May might not have been 'out', but he'd done a lot, joining a Wounded Badger Patrol and funding the Badger Trust's court actions. A lot of ordinary people, though, definitely qualified. Some were described as former hunt sabs, coming out of retirement. One man turned up each Friday with his friends from a London satellite town, pitched the tent, went 'out', came back once to sleep and once to pack, but went 'out' again before leaving for work on Monday. Another had gone further, taking leave, annual leave, compassionate leave, every kind of leave (Fran's rhetorical flourish) to spend time at the camp. Another had simply left a good job and turned up.

But they weren't all ex-sabs. There's "Mr and Mrs 'Surrey', who sat in the middle of-" Fran breaks off: "If you ever see a skinny vegan dressed in black you know it's a sab – sat in the middle of a meeting of sabs and said 'We're not here to do anything illegal'. 'That's fine' – but it works, because they can walk up and down paths... but they've got back-up from the sabs either side of them and the number on speed-dial". For Fran, Mr and Mrs Surrey were talismanic, because it meant she had not just been witnessing the commitment of the committed, but also the commitment of ordinary people. Tories, even.

Their support isn't all far-flung, though. Yes, someone's been delivering cupcakes to the Camp at least once a week from Exeter, but a local woman has gone so far as to name someone she's thinks is involved in shooting the badgers. She's had shit pushed through her letter box and thrown at her windows. Perhaps it's easier to join in at night. Someone's met a local couple, well into retirement, walking the paths they know by heart at two in the morning, guarding their badgers. Benjamin gives me an alternative story about why the camp had been evicted from its original site near Watchet: nothing to do with opposition to the protestors, not even an eviction at all, but the landowner didn't like all the media attention. Benjamin thinks people in the area are not speaking out because they fear exposure, vilification, or even attack. Fran hints at even more, illicit, subterranean support. "There are a lot of pixies in Somerset", she says, with a look on her face (Pixies are beings that undertake "small acts of sabotage" against machines involved in realising threats to the environment or nature; Plows, Wall and Doherty 2004, p. 206).

A couple more people turn up. A woman with a lined face and a look of absolute toughness sits down and starts to take off her boots. She had been with another woman who had stayed back when she saw that a sett would be left unguarded. She'd already done a six-hour stint. Just sat down at the base of a tree with her umbrella. She's got another story, one to grab our attention.

"Thought I found evidence of gassing". She'd found pipes. Could be anything, but she had us for moment. Explosive word that, gassing. Another man has turned up, having walked from Taunton. He compliments me on my coat and starts talking about a few other environmental concerns. Roads, airports.

It's time for me to go. I arrange with Fran and Benjamin to come back in two days and interview them. Fran shows me the easy way out. She's telling me about how the camp attracts a few social care cases who basically come for the food. I think I know who she's talking about. I was once threatened with a sawn-off spoon on a 'peace walk' after a man who had been making inappropriate approaches to a number of women was challenged about his behaviour by a mixture of argument, therapy and opera. I don't like to mention it, so I say something like, yes, open camps often have to deal with that kind of thing. I hope they've got a better idea than operatic singing, though; it didn't work.

Gill (the boots and gas lady) pulls up just as I'm crossing the common at Ash Priors, and offers me a lift into Taunton. She's going home – a long drive – after doing a three-day stint, sleeping in her car. She had tried the Wounded Badger Patrol first, but didn't feel it could be effective. But taking part in the resistance through the Camp had been a positive experience. There's a community now, and a network, people from all over the country had come, got to know each other, and learnt what the resistance involves. You can't just look at the Camp, she warned, to know how many people are there. Lots of people are staying away from the camp, on caravan sites and in cars. She seems strong. Gritty. Worried about getting stuck in Taunton traffic. I get her to let me out sooner rather than later. Station must be over there. Somewhere.

Back on the train, I think about the people I've met and what I've heard. Benjamin and Fran, especially, have broadened and intensified my sense of what is at stake in the conflict. It's not just an animal rights issue, it's also an anti-capitalist issue. It's something with enough breadth to attract and commit people from a wide range of backgrounds. But I'm not sure about some of what I've heard. I don't mean Benjamin's commitment to self-euthanasia – odd as it makes him sound, I'm not too worried about it. I've heard something similar from people concerned with animal rights before. Expressing misanthropy helps to confirm their commitment, but given animal rights groups still exist, and haven't been banged up for random killing sprees, I reckon they don't take it as seriously as it sounds. Bombing, here and there, with low risk to human life, yes. Worse, no. Some of their thoughts, though, did edge closer to conspiracy theory than Anthony and Elizabeth. Hunting, shooting, live animal exports, making money. The trouble with arguments about hidden motives is you've got nothing to go on, you rely on a sense of their plausibility rather than any reference to fact. Conspiracy theories are to politics and crime what *The 39 Steps* is to action-adventure, they stretch the bounds of plausibility (that's why the novel is so enjoyable: it combines almost-implausible action with conspiracy). But as a researcher, it's not my job to dismiss what they're saying as wrong, no basis in fact, mere conspiracy theory. Those tropes would involve me in the political contest. Instead, how can I understand what they're saying? I start thinking about social science.

The most difficult challenge for social scientists is how to balance, reconcile, or order the power of human beings and the social forces that determine some part of our lives. If you can't do that, then you can't come up with an explanation – or at least, an account – of the way things are. The debate so far has swung to both extremes, but one trend in recent decades has been to 'transcend' – get above, beyond - the tension between 'structure' (deterministic forces that make things happen the way they do, irrespective of what people might wish) and 'agency' (human's ability to make choices and take action). It's not one or the other, but both! Structures (such as class and gender) and agents (you and me) are bound in a relationship of co-production! Any academic who pulls this off would achieve the status of sociological Messiah. Anthony Giddens, well-known publicly for his close relationship with New Labour, is a British sociologist who claims his ideas do the job (Giddens 1984). Cue choir music in the corridors of the London School of Economics. Unfortunately for any professor claiming to have all the answers, academics earn their crust by being sceptical about other people's ideas; so much the better if they are put forward as grand ideas. While I was working on my PhD, I came across one such sceptic (accidentally – there it was on the shelf, with an interesting title on the cover). The title of his book was attractive to someone who was struggling to get to grips with sociology – *Sociological Theory: what went wrong?* (Mouzelis 2003). The curmudgeonly author, Nicos Mouzelis (not, as far as I know, a sociological super-star) argued that when looking at sociologists' theories, you had to ignore what sociologists said they had achieved, and concentrate on what their theories in fact achieved. Applying that method to the work of Giddens and another 'transcendental' sociological theorist, he argued that they had, in the detail of their ideas, been forced to reintroduce determinism by the back door. Mouzelis rejected the idea that transcendence was even the appropriate response. Instead, he thought that all you had to do was explain why and in what way people might think their lives are determined by external forces in one situation, and consider themselves the masters of their own destiny in another. The reason, he argued, was hierarchy. People in any position in a social ladder are presented with two aspects of hierarchy, like the two legs of said ladder: its rules and values, and its practices – the way of doing things. At the bottom, we think 'why am I doing this', 'why are you making me do this', or (looking up at someone at the top) 'why on earth are you doing that?'. The higher up we go, the more we worry about how to avoid falling off. Similarly, at the bottom of the social ladder, the values of the system that has put us there is our main object of concern. At the top, we're worried about how to keep the system running, and how to keep running the system. For example, when workers go on strike to defend jobs, pay, and conditions, they often criticise the high salaries and bonuses of company executives, or the company profits. The top brass are greedy. Their arguments are about how money from the business *ought* to be distributed, they are about what is fair. Company executives, though, are not laying off staff, insisting on below-inflation pay rises, or re-writing contracts because they think their employees *ought* to be worse off. They are doing so in order to ensure, as they see it, the future competitiveness and profitability of the business. If employees have very little formal power within the structure of the business, they will tend to see what management does in a morally problematic light: to them, the values look wrong. This could be why the UK loses more days of work to industrial disputes than Germany – around twice as many. In Germany, companies are legally obliged to inform workers, consulting with them, and ensure the representation of their interests. In Britain, industrial relations are dealt with on a more voluntary basis (ETUI 2016; Vogel 2011; Wilson 2012).

So maybe the near-conspiracy theories, perhaps even the protest itself, is a sign that DEFRA and the NFU have failed to consult, and failed to be transparent enough – at least, for the people I have met so far. Or maybe these are people for whom there is no line of reasoning that could justify killing a badger. The 'Badger Killers' website suggests there are people like that involved. Painting the people carrying out the cull as murderers and suggesting conspiracy, the website owners have published a lot of inside information about the cull: maps, participants, emails. They don't seem like the kind of people who might be open to persuasion. But perhaps, whatever their views as individuals, their rhetoric is a social form that helps them perform a useful function, accessing and distributing information the authorities have tried to keep hidden (another example of 'it's not what they say, it's what they do?). My sociological mind kicks in: explaining people's actions by the consequences of what they do is now frowned on in sociology as determinist. It's also the stock-in-trade of anyone that likes to brew a good conspiracy theory. Still, though, bad consequences, even unintended ones, are a good target for criticism.

Protest and criticism is one thing – social movements are another. Instead of standing on the bottom rung and shaking the ladder, participants in social movements get their own ladder, climb up and start causing trouble for people at the top. Social movements offer alternative sets of values and practices, alternative routes to power, and I start to wonder whether the anti-cull protests are part of something bigger. Certainly, the people I've met seem to think so. But who are they? What areas of social life have they come from? How did they find out about the arguments, issues, and problems they've been telling me about? Have they got any alternatives?

That, among other things, is what I want to find out when I return to the Camp, wearing wellies and driving a car this time, to interview Fran and Benjamin. Except, when I reach the marquee using the short-cut Fran showed me before, there's a problem. The Camp is deserted. I stay calm. I don't, at any point, curse the unreliability of activists, or the stupid, lax, self-sabotaging behaviour of a researcher who didn't grab an interview there and then. No, as I said, I stay calm. Maybe there's a hint around somewhere as to where they've gone. I look at the notices taped up on the wall of the tent. The inhabitants of Camp Badger are assigned to looking after the badgers living in Withycombe Wood. There are some six-figure grid references. I whip out my OS map (no print-outs this time) but the northings march off the top of the sheet before they reach the number quoted. Can't be right. There are some other grid references there, other setts. I check again, one or two of them are on my sheet, one near a footpath. It's too much of a long shot – Fran said she hardly ever goes out, I'm not suddenly going to find her sett-sitting the one location I decide to walk to, on the off-chance. I wait for another half-hour or so, trying to make a plan, staying 'calm', and then start walking back to where I parked the car.

As I'm crossing the village green, a muddy Saab packed with adults revs around the corner and disappears down the lane towards the camp. That, I think, was no ordinary traffic. I turn back. Two hours later I'm interviewing Fran in a jumbled kitchen at the back of a terrace cottage owned by a Camp supporter living in another village nearby. I've just interviewed him, and now Fran is ready, hands around a cup of tea, washed and rested, but still knackered. Even though she doesn't usually go out, she has spent the night at Withycombe Wood, taking part in a protection. I'll let her explain.

Could you tell me what's going on with the badger cull?

In what way? They're killing badgers and we don't like it. They've decided, for some arbitrary reason, that they want badgers gone and there's a lot of people who don't want the badgers gone but we're not being listened to because we're not actually a democracy and they are determined, it seems that the powers that be are determined that they want them gone and nothing that science says or reason says or emotion or the public say, makes any difference and they're going ahead with it and it's wrong.

Why in your view is it wrong?

It's completely immoral. The science doesn't add up, the science that they claim, they keep changing the rules, the cull was supposed to be about the efficacy of free shooting badgers at night but three weeks into the cull, they start cage trapping so that shows that it's not effective already. They don't need to finish the trial, to show that it isn't effective, it's supposed to be about the humanity of shooting badgers at night, they're lying, they're saying they've all been clean kills when they haven't, we know very well there are several badgers, I think Badger 102, Badger 103, that were found either injured or dead but had been shot and they've been taken to Secret World and been autopsied but then DEFRA or whoever are claiming, "they weren't shot as part of the cull".

They're monitoring, what, 3%, or something? And the corpses that they're looking at to see if they have been cleanly killed, are being selected by the shooters so they're not going to pick the ones that suffered for an hour or the ones that they finished off with dogs, are they? They're not testing them for bTB so Owen Paterson saying that lots of the animals that were shot were injured and were horribly diseased, is an absolute lie because he has no way of knowing that because the corpses were not tested.

It's a shambles and it's wrong, we can't just arbitrarily decide that this amazing animal that's been here since we were, that has its own culture and way of being, they do have a culture, they use communal toilet pits, they use the same track ways and pathways for generation after generation, some of their homes are hundreds of years old, they get their bedding out in the daylight to air it out, they're intelligent animals with badger culture but apparently unless you're human, you don't have culture and it's just wrong. Wrong.

How did you get involved in the issue?

Because to me, I'm a pagan and the badger is a sacred totemic animal and it's my kind of guardian, my spirit guide if you would and I just couldn't bear, I had to do something and I don't have any money, I don't have any political clout, I've signed petitions, I've emailed my MP who doesn't even bother answering and I'm not quite sure how but I stumbled across the Camp Badger site very, very early into the cull and I had a way of getting down here and I had to come. Once I'd been, I have to come back and I have to do what I can, it's important to (a) try and stop it, I mean we're not going to stop it but we can make it as difficult as we can for them, we can't just roll over, so you can speak up and say not in my name but also to bear witness to this atrocity and it's a wildlife atrocity and it's a cultural atrocity as well, to try and wipe out a creature that's part of our psyche, part of our mental furniture, whether you're aware of its influence or not, our fairy stories, our children's literature especially is steeped in badgers and has been forever.

So did you find out, were you able to find out about the badger cull through pagan networks and organisations?

Facebook and it wasn't pagan network, I don't pagan network, I'm a solitary practitioner, a hedge witch if you will and I'm very aware of badgers in my area, I watch them sometimes, I go out at night and watch them and see them doing their little badger thing. I'm not hugely knowledgeable about them but more so probably than your average.

But yes, I'm not even sure how I stumbled onto the Camp Badger page and at that point it was still an open site and I got a lift share and I came down and I thought, there's something here, there's a role for me to fulfill because I'm not physically in brilliant shape but I could do the support, camp support, I can cook and wash up, I can look after other people who can go and do that stuff so ... and I just keep coming back because we're still here and it's hard and it's getting to the end and it's difficult now.

Have you been involved in anything like this before?

No, never done anything like this in my life. I've been on the odd protest march but that's nothing is it? That's not a ... living it 24/7 activist camp, no I've never done it and I've never cooked for this many people and at the beginning of the cull, I wasn't even vegan but I've had me an epiphany, I did. I've been a long term vegetarian and at the beginning of the cull I decided that I was going to stop consuming bovine dairy as my protest because they're pinning this on the dairy industry, but that's as far as I'm concerned, that's a pretext, there's a lot of hidden agendas as always with this govern-ment, they do not seem to be able to tell the truth.

The night before she'd met up with two other witches and they'd performed a ceremony at Withycombe Wood to ward off threaten-ing spirits, but she's not used to working with other people and the ceremony exhausted her. The tiredness gives her a down-but-not-beat passion to her voice. She has no coyness, apology, or sense that I might not understand or accept her identity as a witch. I try to treat her declaration as unremarkable, but I can hear her disgust at the suggestion of 'pagan networking'. On reflection I can see the resemblance she claims, gruff, anger coming from deep, a concern for the long-term – fundamentals. Regardless of this identity though, she still demands that policy have an evidence basis, and she's one of the few people I interview who has the courage and conviction not just to oppose the cull on moral grounds first and foremost, but also to place that judgement in a political narrative:

- you take away the things that people hold sacred, we did it to the North American Indians, we did it in South America, we've done it all over the world, you destroy the things that people held sacred in order to subjugate and this is, that's what I mean by it being a cultural atrocity as well, it's a psychic attack on the English specifically ... that's what makes it so galling.

In language, her paganism seems scarcely to decorate her criticism of the cull as economic imperialism, with race and nation no longer bastions from which imperial soldiers march, but sources of plunder too. Knowing it's a little unfair to do so, I try to peel away her pagan identity to see what her political colours are. BNP? No. Socialist? No. Come on! Anti-capitalist? Sort of, but it feels all wrong. I let the paganism drop back. A name comes to mind.

Starhawk. Starhawk is an American woman who became politically active during the Vietnam war as a high school student. As a feminist in the early 1970s, she was critical of the way men dominated established religion and the effect that had on women. Interested in issues of personal development and self-esteem she started to explore pre-Christian religions and spiritual practice. Later, she became involved in what she prefers to call the global justice movement, the coalition of Western, Southern, and indigenous groups opposed to economic globalisation that created a wave of protest beginning at the World Trade Organisation summit in Seattle in 1999 that was still flowing at the G8 summit in Genoa in 2001 and was heading for a World Bank/International Monetary Fund meeting in Washington D.C. at the end of September that year – a meeting that was, in the end, cancelled. By then, though, she also identified as a witch and had published a series of books about her beliefs and rituals. In 2002, after the intensity of protest, and trying to deal with the implications of 9/11, she published a book called *Webs of Power* in which she describes her experiences and writes about how she sees the relationship between religion and politics. She's very conscious, though, that she might sound 'way out' to most people.

"Identifying as a Pagan, feminist, Witch, and anarchist is possibly a way to alarm great segments of the general public, but at least it keeps me from sinking into a boring and respectable middle age" (Starhawk 2002, p. 8).

She might be joking but her persistence in linking these identities is reasoned:

"In some places, among indigenous people or among my neighbors in the Northern Californian hills, the integration of the spiritual and the political is understood and expected. In other areas, in Europe with its history of disastrous Nazi meldings of the two, among hard-core militants or Marxist intellectuals, linking the two may seem like a strange and dangerous idea.

"Why bring ritual, magic, spirituality into action? Why mix up a clear, clean militant critique of the world with woo-woo, mumbo-jumbo, New-Age fluffy-stuff?

"The first reason is that a part of our humanity needs symbols and myth and mystery, yearns for a connection to something broader and deeper than our surface life. That part of us is power-ful and dangerous: it can call us to the most profound compassion or justify the worst intolerance, lead us to sacrifice for the greater good or to commit mass murder in the name of our ideals, open us to a wider experience of life or imprison us in a narrow moralism, inspire our liberation or function as an agent of our oppression. Progressive movements are understandably wary of it, for we have all seen the religious impulse fuel hatred and holy wars and justify extreme oppression. But we ignore it at our peril, for if a movement of liberation does not address the spiritual part of us, then move-ments of repression will claim that terrain as their own" (Starhawk 2002, p. 262).

Anyway, I like Fran. She's direct, human, and kind. She seems to have decided that I need a guide to help me through the confusing experience of Camp Badger, and she's decided to be that guide. *He would be a good person to talk to; you should interview her.*

David, the owner of the cottage, was a good person to talk to. While Fran was having a break, I interviewed him in his living room. He too is principled (though not in the same way) and angry. He's also very articulate. I hardly have to say a thing, which is great for a first interview.

From all I have read and information gathered from talking to people, stuff that's been posted on Facebook and on the internet, I have come to quite a firm view that the government and DEFRA are actively misinforming the public about the facts about culling badgers and the control of TB in cattle.

As far as I understand it, TB in cattle is actually falling, thanks to increased awareness and husbandry and biosecurity movements and whatnot, but I think that needs to be significantly increased.

I still don't know why Owen Paterson is as determined to roll out the killing of badgers as he is, I've heard all sorts of arguments about wanting to reintroduce hunting because as far as I under-stand it, when there's a big decrease in badger numbers, there's an increase in fox population, to the tune of 47% as I understand it. Their initial argument for free-shooting badgers was that it was cheaper and so say more efficient and more humane to shoot them, while they're out foraging and they dismissed cage trapping and shooting because that was going to be too expensive.

However, it became very clear in the first few weeks of the cull that they weren't getting anything like the numbers that they wanted to get, I think that was probably significantly affected by the protestors and so since then, they have resorted to cage trapping and shooting, which begs the question well if you're going to go to the expense, it shoots the argument in the foot that it's too expensive to cage trap them to vaccinate them because cage trapping is too expensive, if you're then going to have to do cage trapping to shoot them, you might as well vaccinate them and let them go.

I have seen graphs that show that the so-said massive increase in TB incidence in cattle, actually correlates to the increase in testing of cattle and actually if you look at the proportion of incidence of TB in cattle, it's pretty much in direct proportion to the number of cattle you test, so that kind of questions whether the TB is spreading, is increasing as radically as the government claim.

Owen Paterson has been on the television and talked about sick animals which is, as far as I understand it, rubbish, he's talked about all sorts of things which are quite inflammatory and I think quite misleading. As far as I'm aware, the purpose of the pilot of the cull was to test the efficiency of free shooting of badgers as a means of culling and very quickly I think that was shown that it doesn't work. But of course, as usual, the government have been determined to do anything rather than admit they've got something wrong.

There's two primary things which have made me angry, one is that I strongly, passionately believe that democracy completely depends on our ability to trust those in government and those that we elect into a position of responsibility, have an absolute duty to be honest and upfront with their public and I think this exercise has clearly demonstrated that they have no problem at all with distorting facts, selectively presenting information and deceiving the public, which I think is abhorrent and needs to be stopped and it needs to be stopped right now, very, very angry about that.

I think that spills out into HS2, I think it spills out into fracking, renewable energy, I think the big corporates who are involved in the energy business, putting on a lot of pressure to sort of play down the renewables and to keep pumping out the coal and the gas and the nuclear. I think it applies to things like GM crops and anything where big business is involved and I'm very concerned that the government is getting away with lying to the public.

The second thing I think is of paramount importance is I think it defines us as human beings, as to how we treat our environment and the other life-forms which share this planet and I think it is high time we grew up, stood up and stopped treating animals, insects, wildlife, plants, weeds, whatever, as wholly our right to control as we see fit because it doesn't fit our economic or business model.

I think we have a duty to basically nurture and use our intelligence to learn to live in harmony with our environment and with all living things, without just going round destroying them because they don't fit with what we want to do. I think we have the technology to do that and certainly the technology is growing very rapidly, we're in an exponentially better and better place to be able to act wisely, so this badger cull is a prime example of an area where it's draconian, it's crazy, it doesn't make sense...

The other thing that I think is highly relevant, is the divisive effect that it's had on the communities around here, I've lived here for the best part of 10 years and the things that I have seen going on and the things I've heard about going on, are completely ruinous I think to a rural community.

Rural communities I think are quite sensitive environments, they're not like a town or a city where there's lots of influences and people are more adaptable, I think people who live out in the countryside, they're very set in their ways, they're used to living a certain way and to have this sudden disruption, has polarised opinion, it has caused an awful lot of animosity, it has caused a lot of hostility between people who before the cull were perfectly good friends but since the cull started, have become quite hostile towards each other.

I think it has raised the game in terms of the hostility between those who purport to be country people and those they label as townies, it has amplified this perception by country people that townies don't know what we're doing, don't know what we're talk-

*ing about, we don't understand country issues and it's just im-
mensely damaging, I think it's done immense damage.*

*... now I just feel differently about living here because I'm driving
around looking over fields and hedges, looking for traps, I'm looking for
farmers gassing badger setts, I'm looking for people doing things that
they shouldn't be doing and it's very bad, it's very, very bad.*

It's getting late. I still have to take a load of water cans back to the
Camp and meet Benjamin up at Withycombe Wood. Fran's met up
with a friend, a sab in a Saab, and they show me the way back to the
Camp. There's half a chance I could interview the sab before I go,
but she disappears for an hour while Fran lights candles and I try to
help clear up and chat about the Camp and paganism. By the time
she comes back, it's about half-nine (feels like midnight) and I really need to go. She had been talking about going to Glastonbury for a
party, but Fran begs her not to leave her at the Camp on her own.
It's Hallowe'en. They decide to have a bonfire. Sounds toasty, but I
leave them to it.

Benjamin is on Stripey Gate. It's the activists' name for one of the
entrances to Withycombe Wood, according to Benjamin, one of the
oldest and largest badger setts in Britain. That's where I'm going to
meet and interview him. But, it turns out, the wood is miles away.
After driving for about forty minutes I miss it, right up against the
dual carriageway just outside Carhampton. I turn round and park
up in a gateway at the end of the dual carriageway, dash across,
check my map, and start walking along the verge. This is grim. Cars
rip towards me in the dark, blinding, then leave me blinded. I concentrate on not stumbling into the road, and try not to wonder too
much what the drivers make of this lone walker bumbling along the
edge of a busy main road at ten, ten-thirty at night. Do they even
know what's going on here? I have this feeling of being on the edge
between two worlds, about to pass the gate and move from the
bland, banal, passive everyday life of ordinary Britain as viewed
from a car window into...

There's a word for this, volunteering itself as a description of the
feeling, even though I don't know why. And it comes associated
with something that doesn't fit this setting at all, the city. Uncanny.
The 'urban uncanny', some odd pair of words I've picked up somewhere along the way, now repeating themselves in my mind without much invitation. I guess I could ignore it, but it doesn't leave
me. It gets written down somewhere in my notes and eventually I

come back to it, scratching. I find an article by a lecturer at my first university about the urban uncanny. I can picture him, speaking these written-out sentences or something like them; or at least, I can recall my incomprehension. The article tells me that it's safe to take the urban off the uncanny, and points me towards an essay by Sigmund Freud for more (Freud 1919). In German, he writes, uncanny is 'unheimlich', or literally, unhomely, but as heimlich isn't just 'homely' but something to do with 'secret' – in the way, I suppose, that the domestic and the private go together – unheimlich carries a sense of alien and revealed. Freud wants to go further and say that uncanny is the feeling we get when experience is triggering some unnamed, repressed fear. Like lovers heading upstairs at a party, his essay heads towards sex and the fear of castration with comic inevitability (for this, if one knows anything at all about Freud's thinking these days, is what one knows; that human psychology comes down to sexual desire and the fear of castration, and it's just uncanny, the way, when we open his work up and actually read it, there he is, *at it*, when we feared it would be something so much more difficult and unfamiliar). But his version of the uncanny is broader than that.

"...the uncanny is that class of the terrifying which leads back to something long known to us, once very familiar" (Freud 1919, p. 123-4).

The feeling you get just before rational thinking kicks in, when you think you caught that ventriloquist's dummy move all on its own, or that very weird moment just before you realise you're having a conversation with a sleep-walker-talker; both take us back to the fear of death by shaking our confidence in the exclusivity and necessity of our conscious selves. Does a witch play with the uncanny as a feeling at Hallowe'en, or, overwhelmed, refuse to by refusing to be left alone? Play, the wrong word perhaps. Is it 'aesthetic'? That's the word that lecturer used in his article – a way of thinking about what is beautiful and what ugly, disgusting, frightening. Aesthetics, not just about how things look but also the sensations, feelings we have in relation to what we see, or think. He calls the uncanny 'a boundary aesthetic' (Gandy 1999, p. 34): a sensation we get as we approach some boundary between things we think of as beautiful, good, rational, clean and ugly, bad, irrational, dirty; or between life and death, or short of that, ourselves and the unnegotiable, unremitting, undeniable, other.

What's going on here? I'm hardly afraid I'm about to die, at least not very afraid, as I carefully try to avoid tripping and becoming roadkill. But I'm aware that I've marked this boundary three times now, once tonight, once as I superstitiously crossed Loch Lomond, and once in the car park in Newent. Initially, was it fear of rejection by the activists, not wanting to be studied? Fear of exposure as someone different, not one of them? Fear of failure? Or of this other person that I could be, putting myself in the way of the law, or in an off-track life, again? There's another line in that article, though, that brings me to a stop. The lecturer says that the urban uncanny is an experience that makes a play of the fact of the absence of ugly, bad, irrational, dirty things that are kept out of sight and out of mind, just as now that we don't have to experience or think about death so much anymore, we play with Hallowe'en (except he doesn't write 'play', he writes 'fetishism' – placing an unreasonable amount of value or emphasis on something, or obsessing about it; Gandy 1999, p. 35). So what, if not my repressed feeling, is being kept out of sight, out of mind, here? There's the unknown – am I fetishizing the process of research here, not just in writing, but in myself, getting too attached to my role as both observer and uncoverer, getting in the way of what's really going on? There's the action itself, the protection of the badger sett, occurring at night. If it's an act of protest then the absence of political protest from everyday life, not usually or consistently reported in the media, deprecated if mentioned at all by many people, is dramatised by this darkness. Or it's another kind of act as well, an act of relationship, one we don't think of too much, or if we do, we minimise: our relationship with nature.

Is this it? Gate, muddy tracks, footpath sign. I shine my torch on the gate. There are three stripes of paint on the bottom bar. Not overwhelming, but probably it. I climb over and start to look for some sign of a path going in the direction the signpost is pointing, but I don't need to. Someone's just flashed a light.

It's Benjamin and another man who has turned up for the first time after hearing Dominic Dyer (ex-DEFRA civil servant, policy advisor at Care for the Wild, soon to become CEO of The Badger Trust, leading opponent of the culls) speak at a protest in Derby at the weekend. I met him earlier at the Camp, after I had turned back. In his fifties, he talks, and fixes you with these wide-open, rigid eyeballs as he does so, which does nothing to help me come up with a generous assessment of him. He's a crank; that, or a ham-fisted under-cover police officer nearing retirement. Apparently, people are feeling pushed and it might just spark into violence, big riots, something. Sounds like he's warning about what he most desires. I can't imagine he's done much to help Benjamin's ready misanthropy, so I'm glad he quickly volunteers to go for a walk to let us complete the interview. The word 'hike' comes to mind.

We sit beside each other in the dark, on a fallen tree trunk or fence post – I can't tell what it is, except that it's uncomfortable. The only light is the LED on my voice recorder, my torch when I need to check my questions, and the car headlights, sweeping by a few metres away on the road. Their noise obliterates the sound of our voices and now and again our words are lost to the recording. The great thing about interviews like this, though, is that they are very flexible. If someone brings up a topic you were planning to explore later, you can go with the flow and talk about it now. If something interesting comes up, you can dig a bit more. As Benjamin is talking, I begin to realise that I've got a problem that I have to solve within these interviews. Basically, Fran, David and Benjamin are being vague about how they got involved and the nature of their previous political involvements. Maybe I'm just finding it hard to believe that people committing to weeks and weeks of grotty conditions such as those at the Camp have little or no political hinterland to explain their commitment. As I'm talking with Benjamin, I decide to try a bit harder.

Can you tell me about what's going on with the badger cull?

The badger cull is a sop to the NFU which represents 18%[4] of the farmers of the UK, more as an electoral bargaining chip to allow

---

[4] I've now collected two different numbers for the proportion of farmer represented by the NFU, 13% and 18%. It's true, a 3 could look like an 8 when hurriedly scribbled in a notebook. Maybe it's best to double check. Assuming that what is being talked about in the source I've found (NFU 2016) is members across the whole UK (it's not clear), then the NFU has 47,000 members. Latest figures suggest there are 214,000 farmholdings in the UK (DEFRA 2016a), so that makes the NFU representative of 22% of UK farms (unless there are more subtleties about NFU memberships that I'm not aware of, such as it not being sensible to assume that one member means one farm). This exercise tells me that all of these figures should be treated as being *very rough*, no matter how well referenced they are!

the Tories to regain power. It was "you vote for us and we'll do something to make it look as if we're going to try and deal with the issue of bTB" but the badgers are the scapegoat for this.

What's your sense, how do you feel about it, it's a moral, ethical thing, unethical thing?

I don't want to see any badger killed, I don't want to see any of our wildlife suffer for what is essentially a solely farming issue, it's about biosecurity but ensuring that the cattle are kept in a clean environment, not having to live in silage, spending the days walking through it like they do, better maintenance of where they store their feed and general better land management by farmers.

... [We talk a bit about biosecurity. He gives me examples of when it has been lax. Then I ask him more about his view of the cull, before having a go]

How did you get involved with this issue?

Initially through Facebook, I signed up to Facebook purely to fight against the badger cull.

So you knew about it before, how did you find out about it?

I knew in the general media, I knew of Brian May's actions against it, I knew of his petition, I was also angry about the fact that the BBC failed to objectively, to cover any of it within the Springwatch programme, when historically Springwatch stemmed from a programme called Badger Watch.

I think the BBC have been gagged by the government and they published information online but they've toed the party line because all the evidence does not support a badger cull.

Can you tell me some more about the sources you've used to find out about the cull?

Through Facebook? There's various groups through Facebook that have been set up to protest the cull. There are Facebook groups from different locations in the country, there's been overall stop the cull groups, there's also been other websites that have been used to promote action against the badger cull, primarily one that's ... in the United States because it was hosted over here in the UK but it's transferred to the United States because they have freedom of speech, looks as though it's part of their ... like the First Amendment, so you can't not have free speech in the States, so when the government from here in the UK said, "we ..." "no over here we've got freedom of speech", they can't stop it.

Is there a source that you prefer?

No, I think it's all equally valid information sources.

Are there sources you dislike or avoid?

I think the government's point of view is, it's biased but they've cherry-picked evidence to suit their argument, when if you look at the full evidence, it goes against everything that they've said about it.

And you mentioned the BBC ...

I think they've been effectively gagged because they are highlighting the same cherry-picked data, cherry-picked information instead of giving the full information. Owen Paterson's research that he's done, he hasn't done research at all, he's cherry-picked details from other countries and failed to give the full information.

... [We talk some more, and then I decide to have another go]

A couple of things I want to backtrack on. Have you been involved in anything like this before?

Not anything to this level, no. Not to this intensity. I've signed petitions against vivisection and I don't agree with animal experimentation at all, I don't think there's any justification, be it for cosmetics, food, medicines, none of it is justified.

Have you had contact with any animals rights organisations?

Not on a personal level, no, as I said I've signed petitions by the League Against Cruel Sports.

So you're aware of them, you'd go to their websites but you don't join them?

No, not up to now but I am planning on doing that as a result of being here, I'm planning on joining the HSA which is the Hunt Saboteur Association because illegal hunting still takes place because the police fail to uphold the law.

I sort of asked you this before and you told me about how you found out about it, but what made you get involved in this?

Because I think that ultimately, the badgers have been scape-goated to suit political ends, not for any true ... solving of the bTB problem within cattle.

...[I start to wrap up the interview, but before I do, I come back to the question that's bugging me]

I'm fascinated by you said previously where you'd signed peti-tions and been to marches and things, could you say what made you convert this time to coming out into Somerset and commit-ting to ...? You were saying before you've been at Camp Badger for quite a long time.

I've been at Camp Badger on two occasions, initially for a short number of days and then for a long period of just over two weeks.

Did you intend to do that initially?

I wanted to spend as much time as I could to actually ... to take part because I couldn't have lived with myself if it had taken place without me attempting to do something myself.

If it had been hedgehogs, would you have come out? Is it some-thing to do with badgers or is it something else?

It's not just badgers. My personal opinion is that all life should be free to live its life, to the full extent of its life, especially wildlife. I've always cared about wildlife and animals in general but it's almost this is like brought it to a head, where enough is enough.

Damn Facebook. Before the ubiquity of the Internet, people might have said that they met so-and-so or got chatting to such-and-such at work and they invited them to come to a demo/meeting/film and they went along, got really into it, or that this was something that was important at their church – in any case you'd get a sense of people's ideas and commitment developing as they move through the social networks they are embedded in. They might even have been able to talk about the experience of moving towards a threshold between everyday life and political mobilisation, experiencing something like the uncanny, perhaps, and then moving beyond it. Even in the early days on the web, people mobilized through social networks (this is difficult these days, but here I mean, literally, *social* networks, rather than 'social networking sites'), and then used the web to publish what they were doing, or discuss issues with other committed people in forums you would only ever have heard about if you were already involved in some way. Now, people go on Facebook, find sites and groups that somehow express their values and concerns, and some of them shift from strong values and low-level action to strong values and strong commitments in next to no time at all. The sudden epiphanies aren't new; it's just that patterns of human and traceable interactions are now merged into one, possibly two online platforms. There seems to have been a shift in which things like this happen not in relation to some possibly vague sensation or experience, but in relation to some possibly vague information. Fran, David, and Benjamin can't even tell me what groups and sites they've visited on Facebook or anywhere else. It all seems to merge into one Internet soup of information.

But there must be some common sources for their ideas somewhere, even if they are developing them from reading different websites and Facebook pages. All three of them raised concerns about the numbers of cattle being culled for infertility, mastitis, and lameness. All three argued that the cull wasn't going to have been cheap and that cage-trapping to vaccinate would have been cheaper. All thought vaccinating the badgers was the way to go, along with vaccinating cattle as soon as it was available (and thought it should have been available ages ago). Fran and Benjamin both criticised the NFU for being unrepresentative of farmers, and referred specifically to the Hunt Saboteurs Association website as a source of information.

Our cheerful friend is back. He's been visiting the gate-sitters at the top of the hill, and someone showed him around the wood. He's full of his discoveries. One of the others is coming down through the wood itself, no torch, and duly she arrives. After talking for a bit it looks like she might have half a lead for another interview and we exchange numbers. After she's gone, Benjamin and – let's call him 'Ed' – Ed begin to reprise an argument they had been having before I arrived. Benjamin thinks the government should do X, Ed just thinks that's just not going to happen, is it? More covert justifications for violence. I'm off, trying not to think of how long the night is going to seem to Benjamin, passing the time with this irritant, flashing a torch on and off as he talks, spoiling Benjamin's night-vision as well as his mood. I quite like Benjamin, too. He seems gentle, honest, earnest, if a bit unworldly.

Their voices fade behind me, and I tramp back along the now near silent road.

Chapter 3

The Wounded Badger Patrol, Gloucestershire

Back on campus the next Wednesday for a team meeting. Steve and I sit facing the screen in his office and talk to Clare and Robbie in Cornwall over a Skype connection. Not ideal, but it's the first time we've all met. Or, given that the others have been working together since they first had the idea for the bid, the first time they've all met me. Robbie is the new face. He's a mammal ecology expert, especially disease, especially badgers. One of his PhD students' work is featured on the front page of the university website. It's about the social structure of badger communities.

Steve is a human geographer interested in 'geographies of nature'. In the last thirty years or so, within philosophy, science and technology studies, and, more recently, geography, the idea that there is such a thing as 'Nature' has been under attack. Some academics have suggested the notion should be junked. Instead, Steve tries to rethink 'nature', and work out the implications of that new way of thinking for environmental politics and policy. He's interested in "how nature is 'done', how it is practised, how it materialises as an active partner in and through those practices", (Hinchliffe 2007, p. 1). The ideas he's interested in overlap with strands of thinking that have been labelled in recent years as 'new materialisms' (Coole and Frost 2010; Van der Tuin and Dolphijn 2010; see also chapter 6 for a more detailed account of some of these ideas).

Clare is a political sociologist, but as there are only two universities offering political sociology in the country, she usually ends up in the politics department. That's where she is now. She's interested in environmental politics and protest, the UK environmental movement in particular. She's been involved in a lot of survey work, gathering data on protest from newspapers, or from the protests themselves, or campaign organisations, as well as getting involved in arguments about how to define a movement. In the last few years she been getting more involved in policy-related issues around climate change, energy efficiency, and now, badgers. So although she started out identifying with the radical-ish, romanticism-inspired, eco-centric politics that (re-)emerged at the time of the roads protests in the 1990s, she's developed a strongly empirically-led way of researching the area around it.[5]

I wonder how this is going to work. Interdisciplinarity is all the rage in academic funding at the moment, and the variety of interests represented in the project is almost certainly one of the reasons why we got the money. But, looking at the bid, it looks like this is not so much interdisciplinary working, as disciplinary parallelism. Each investigator is going to write about a different part of the project. Perhaps it's just as well. Robbie's scientific-mechanical view of nature, Clare's romantic one, and Steve's alternative are not just different, they're in conflict. Romantics criticise scientists for the technological consequences of their work, and their failure to give moral weight to living non-human beings. That said, I'm sure Robbie's involved in mammal ecology because he likes mammals – but is he maybe too tempted to think of them as mechanical, un-feeling objects – a little too quick to accept that wildlife and whole ecologies should be managed here, culled there, or moved or re-placed elsewhere? On the other hand, scientists reject a romantic-political point of view because it seems too quick to accept tradi-tional or received wisdoms. The human geographer rejects both views, because there is no such thing as nature, or in Steve's case, there is, but it's not straightforward to pin down. Science is as much a political ideology as the green values of the romantics because it claims to speak 'truth' while at the same time hiding the real me-thods by which their privileged-status knowledge was arrived at. Meanwhile, the romantic suspects that Steve's alternative is in fact a depoliticised, conservative cloak, and the scientist steps back in horror and yells "*Relativism!*", or just "*WTF?*". Forcing Clare, Steve, and Robbie to agree on fundamentals would put at least two of them under pressure to make a career change, or maybe just put them into rehab.

---

[5] For a detailed look at the relationships between romanticism, ecocentrism and more mechanistic views of science see Pepper (1996, chapt. 4).

Accidentally, I should be well-placed to work with the three of them at once. I've always been interested in what ordinary speak calls 'the relationship between humans and the environment', and back when I was a Bachelors geography student I tried to mix 'physical' and 'human' studies, confounding academics whose teaching and administration was built around the idea that you would be either a budding natural scientist or a budding sociologist. I've taken samples from muddy ditches looking for invertebrates, done street protest surveys looking for first-time protestors and inveterates, carried out observation and invented interpretations of what I was seeing. Jack of all. OK, I admit, I'm not that familiar with scientific ecology beyond a low level, I'm not that enamoured with surveys, and it's a long time since I read any of the new literature on nature. Master of –

Sociology, I guess, although there isn't even agreement on that. The alternative 'social science' has become fairly ubiquitous but for some it isn't broad enough. The American sociologist, if I can call him that, C. Wright Mills, preferred 'social studies' to allow space for, in particular, a more broad, more exploratory perspective (Gitlin 2000), but it hasn't caught on. 'Social research' has though, although I've never been too sure why. It's even more open than 'studies' and is more practice-oriented, not necessarily aimed at drawing academic conclusions but also for business or charities. It seems as though people can become very committed to their version of what they do, to the point where the department – school – I studied at in Kent was called, without apparent self-satire, the SSPSSR – the SP stands for social policy, there's another one.

It's the word 'science' in relation to studying things social that's often been controversial, despite the widespread use of the moniker 'social science' by all kinds of different academics. What should science be, when it comes to studying societies? One of those who is seen as a founder of sociology, August Comte, envisaged a discipline that could provide the solutions to social problems. He wanted his sociology to make a positive contribution to society rather than merely being critical of it. His approach and his idea of a social science that reflected the exactness of the natural sciences became known as 'positivism'. In the 1930s, Comte's aim to study society in a scientific way was reflected in what became known as 'logical positivism', which in its later versions insisted that statements could only be meaningful if based on things that were publically observable.

One of the most famous philosophers to emerge after logical positivism developed was called Karl Popper. Popper disagreed with logical positivists about the principles of science, arguing that the important thing was whether or not it was possible to test a claim to see if it held true in practice; in other words, whether the claim was falsifiable. A falsifiable statement is known as a hypothesis, and the practice of formulating such a statement and then testing it is known as the 'hypothetico-deductive method'. Popper propounded this model as the key means to progress in science. He took part in a debate with what were thought of as his key opponents, a group of German philosophers and sociologists who were known collectively as The Frankfurt School. Their style of sociology was called critical theory and they looked to different sources of inspiration, among them Karl Marx, whose 'structural', economics-based projections for the way human society would develop did not seem to be working out, and Max Weber, who emphasised people's 'agency', their motivations and the meaning of their actions, to explain the way society developed. The critical theorists' key argument (in relation to 'social science' and how to do it) was that you couldn't take the hypotheses set up in a positivist research project for granted, as they are influenced by assumptions and blindspots coming from the prevailing culture of the place and time. The real task, they argued, was to open up those aspects of our social and cultural life that we take for granted and ask 'how do we completely change society?' Popper agreed that values were embedded in scientific practices, but believed that the scientific method was still valid, and that it was better to ask questions like 'how do we improve society by degrees?'

In the 1960s, Thomas Kuhn, an American physicist who became more interested in the history and philosophy of science, proposed an idea that seemed to reconcile the contending arguments of Popper and the Frankfurt School into one system (Kuhn 1962). There are periods of 'normal science' in which scientists work to build on a widely accepted foundation of existing knowledge and exceptions to the rules of their knowledge are seen as aberrations, and 'revolutionary science' in which those irksome exceptions can no longer be ignored and threaten to alter the very terms within which knowledge is established. The reliance of knowledge on consensus between scientists meant that science was seen as an inherently social process, and this led to a growing number of studies into the ways in which knowledge was socially constructed. Social dynamics such as gender, race, or what was presumed to be the normal relationship with (the rest of) nature were argued to be integral to the fields, directions, styles and conclusions of research. As this type of thinking developed, and in a significant reversal to the earlier relationship between natural and social science, writers began to draw on theories in physics such as Einstein's theory of relativity and Heisenberg's uncertainty principle that they argued showed that the universe, and not just the social world, was inherently relativistic, multi-perspectival and relational. This had what can possibly be described as an unintended consequence.

This is what happened. An American physicist called Alan Sokal became so annoyed with the way what he saw as hard scientific ideas were being misappropriated that he wrote a spoof of the kind of work that most got on his nerves and submitted it for publication in a sociological journal (although not one that ran a peer-review procedure) as if it was a serious piece. He pitched it perfectly so that it read like a plausible example of the new brand of sociological discourse, but was clearly, to anyone with enough scientific background, complete bollocks (Sokal 1996a). It was accepted and published.

After a brief pause, during which time the editors of the journal discovered their blooper, Sokal penned a commentary revealing the deception and tore into those he viewed as the worst culprits of this variety of pseudo-scientific nonsense (Sokal 1996b). He wrote

"In short, my concern over the spread of subjectivist thinking is both intellectual and political. Intellectually, the problem of such doctrines is that they are false (when not simply meaningless). There *is* a real world; its properties *are not* merely social constructions; fact and evidence *do* matter. What sane person would contend otherwise? And yet, much contemporary academic theorising consists precisely of attempts to blur these obvious truths – the utter absurdity of it being concealed through obscure and pretentious language" (Sokal 1996b, p. 4, original emphasis).

The 'Sokal Affair' became one of the early battles in the Science Wars, a massive escalation in the scale and depth of the contention between 'scientists' of hitherto social type and 'anti-positivists'. In scale, because a whole new set of combatants felt compelled to take part – natural scientists infuriated at the hijacking of their work; in depth, because now at stake was not just how sociology ought to be done, but the very nature and possibility of truth. And, as the war has gone on it has become difficult to work out which side is which as they have reformed allegiances and swapped tactics. This is one of Sokal's key targets, Bruno Latour, commenting on the attempts by US Republicans to undermine climate science:

"While we spent years trying to detect the real prejudices hidden behind the appearance of objective statements, do we now have to reveal the real objective and incontrovertible facts hidden behind the illusion of prejudices? And yet entire Ph.D. programs are still running to make sure that good American kids are learning the hard way that facts are made up, that there is no such thing as natural, unmediated, unbiased access to truth, that we are always prisoners of language, that we always speak from a particular standpoint, and so on, while dangerous extremists are using the very same argument of social construction to destroy hard-won evidence that could save our lives. Was I wrong to participate in the invention of this field known as science studies? Is it enough to say that we did not really mean what we said? Why does it burn my tongue to say that global warming is a fact whether you like it or not? Why can't I simply say that the argument is closed for good?"
(Latour 2004, p. 227).

So, when I say that the members of the team see things differently and that this might be a touch difficult I'm downplaying things a tad. They each present profoundly different intellectual commitments for whom any kind of root agreement is probably out of the question. And when I say I should be 'well-placed', I don't mean 'comfortable'.

*

I put on a positive schpeal about getting three interviews in a short space of time, the leads I've got, and the arrangements I've made for more in Gloucestershire. Still, though, recruiting participants is a worry, especially farmers or anyone remotely connected with the cull. I suggest a ventriloquist approach, sending letters from the professors in the team to people I think might respond to the status symbol of their titles. The arrangement feels uncomfortable, given that Clare, who is the 'Principal Investigator' – the one running the project – isn't a professor, and the professors are both men. Anyway, they agree. We run through plans for the rest of the project, and how we're getting on finding people to set up an online discussion forum for us, and also to run a face-to-face discussion session. Early days. After the end of the call I remember something I wanted to ask about, so I run it past Steve. I'm going to Gloucestershire tomorrow night and joining the Wounded Badger Patrol again, to see if I can get more leads. But I want to stay the night in Newent. I explain why. He thinks it's OK.

It's a sociable day. I meet up with my neighbour; he's got the office next door to me. He's a teaching fellow, which means he has to do all the teaching someone else doesn't want, or doesn't have, to do. When an academic gets a research grant, sometimes they're able to 'buy themselves out of teaching', which means the courses will have to be taught by someone else, usually a junior member of staff hired on a short contract who is given very little time or opportunity to further their career by the only measures that matter to universities now, research grants and publications. The only way to jump from being a lowly teaching fellow to becoming a lecturer is to work for as long as you can stay awake. Meanwhile, you have to face students who feel that, for the money, they should be taught by the professors doing the research, not some rookie who's hardly finished his PhD. It's possible, if, like Andrew (or indeed, 'Andrew'), you're teaching in a politics department, you sympathise with their point of view while being that rookie. Except, of course, that the professors aren't really doing the research, they're managing it. The research is being done by some rookie who's hardly finished his PhD. Like me. The only way to move from being a researcher, ever dependent on the next research contract, to a lecturer, is to publish, publish, publish – in other words, work for as long as you can stay awake.

Life is too short. Andrew gives off an exhausted, tense buzz as he talks about the conference he's going to, the paper he's writing, the slides he has to prepare, the marking he hasn't done, the data he's behind with analysing. I feel guilty, as if I should be using my opportunity in the same way; I feel privileged, somehow, even though this feeling is vapour. If I don't answer the 'what next?' question in eighteen months I will be in trouble, financially speaking, and the consequences, the responsibilities - I try not to think about it. My views on the relative value of salaried labour and human life are hardening off, and there's not much I want to do about it.

I hurry off to my next appointment, a meeting with my dissertation supervisor from years – ten years back, Gail Davies. She's also moved from London to Exeter, being part of the 'rethinking Nature' school of cultural geography that they've developed there, and when I heard she was there I thought I should at least say hi. She ran a Masters degree at UCL called the 'Public Understanding of

Environmental Change', although that name, understandably, has been changed now. It was a pretty important course for me, where I felt like the effort I expended during the Bachelor's degree was converted into some kind of awakening. A limited one, but nonetheless. It was also where I met my wife-to-be. Anyway, we reminisce in a slightly 'who the hell are you?' kind of way, and eventually get talking about ideas. Gail had given a talk that lunchtime about her inquiries into 'GloFish', the first commercially-available genetically-modified being. It's a fish and it glows, which is useful when you want to look at the development of the embryo under a microscope. It's also for sale as a pet in the US. She goes through the different regulatory and cultural regimes in Europe (biohazard - strict), Singapore (regulated, but in aquariums), and the States (consumer item, free expression), and points out the way the ethical status of the fish and the way it is treated shifts as she moves her perspective to different cultures. She wants to say that the world is so complex that it is impossible to bring what's going on into a coherent whole, which she's calling 'baroque complexity'. My head hurts, but it's not a headache. If there was a '*WTF!*-index' this would score high. I'm trying to work out how I can read badgers into this, and what the use of reading badgers into this would be. The questions afterwards are off the *WTF!*-scale, so, entering into conversation with Gail – or, more to the point – Professor Davies about this is nerve-racking. As back-up, I find myself citing *The Great Gatsby*, one of my A-level English texts.

The narrator of *The Great Gatsby* suspends his judgement of the characters in the story. In part, that what makes it a great novel, as he allows the nature and quality of each of the other characters to come through, along with the atmosphere they create around and between them. But he's also weak, passive. There's this ethical difficulty as a result – instead of just observing, couldn't he change the course of events if he intervened – if he pointed out that Gatsby is deluded, Daisy shallow, Tom a bully? He doesn't, perhaps he's like that and it never crosses his mind. Meanwhile, he enjoys his association with some of the wealthiest people in the country. I get as far as suggesting about a tenth of that – that suspending judgement is weak – isn't that a problem?

Of course, though, in academia, lack of judgment is not the problem. Even academics with next to no training in critical analysis have a view about what the problem is, and what should be done. An 'evidence-base' is now a readily available weapon in policy warfare, and there's often a 'scientist' available to talk the public through the implications. Away from 'hard' science, academics rush to claim theoretical perspectives and construct careers from arguing the toss between them. Climate change is happening! No it isn't! Or if it is, it isn't important (Bjorn Lomborg vs rest of world). Globalisation is here! No it isn't (Hirst and Thompson vs received wisdom). In the case of animal geographies – Gail's field – it's 'this is all the result of capitalism' vs 'this reflects the extension of government to control of the body and the biosphere': the technical terms are 'biocapital' and 'biopolitics'. Gail says she is trying not to fall into either camp, trying to make people think, to say 'it's more complicated than that'. Well, it's working. But then she says that she's also on a Home Office panel on biosecurity and if they asked her what they should do about this new genetically-modified fish, she would say 'ban it, don't let it out'. She's aware of the problem, concerned by it. Somehow, the sophisticated thinking and the right action don't match up.

So when I get back in a car on Thursday morning it's a release, even though it's taken half an hour to prise a car off the hire firm, who are still convinced I should be paying for it, not the university. Contact my administrator. I've got two interviews lined up today, and then I'm going to Newent for the Wounded Badger Patrol, and to execute The Plan. Both interviews are in Gloucestershire, though outside the cull zone. The first is Elizabeth, and the next are two people Anthony suggested I contact, though I've no real idea who they are. Anti. Involved. You should get in touch with them. Fred and Grace.

Elizabeth lives on the edge of a pretty Gloucestershire market town. Her house feels older on the inside than out, if you misread open-plan as old. We settle down on bar stools at the kitchen counter – the dogs get the sofa – and go through the legal procedure before the real questions. I'm not expecting any real surprises. As we've already met and I've listened to Elizabeth speak at length about what's been going on this, I think, is more an exercise in getting her story recorded. I'm keen to make sure I get down the basics. What have you been doing?

It's a wounded badger patrol, so you're looking for wounded badgers, what are you doing, what are you trying to achieve?

That's basically the whole remit of the group, is to look out for wounded badgers, I haven't actually seen a wounded badger I have to say!

Has anyone seen ...?

Oh yeah, I think they have and I think a couple have been picked up but I know the gunmen have to bag and take the badgers away so I think they're trying to do it as surreptitiously as possible, so they're not left wounded.

And is there another side to it?

You mean the ...?

I thought there was something to do with the element of being there, so you're walking around looking for wounded badgers but there's the sense of being there on the paths and if that path happens to be near enough to a set, what's that ...?

I suppose this is my impression of it, I'm not sure what it says on the wounded badger website, but I think we are there to be visible and to be seen by farmers and the community too. We are there to prevent the gunmen from shooting because some of the setts are, they're either right on the road or right next to the footpaths and the gunmen aren't allowed to fire when there are people nearby so by our very presence, means the gunmen can't fire.

In your experience, has that happened? Have you arrived on a footpath, near a sett, there being a shoot ...?

I've bumped into a lot of policemen, I've only bumped into a gunman on one occasion and that was on the Forthampton Estate, didn't see any badgers but they were there and we just kind of stumbled into something that they were doing.

You can't tell whether that was related to there being a badger sett there? What were they doing?

... on the Forthampton Estate they have these shooting platforms in the trees and we were actually walking up a sort of hill, a field that goes up a hill and then at the top of the hill was a wood with

these shooting platforms and then on the other side of the wood, there was another field going down the shooting platform so I think it's really designed for shooting pheasants, with the shooting platforms and the trees but we were doing a kind of a square walk, sort of up the hill to the top, down the footpaths and when we got to the footpath by the wood, it had just been removed, it wasn't there anymore and there was a big fence with barbed wire on the top and we were just standing there saying, "God, this is appalling that they've taken this footpath out" and we noticed there were lights up in the trees and you could hear a couple of sort of gun dogs barking.

We knew they were there and then that was one of my early weeks but we weren't quite sure what to do, particularly because the footpath had been barbed so we couldn't possibly get over it, if we'd have tried to get over it, if we'd have tried to get over it, we'd have gone over the barbed wire and we'd have cut ourselves.

And they were on the other side of the fence?

Yeah.

What happened next? Did you make your presence known?

We did and we had a bit of a debate about what we should do because there were a number of different opinions about it and we decided to go back to a place of safety, which was on the road and when we did that, the gunman had called the police and the police had arrived there to talk to us.

At the same time, a load of hunt sabs had come as well, so it was kind of mayhem at that point, there was just lots going on. The sabs asked us if we would stay on the footpath and be witnesses, just in case any violence occurred, which we did and we didn't see anything.

It was dark, there was no-one there or ...?

It was just dark, there was stuff going on, there were whistles being blown, I just don't know ...!

More exciting than my first time on Patrol, then. Hunt saboteurs, though, are not the only hunting link Elizabeth tells me about.

- there is definitely a strong link with Ledbury Hunt in Red Marley and what does seem to be coming out is that the cullers are

being sort of supported by the hunt and the hunt servants are going out and are intimidating people.

I don't know if you saw it on the night that you came out but they're sort to following the patrols round and ... was out one night, they were following him in a vehicle with the lights turned off, nose to tail behind him, so they're intimidating but what's certainly been happening is I think you could say there isn't any clear proof that it's the hunt, apart from one incident where it was photographed and the police have charged them.

In a few weeks I'd find a plausible reason as to why the hunt was involved. The farmers taking part in the cull preferred to know who it was going to be on their land at night. They wanted to be confident it would be someone they could trust. So they tended to employ local contacts – and who else were those local contacts likely to be, but hunters?

One of the things Clare and the others are interested in is the character of the conflict between cull supporters and opponents when they meet, so I focus in a bit more on these patroller-gunman meetings. Inevitably, the topic of the police comes up. As background, Elizabeth has been helping to report blocked footpaths to the county council, to get them cleared. What's that got to do with the police? Wait for it...

There was an incident where one of [the gunmen] left some cartridges, which were found, I don't know if you've seen that, that's on YouTube as well[6], they left a little thing of cartridges which were found by one of the patrol members and they filmed it and ... the police were there at the same time and escorted this person away and ...

Why did they do that? Were they off the path? Why were they escorted away, for their own safety?

They escorted the gunmen away and they wanted the cartridges to be handed over immediately and the people that had found them,

---

[6] I've looked, but I can't find it.

filmed it before they gave them to the police and the police then did issue a report to say that this gunman had had his licence changed, to stop him being able to do the badger cull shooting, so they sort of had removed it because he'd acted inappropriately.

Which involved leaving his cartridges behind?

In my view, he'd done two things, he'd left his cartridges on the footpath which was a careless mistake, which if he'd had a sort of partner with him, he probably wouldn't have done it but what he did which was really negligent, was he went out without a partner to do the shooting and that was a really serious breach of his shot-gun licence and the police didn't do anything about that because they didn't understand that he shouldn't have been there alone and I think there have been quite a few incidents like that, where the police haven't understood the law and they've tried to do something or tried to put it right but in putting it right, they've sort of shown their lack of understanding of the law, which has been the same with this issue about the injunction and whether that's a crime or a civil matter and they've not understood that.

I think they are understanding it now but it's taken them a long time to understand and again, it's a sort of ... from my point of view, I've had very little contact with the police in my life and I've had quite a lot now and it is really surprising that they don't understand the law.

Tell me about some of those interactions, what have they been like?

It's been varied, hugely varied. They normally have a male and female liaison team out in the evening and they're very good, they will come and have a talk to you and they've got really good people skills and they'll talk to you, that's fine and then you'll come across others, I think the difficulty is they're being called in from all over the place and I think they're just called in and they don't necessarily know how to deal with peaceful members of the public doing something legal and I think I told you, when I was on the Forthampton Estate, it was about half ten at night and I was just taking my boots off on the side of the road by my car and another lady was doing the same, we were the only two people there and we got surrounded by this riot van, shining all these torches into our cars and demanding to know who we were. That really annoyed me, that they would do that to us and I think they just didn't know what to do, I think they thought, "we'd better treat them as if they're sabs and they're here illegally" and that really annoyed me.

Another evening, they obviously got my registration then and they did a full, they didn't search my car but they did a vehicle check on it and then I got picked up on the motorway a couple of days later and I was followed home. Somehow, my number is in the police computer and I've been picked up as a suspect person and I haven't done anything illegal, so that's quite annoying and I've been followed a couple of other times as well, so that's just annoying.

I'm now very careful about what I say to them because I'm assuming that it's all being fed back to some database and they have some database on me. I was saying with ... this farmer, the first one that wouldn't come out of the house to speak to us, reported me to the police and at the time I was talking to someone at the county council and he was being very formal with me, then the police contacted him and he was quite horrified, how the police had got involved in something that was completely legal.

The police have been putting pressure on the county council to delay dealing with the public footpaths, which I think is really inappropriate and the council I think also thought that, so have not taken any notice of them.

We've had something put on our computer and I don't know what that is either.

What do you mean?

I think the policeman that wanted to investigate me, contacted the person at the county council and asked me if he would asked sending on my email details and I said "no, I've got no problem with that at all", it was all sent onto the policeman and then I think my email was hacked into, my husband ran this sort of diagnostic thing on the computer because we just had a few peculiar emails come through at that point, we thought "this is really strange" and my husband ... did a diagnostic thing on the computer and found these spyware programs were on the computer, which was, we felt we've only put 2 and 2 together because we're not doing anything else ...

Were you able to identify when those programs had been put on?

It was very shortly after I joined the wounded badger patrol and started getting involved with the footpaths, so I don't know. We suddenly realised that there was something not quite right because it started running really slowly. We've got two computers so [my husband] did a diagnostic on both and found this spyware stuff that was on it and I don't know what it was, he'll know the name of it. Since he's removed all of those, they've been fine.

It's kind of annoying and I think it's the police that have done it but I've got nothing to hide, I'm just investigating footpaths and so I think that's what it relates to, which is just really peculiar! But I haven't mentioned that to anyone else in the badger control and I assume if you're in the police, it's quite easy to get permission to get into people's computers... so I don't know.

Have you had any sense of the view of the police in relation to the cull itself, or how do you view them in their relation to the cull? I remember when we went out on a walk, we met some police liaison officers and they would say "let's stop talking about this", at the point at which the question was hanging, "what do think you about it?", so what's your view and experience of that?

I think that's right. I think they're probably advised not to get into discussions with us. I'm sure they do all have views but they are doing their job and they're doing what they're told to do. I think it just, they're people like anyone else and I think they do have their views. ... was out one night and one of the policemen shook him by the hand and said, "you're doing a really good thing here". So I know that there are some of them that are sympathetic and others that aren't, equally I know there are some that are quite pally with farmers and that's been spotted and there are others that aren't.

I think probably it's a benefit, they are calling in police from other areas and I think it's a benefit that they're doing that.

Do you have a perception of more generally, the overall way in which the cull is being policed, would you say the cull has been policed neutrally or ..?

No, I don't think so at all actually. I think it was very one-sided at the very beginning and I think it's got progressively better and I

think that's because GABS [Gloucestershire Against Badger Shoot-
ing] have been taking a very strong lead. I gather one of the people
in GABS is a retired police officer, there's some connection but I very
much got the impression at the beginning that we were being
treated as criminals, which is really insulting and I think ... I gather
that it's at the Hereford & Worcester Police, I'm not sure what the
formal name for the force is but I understand they were particularly
bad at the beginning, that incident I was talking about with the
riot van, that was them and what's been happening since then is
that we've been asked to check the number plates of the police cars,
ask the policemen for their badge numbers, so we've been keeping a
record of all the incidents and then after each evening, the appro-
priate person at GABS then goes to the police liaison officer and
says, "last night this occurred, this didn't occur", so I think gradual-
ly, the police have realised that the wounded badger patrol are
honest, law abiding people and I think the opposite of that has
probably happened – but this is only my view – that the farmers
and the hunt have been very violent and aggressive and the police
have started seeing that, I think they've seen it on several occasions
and they've had to caution them. I think they're building up a bit of
a picture as to what has been happening.

Elizabeth doesn't know, I don't don't know either, but sometimes
it seems difficult to believe in coincidences. Despite her suspicions
about police surveillance – and her experience of it – she seems
quite balanced. She's not raving about 'cops this, cops that' like an
anarchist for whom 'the state' and its arms preside over all ills.
Covering this event the police might expect, perhaps even hope,
that neither side sees them as neutral – on the other hand, why
would you dismiss the evaluation of an intelligent, professional
person such as this?

For a few hours, as I ate a jacket potato and then drove on through
the spectacular Gloucestershire autumn, I took Elizabeth's view and
experience of the patrols, the farmers, shooters and police as the
GABS view. I would soon find out I was wrong. Why would it be? It
was just my first interview with someone involved with them. Meeting my next two interviewees, I was quickly put straight.

Can you tell me a bit more about this idea of the wounded
badger patrol? Where did that come from?

...[Grace] - we knew that all the footpaths in Gloucestershire were
literally in the firing range, we established that as a fact because we

were trying to point out the danger of having these high-velocity bullets if you're out walking your dog, for example. We knew that they were all in the firing range ...

[Fred] We got an FOI [Freedom of Information[7]] on that one and things like that, so it was clear that all the shooting would be within two miles of a public footpath.

[Grace] But that didn't seem to make any difference to anybody, given that we're so obsessed by health and safety, this important fact seemed to be not important so we thought let's exploit that in some way. We've got lots of footpaths in Gloucestershire, we know they're in the cull zone, why can't we walk round the footpaths in the evening and we also knew that it wasn't going to be a humane way to kill them, so there could be wounded badgers ... it gave us legitimate authority to be there. Then the sabs are there, but the wounded badger patrol, we wanted to attract Middle England ...

[Fred] That was a key thing really.

[Grace] We needed the numbers of people, we needed credibility.

[Fred] We knew that you wouldn't get sort of "normal" people shall we call it, going out doing ..., so we wanted some sort of mechanism whereby we could engage just the average Joe Public, in doing something to stop this happening and that was our solution to it.

[Grace] The wounded badger patrol, that could work because it immediately draws you in, so that was it ...

Has that had any effect?

[Grace] Well yeah because we've had hundreds of people out over the weeks.

[Fred] It's just absolutely been amazing, the people that have come from all over the country.

---

[7] The method by which British citizens get informational blood out of the governmental stone.

[Grace] People that have never done anything like this before, you hear that time and time again and they were really ... pleased that they had that mechanism, they wanted to be lawful because a lot of them are working, they're professional people and they couldn't really do anything sort of illegal, so it gave them that ... mechanism.

[Fred] What we haven't mentioned is we've developed a protocol which everybody that joins the wounded badger patrol has to sign, so it says legally they can't intimidate people, they can't trespass, all those sorts of things.

[Grace] We spent a lot of time on the protocol and we had some workshops with just general members of the public, seeing what they thought of was it reasonable, did they understand it, could they sign up to it? We also engaged the police, we showed them the protocol, they were happy with it, so again it's about legitimate authority, that's what we felt it would give the patrols.

Some people have said "this is not for me" and they've ripped up the protocol and we haven't seen them again, which is fine but then it's clear, we wanted that clarity so that they knew exactly what the purpose of the patrols were for.

What would count as success?

[Fred] The overall purpose of GABS was to stop the badger cull. That was through whatever legal means we could do that and we made it on politics of all of that to start off with and various routes we could mention if you wanted us to. But then more recently, the only thing we could do to raise the profile was the patrols.

The patrols haven't been set up to stop the cull because that would be illegal, all we've done is to go out on the footpaths and look for wounded badgers.

Now one of the side effects of being out on the public footpaths is the guidance for the shooters is that if they are aware that there are people within close proximity, they have to break their guns and walk away, so that's happened as a consequence of us being out there and looking for wounded badgers.

[Grace] We knew that was the guidelines so we thought wounded badger patrol, we could legitimate be there and legitimately, the shooters would have to stop.

[Fred] But that's never been our key purpose because that would be illegal and also people will be aware that the NFU took out an injunction just before the cull started, we sort of ... even more basically really, where the NFU did send us letters from the injunction, well with the injunction saying that if we did a range of things that we would be liable to arrest but of course, we've never been arrested, there's not a single wounded badger patroller has been arrested throughout the whole process, although other people have and that's just shown that what we've done has always been legal and the police have confirmed that everything we've done has been within the law and they've had no problems with us and in fact, we've got an ongoing, regular liaison with the police about the whole issue because one of the things they're keen to do, is to avoid this thing causing a breakdown of law and order. So we've tried to assist with that process.

[Grace] They say they find it quite helpful because we're almost like the trade union, we're one form of communication, a single form of communication rather than having hundreds pile in, we try to control all the issues and make it manageable.

Tell me then, the case of the badgers. Why do you think it is you got involved? What was it about the case of the badgers that kind of got you into it and ended up with you ...?

[Fred] I think it's three things, one is the time, we'd just finished work and we'd been involved in caring for a relative who had died, so we had some more time. The second thing was that we quite like badgers, we used to have a badger which came through our cat flap and would steal food in the house for two or three years, so we do quite like badgers but we're not badger specialists or badger obsessives.

The third thing was then as [Grace] said earlier on, the more we got into it, the more ridiculous the whole thing seemed because the policy seemed to be contradicting what the science said and as [Grace] said, we've been introduced to it by this guy called Chris Cheeseman, who had spent 35 years working on badgers, he used to kill badgers as part of his work, he is a person that still engages in killing other forms of wildlife so he's not aligned with some of the bunny hugger sides and he says that himself, but he was saying "this is a total nonsense".

[Grace] He's a senior scientist, have you heard of Chris?

Yes, he's been mentioned.

[Fred] So from the scientific point of view, it was clearly not right because he was saying that and then the more we found out about it, the more wrong it seemed to be and we just felt an injustice. Just as an aside, you think to yourself, "if this happens over badgers and the amount of lies the government produces and the way it distorts information as it has done over the figures, just in the last few weeks even, what on earth are they doing with everything else?" It's been an interesting, perhaps for one of your academic colleagues there, we have started with sort of lots of Middle England people and whether you go out and see them in the middle of the night in the fields, they become, the only word is radicalised I suppose.

[Grace] They change literally within about a week, they start off as this fairly innocent almost, accepting and jovial and a week later, they can't even look at the police officer because they've never come into contact with a police officer before and they regard it as a whole negative experience and they loathe politicians, loathe the BBC, you name it! They switch quite quickly, they just see it almost a different side of life.

I'm struck, though, by how my two interviewees – Frederick and Grace – are saying they're not quite like that. They're distancing themselves from the ordinary patrollers, and describe themselves as union representatives with a collaborative relationship with the police. Looks like hierarchy again, they're more on top of things, working out how to get things to work, less worried about the in-transigent-looking obstacles they're presented with – even though they're also presented with a few themselves. But they have been radicalised in some sense – against the government, or at least, the Tories. Against the media too, and against journalists who might be masquerading as researchers to get a story. Before the interview starts I'm subjected to a quick-fire round of questions about the funding and aims of the project, none of which seems to get the time for an answer. They're tense, aggressive even, but settle down as soon as we start, saying "we're very suspicious about people – now".

Fred and Grace must be every local government's worst night-mare. Former insiders, they know how this type of policy works. They can imagine the minor technicalities that could cause major hiccups, they're articulate, skilled with information technology, unafraid of speaking in front of large crowds or cameras, they can understand a complex brief, they are socially embedded, able to link local networks with the national animal welfare elite, Team Badger, and, most of all, they have bags and bags of spare time. Apart from the Wounded Badger Patrol, they've been trying to block the cull from going ahead in other ways. Before they knew where the trials would be they were getting landowners in their local area to sign up in opposition. Then they focused on local councils with land in the cull zones, and then they focused on the National Trust, the biggest landowners in the country. They also tried to unseat the local Tory council with the slogan 'ABC - Anyone But the Conservatives' (and almost succeeded). The point of these campaigns was to try to make it more difficult for organisers to achieve the 70% of the land needed for the culls to go ahead. Except in their local area, they didn't manage it, but their campaign, as well as the position of other landowners in the area, such as the Wildlife Trusts, did have consequences for the cull later on, as I would discover. "We are quite awkward!" they admit, after running through a few of their other, unrelated political activities.

I'm not sure why, but for some reason, they take a step further than the other people I've spoken to so far in the way they link the science and the politics of the issue. The others would point out that as far as they understood it, the science doesn't support the cull. I don't know anything much about 'the science', but I do know that a number of 'scientists' have spoken out against the cull, which is not quite the same thing. Why the scare quotes? Because I know Steve, at least, would have a problem with talking about science and scientists in this singular way. But I'll come to that later. For now, I just wonder about how far my interviewees' logic goes. *The science doesn't support the cull, so why is it going ahead? It must be something other than the problem of badgers giving cattle bovine TB. Which anyway, they don't because they don't have it, or if they do have it they don't give it to cattle because how does a one-foot badger pass bacteria to a five-foot cow? Or if they do, the risks should be better managed with biosecurity and vaccination. Culling could just make matters worse.* So far, people have gone in a circle. 'It must be to do with something other than bovine TB' leads to offshoots of reasoning, guesswork, but in the end, they all ended up saying 'the science doesn't support the cull because the science doesn't support the cull'. Frederick and Grace, however, have moved on.

[Fred] We started off for the first six or nine months, thinking it would be the science of the stuff here because we assumed that there would be some academic research ... and that would be produced and the government would then say "oh yeah, this is not right", but it became clear after a while, when we used to read those reports, that actually it's a total waste of time because the government has ignored anything which hasn't suited the policy decision it's taken. So to be fair, we've stopped reading policy documents and new research because we know that that won't stop the cull, it's pure politics now and that's the only thing that really, which would stop the cull.

[Grace] And the ethics, there's no concern about ethics either so it's about some form of power issue going on, that's the only way we can actually analyse it isn't it?

[Fred] There's no other rationale for it really.

[Grace] It's about prowess, macho power and they will do what they want. They have a horrible expression about "bearing down", bearing down on wildlife and they use that expression in the economy, bearing down on certain parts of the economy and it's this bearing down, they're obsessed about bearing down and that's what it is, that's what it's all about. And it's also about who owns and runs the countryside, the government have never really accepted the fact about fox-hunting, they've lost that argument on fox-hunting with dogs and they were going to lose ... badgers, there was no way, so they had to win on that, this bearing down concept.

You see Paterson talking ... he bears down on the interview, he will win because he just repeating the same mantra, they don't actually understand a lot of the subject but they use the same expression, the same phrases and it's quite effective isn't it? They've used four words, they want healthy cattle and healthy badgers and they've used that constantly for about a year and they're still using it.

It's quite clever because it makes you think "oh they care about the badgers" but you don't make a species healthy by slaughtering them do you? But it's these four words they keep using.

We spent too much time, we were trying to be conscientious in getting the information out and the correct information and it's counted for nothing has it?

[Fred] No, not really.

I manage not to leave tyre prints in my kind respondents' lawn and, ignoring their advice, head cross-country to Newent. Meeting the prime movers in the Gloucestershire campaign against the cull has changed my feeling of what's going on. In Somerset, at Camp Badger, I got this sense of very loose networks of people coming together because they share a concern about badgers, but going about things in different ways. According to one version of a movement, it fits. Here's my former doctoral supervisor, Christopher Rootes:

"a loose, non-institutionalised network that includes, as well as individuals and groups who have no organisational affiliation, organisations of varying degrees of formality; that is engaged in collective action motivated by shared environmental concern; of which the forms and intensity of both action and concern may vary considerably from place to place and from time to time" (Rootes 1997: 326).

Ok, so maybe Camp Badger didn't represent a whole movement in and of itself, and the 'environmental' bit is something I know Chris would quibble with (more, oh much more about that later!), but looking at the response to the cull as a whole, from Brian May and Team Badger to hunt saboteurs and Camp Badger this sounds about right. Of course, the entire discipline of social movement studies has not rallied around Chris' idea. This one's much more popular.

" - a sustained challenge to powerholders in the name of a population living under the jurisdiction of those powerholders by means of repeated public displays of that population's worthiness, unity, numbers and commitment" (Tilly 1999, p. 257).

Basically, Charles Tilly thought a social movement was less like a network and more like a campaign. And Fred and Grace seem more like campaigners – except they're not just running one campaign, they're having a go at, by my count, four. Worthiness? Yes, they emphasise how the patrols are legal. Unity? You take part in a patrol, you sign the protocol. Don't like it? Don't take part, no hard feelings. Numbers? They've got hundreds involved. Commitment? Do I need to answer that? So maybe a movement is a campaign, but it feels less movement-y to me. More formal. Ok, maybe this is just one of the more formal bits.

I'm interested because this is what I do. Used to do. Did. I spent my PhD studying the environmental movement in the UK. Thinking about how to think about it better. I'm not sure I got very far, but if what I'm looking at now is a movement, or at least part of a movement, I can start to apply some of what I know. Anyway, movements are interesting – if an episode or group of actions add up to a movement then there's a chance of change, not just change to one specific policy but more – people changing their attitudes, their habits, changing that tired old 'political landscape'. Could the resistance to the cull signal a change in political assumptions about acceptable attitudes to – what? Animals? Wildlife? The countryside? The environment?

The question is not just about how a big a conceptual box the cull's opponents fit in. It matters because the protests and patrols will be treated differently by outsiders – the 'public', the media, politicians, depending on which box they get put in. Animal rights protests are associated with violence and intimidation, environmental protests are not (generally). If this is an animal rights protest, it's likely to have a much narrower scope for acceptance than a conservationist or environmental protest. I think my 'old' supervisor would quibble with me over whether this is really an environmental protest, because in the past his research has shown that animal rights and environmental activists are not connected (Rootes and Miller 2000). They're not part of the same network, so they're not part of the same movement. But, thinking about the people I've met so far and what they've said, I'm beginning to wonder. There are definitely animal rights people involved: the Badger Killers website demonstrates a number of classic repertoires that have been used against people involved in animal testing. Naming and shaming. Encouraging people to set up nuisance phone calls. There are hunt saboteurs – historically they have been closely linked with other kinds of animal rights groups.

But there are also conservationists, and people for whom this is not mostly about badgers, or even badgers and cattle, but about the countryside.

Detecting movements – their creation, growth and decline, is a bit like detecting the culprit in a murder. You look for means, opportunity, and motive. MOM. Well, it's mobilising structures, political opportunities, and cultural framings (McAdam et al. 1996), really, but MSPOCF is not a handy acronym. For now I'm interested in 'opportunity'. What if this cull had created an opportunity for animal rights-, conservationist-, and especially, environmental-minded individuals and groups to come together? Now, that would be -

I squeeze the car under the archway beside The George, park, and go and find the barman to check in. There are a few other guys in the bar, having a drink and watching the football. This is the set up for 'The Plan', but first I'm going out on Patrol again.

I'm more relaxed this time, this all seems familiar now. There's a police car circling about, and a black pick-up has parked. A man gets out and strides over to the Co-op. The patrollers nod to each other – they recognise the van. But there aren't as many patrollers tonight – seven – and only two I haven't seen before. One of them seems to be a local, knows the area well, and is prepared to go off on his own. He's regailing the group with a story about being followed by the police, something that has happened to him a lot. This time he challenged the officer to give him his name and station, but the officer would only give his number. The man said 'you may only refuse to give a name and station if you are dealing with me under the Terrorism Act', so when the officer refused to give his name and station again, he concluded, 'so you are using the Terrorism Act. Right.' The others join in with accounts of being followed by police cars outside the cull zones. All the way home in some cases. They didn't think the police were allowed to do this, but someone had heard that they had been given permission to do so by a Chief Constable. A little later on, the man is talking about traps. He whips out his phone and shows us a picture of a snare that had been found.

This man is planning to act as a link between the hunt sabs who are somewhere in the area, and the patrollers. This connection seems to give him some cachet, and the co-ordinator for the evening defers to him. The co-ordinator is Attenborough (no, not *really*). Thursday nights are his turn to organise things. Elizabeth is there too. We team up again, with another man I haven't seen before. We share a car (His. I'm not that relaxed.) and follow Attenborough to our first stop. It turns about to be our only stop. Attenborough wants us to split up, but no-one is confident enough to say they will lead another group. We split into two groups and walk along the field edges, using our torches to keep a look out for traps and keep track of where the other group is. Nothing much happens. We lose sight of Attenborough and the others as they take a different route. As we come out of Greenaway Wood and cross the road, a police car pulls up. There are three officers in there. The one on the passenger side winds down his window and starts questioning us in a vaguely threatening, patronising, macho tone that suggests he's not a liaison officer. He embarks on a poorly-disguised fishing expedition which my companions divert, smiling. I think Elizabeth's enjoying herself.

It's the second time we're walking through Greenaway Wood when it happens. As we're approaching the exit there's a bright light shining down the path. Almost before any of us can ask 'what's that?' the light snaps off and we hear an engine being gunned, a scratch of gravel, and it's gone. Shooters. Or if not, someone out for a quiet spot of 'lamping', using the bright light on the back of their pick-up to find prey, make it freeze momentarily in the glare, and shoot it. We reach the lay-by where the vehicle had stopped. There's a deep rut where the driver spun a wheel in the hurry to get away. We've heard that shooters will leave a site now if patrollers turn up. They didn't use to, they used to wait, expecting the patrollers to get bored and move on. But why the hurry? We're wearing reflective vests, so we would have stood out. Could we have been mistaken for police? It's as if they were doing something wrong. Or maybe they knew about patrollers – knew we would also be wearing high-vis clothing. Elizabeth thinks it's strange. Isn't this wood Wildlife Trust land? Culling isn't supposed to happen on their land because they're not supporting the cull. They're not opposing it either, but they haven't given permission for culling to take place on their land. We try to find a sign that might help us, but there's nothing clear. This bit is run in partnership with one lot, that bit in partnership with another. We're not sure. We're assuming it was a shooter. We need to know if they come back, but we need to keep moving so we can cover the whole wood.

I pick up a light stick and prop it across the gap in the barrier where walkers can enter the wood. As I do so I feel I'm crossing a line. It's silly, boy scout stuff really – a trick to see if someone comes into the wood while we're away. But I'm not just an observer now. I don't want people to come here and kill badgers. It feels like I'm doing the right thing by helping to stop them.

We're back by the cars at the entrance to Betty Dawes Wood when things start happening again. We're just deciding what to do next when there are headlights, a revving engine, and a small car skidding to halt on the gravel, nearly running us over. Two women. Open window. Passenger: 'This van's following us' – a black pick-up fires past, accelerating, headlights flashing on '- and now we're following.' The car pulls back onto the lane and we watch them as they try to catch up with the pick-up. Maybe they want to read its number plate. But it's too fast and I can see it roaring away from them up the lane.

Attenborough's on the phone. Within minutes, the sab-liaison man turns up in his car. Apparently, this wood is 'hot' – a badger was taken from there the night before. That would explain the pick-up; we wonder if it also explains the presence of the police. The best thing we can do is hang around, walk through the woods again and try to keep tabs on whether anyone is coming in. A van could drop a shooter and drive off, leaving the shooter in the woods and unless we were there, we would know nothing about it. Until something went bang.

For a couple of hours the tension keeps us going as we go around the wood again, putting up sticks, checking, reporting to Attenborough. But nothing. The sab-liaison man is there again, he's being encouraging, saying we're really helping by being there. It's getting on for eleven o'clock. Elizabeth and our other companion need to go home. I can hang around for longer, so we arrange to meet Attenborough back at the car park. He and his colleagues turn up shortly after us, and they wish each other goodbye warmly. Attenborough and I head back to the entrance of Betty Dawes Wood. Liaison-man is convinced this is where we can do most good – but we need more of you, he says. It's true, there aren't enough people out tonight. He tells us that there's a sett in the field beside the wood, in a bank that used to be part of a railway. Loads of entrances – big sett. Probably why there's so much interest in the area. A couple of sabs come by and Attenborough chats to them, and then they disappear into the field. We carry on eating oat cakes and flap jack in his car for a while, and then Attenborough calls in to liaison-man. When he rings off he says 'What's that?'

It sounds like shouting. We're out of the car and down the road. It's stopped. What the hell was it?

We walk down to the entrance of the field. After a few minutes one of the sabs turns up. Did you hear that? Turns out it was them. He says that they'd heard that screaming near to a sett would scare any shooters off and draw the attention of the police, so they were giving it a try. Could have mentioned it before.

We decide to move the car down to the field gate. Facing up towards Betty Dawes Wood we can cover the two entrances at once.

We carry on snacking and drinking tea. Attenborough used to be a wildlife cameraman. His first experience of filming had been with badgers – back in the day when film meant film and the camera made a loud whirring noise as it passed film from reel to reel. It would take a while just to get the badgers accustomed to the noise. Why was he here? He said he felt the cull had gone too far. The barn owls were gone, hedgehogs and other species were now scarce as a result of human activity, it was wrong to attack yet another species. I mentioned that people were saying how badgers had had a bad year last year, because of the bad winter. Attenborough dismissed the idea – he'd seen badgers playing in the snow at high altitude in Tibet, a bit of rain and cold weather wasn't going to bother them; they'd evolved to deal with British weather. What did he like about badgers? His voice – already friendly, enthusiastic, even affectionate – softened. They're so playful.

The two women (besides Attenborough they seemed very young – sabs though) we had seen being chased earlier stopped a couple of times, circling around to make sure no-one had entered the wood while no-one was there. The second time they come around Attenborough leans out of his window and says, next time, I want to do what you sabs do. Sett sitting.

It's getting on for one. After a quick call we're given a route passing by a farm known to be actively involved in the cull, and then we drive up to meet liaison-man at his look-out post. He's found an amazing spot. From here, at night, you could see any car that moves (as long as it's got it's headlights on). Using mobile phones, a small number of people could cover a large area effectively, turning up exactly where they were least wanted. I look out over the dark valley. Nothing. Time to stop. Attenborough drops me off in Newent. No short drive home for him. I hope I'll meet him again one day.

No rest. I must have slept between 2 and 5 but I'm tense, gearing myself up for the next stage of my trip. The Plan. At half 5 I'm woken by a series of heavy footsteps and doors banging along the corridors of the old pub hotel. I get up, go for an unnecessary piss in the toilet al.ong the corridor, keeping my ears open, and then, back in my room, check the street outside. Nothing.

At about half seven I go out to the car, without really needing to, and peer in through the windows of the breakfast room. Shit, there are people in there and one lot looks like a very likely bunch. Ok. Time for breakfast. Four men sitting at one table. Two at another. Not sure about those two. Concentrate on the four. One in his forties, wearing a blue sweatshirt with 'Quiklift' written on it, the others – two in their late 20s, 30s maybe. One with a top with 'CL' on the back. One in his 20s. These three dressed as... what? Decorators? Bottom half looks like paint-spattered overalls. They chat in northern accents over a cooked breakfast. I can't hear anything specific. When they're finished they get up, collect bags – large holdalls, and after a bit of hanging around, a cigarette, disperse. Only one of them drives off in the van parked opposite the hotel. It's an old Quiklift van. Old in both senses – battered, and clearly not a Quiklift van anymore. The stickers have been removed, but the sticky stuff has stayed behind. 'Quicklift – plant machinery moves'. The others seem to disappear on foot.

Trying to make sense of what I've just seen I eat my breakfast slowly, pack the car and go to the bar to pay. The accounts book is sitting open on the bar. I glance at it as I lean over the bar to type in my pin. 'Quiklift' checked in Sunday night, checked out Friday morning. Coming back Sunday night. Another set of regular entries for a couple of first names, but I don't have time to register them. The other two guys?

What, I ask myself, are four guys dressed as decorators and claiming to be with a plant machinery transport company doing for four days, five nights, week in, week out, in the industrial heartland of Newent that gets them accommodation on expenses in The George? How did the other three men get back home – at a guess, a long way away – without a lift or a car?

I hold my breathe as I ease the car out under the archway onto the street and try to work out what I should do next. As a researcher I have freedom of movement. Perhaps I should have just sauntered up to them over breakfast and asked them if they had anything to do with the cull. Something tells me that might not have gone too well. *If I could just confirm they are who I think they are.* Shooters. Then the idea hits me. I could phone Quiklift (if it exists), and ask them about their operations in Newent. Extract a 'what operations in Newent?' response. I could, if I was a journalist.

I decide to take a drive up to Ledbury, get a map and head past Red Marley and Forthampton to see if I can spot anything that suggests a link between the hunt and the cull, or find a lead for an interview. There was a farm Elizabeth was talking about. I click on my voice recorder. Driving and talking on the phone are illegal. Does a voice recorder count? I have no idea, but I need to make a record of everything that has happened soon, or I'll forget it, forget the details. Memory is the anthropologist's bladder, they say. I'm not an anthropologist. I go over the events of the night for half an hour, and once I think I've covered everything, I'm ready to make an admission.

I have to admit at this point – and I don't know how much of this I'm going to record as part of the project – is that I'm beginning to feel quite a strong sense of what do you call it? Co-option, or alle-giance with the anti-badger, anti-cull people. I'm meeting people who are my parents' age, above and below, who are very sympa-thetic, engaged and concerned people who are just really easy to get on with, whose issue I'm very sympathetic to, and I'm already hav-ing ideas about ways they could advance what they're doing, par-ticularly if there's going to be further culls in the future –

And no, I'm not going to record everything.[8]

---

[8] For a reflexive look at the issue of 'going native', see Fuller (1999).

Chapter 4

Farmers

I have a problem. I need to talk to farmers who are involved in the cull and who farm in the cull areas, but no-one seems to want to talk. They're afraid of Stop Huntington Animal Cruelty (SHAC)-style attacks on the person, family and property, so they're trying to stay anonymous. They've failed. The 'Badger Killers' website has been acting as a part campaigning, part 'wiki-leaks' site, reporting details you can't find elsewhere, including lists of farmers allegedly involved. Not good for the farmers if SHAC-style protestors are using them to target farmers, great for an innocent researcher. I make a list and cross-check the contact details on a directory website before trying to ring them up or send an email, but no-one answers. Except the NFU reps. I'd already been tipped off by my interviewees so far that these men might be good to talk to, but I'm initially hesitant – neither of them farm in the cull areas and I'm not keen on having a load of PR schpiel. But it's all I'm getting (maybe that's the deal between the cull participants and the NFU. Let us do the talking), so I don't have much of a choice.

I call one of them up. A rich male voice comes on the line. I explain who I am and what I want. An interview. The voice wants to know why he can't be paid consultancy fees for this sort of thing. I try to explain that people aren't usually paid for an academic interview without going into details, as this doesn't seem to be going too well, and to the individual the reason that comes to mind could sound insulting. Basically, I think, we want genuine views, not rent-a-quote, but saying so to the individual would imply that we think their integrity is so flexible that they would be quite happy to argue for the return of capital punishment for minors for ten bob. But then, psychologists pay participants for research – students routinely eat out on it. Yes, but psychologists are researching the unconscious, they're interested in what you do, even what you can't help doing, or can't help thinking, not in what you think you think. This guy is calling it consultancy, but it isn't, it's just an interview. Maybe he's just got the wrong end of the stick. Doubts are swirling around my head, and he's insisting I explain why we're not offering to pay him. I go for cover. 'I'll check with my colleagues and get back to you' I say.

On reflection, the issues around payment are more complicated than the 'rent-a-quote' problem, which counts as the first thing that sprang to my mind when caught on the hop. Perhaps I should look it up. Here we are, 'Paying for interview?' the journal article title says (Hammett and Sporton 2012). Turns out not to be quite what it says it is, as it explores the issues around paying interviewees who give interviews to UK students on field classes in Kenya. There is a more general overview, though. Social researchers are always very worried about the relation of power that exists between them and their interviewees, and most of the time they assume that they are going to be the more powerful ones. A payment might help to balance out that relationship a bit, or recognise, as in the case of the people living near a Field Centre for UK students in Kenya, that research is making quite a large interruption in their lives, or indeed, the time they spend making a living. I'm not sure I feel as though the 'power' in this interaction is going to be all on my side,[9] and there's another point of view that suggests just the opposite, that by paying people you just repeat the pattern of 'all-knowing academic, dropping in from utopia-towers' (putting oneself in serious danger of paying for what people think you want to hear, or rent-a...). Perhaps, though, if this man receives a lot of these requests, he might ask for, if not consultancy fees, then at least the cost of his time. But then again, I'm only contacting him because he's the public face of this section of the NFU – speaking to people about the issues the NFU is involved in either is or is not his job. If it isn't, then he could just politely steer me somewhere else, and if it is – well, I don't know if the position is paid or voluntary, but it doesn't look like it makes any difference.[10] Above all, though, as

---

[9] For more on interviewing elites, see Ball (1994) and Harvey (2011).

[10] Later, when we offer some money to those who take part in an all-day workshop, many of those associated with some formal organisation – professionals, in other words – don't take it, because the hint of financial association with an organisation outside of their core business would threaten their independence. Rent-a-quote again, but backwards. Or maybe they just couldn't be bothered.

paying for these interviews has not been planned or costed into the project, no-one else has received a payment, so why should any one of the respondents get paid just because they felt powerful enough to imply they should be, and the others not?

Anyway, the phone call continues. When could we meet? We find a date. What time? I suggest the late morning. The conversation takes another turn. 'I'm self-employed', the voice announced, 'and if this was me, I would get up early and make sure I was able to get to my meeting by 9 am." I explain I need to get a hire car in the morning, and I've no wish to arrange an early meeting time only to keep him waiting. "So, you're also hiring a car, and driving up during the day, so that's 400 pounds before you've even started". He's assuming I'll be driving from Exeter, and I'm not about to disabuse him of that thought, even though explaining about the rush hour in my hometown would help my case. I explain again about not wanting to be late for our appointment. We agree a time, and hang up.

Shit, what a nightmare.

My mobile rings, declaring that the number is 'unknown'. I don't usually answer 'unknown' calls, but, so soon after that last call, I'm a bit unsteady and assume it will be the unpleasant voice again. It is. "How did you get my number?" punches into my ear. I can't remember. The last few weeks have been an Internet soup of different sites. The NFU site flashes to mind, and I tell him. He checks it, can't find his phone number, and then I realise it was Badger Killers. There's something awkward about this, but just right now, I can't put my finger on it. "I guess you know about the Badger Killers website" I say. "Oh I see," he says. "You realise that they are not our favourite people?" I say something like 'er'. "Well done," says the voice, and hangs up.

Shit. *Shit.*

This is really getting to me. Following a hunch I search for the man's phone number online. As I thought. If I hadn't got it from Badger Killers, I could have got it from any number of telephone directory sites, or even – what's this? - his own website! Advertising holiday accommodation. The seed of guilt dies at germination. Feeling angry, I check my emails. There's something from Steve about the Professor Letters. He's got one for Angry Voice, but I've asked him not to send it yet, while I try phoning. "I wish I had asked you to send that one now" I write, "having spoken to him". I leave my computer, trying to do a few other jobs to take my mind off it, cool off. Check my emails. Another from Steve. 'Have now gone back and sent that letter.' No. No, please. You've just sent an invitation letter so someone I've already invited. To, in fact, the only person a mistake like this is not just going to be embarrassing, but excruciating. Did I really give you the impression I wanted you to do that?[11]

Shit. Shit. Shit.

The interview is a few weeks away, and I try to keep my mind off the impending disaster that has to be actually meeting this man, but it doesn't really work. In fact, things are going quite well. A few more farming leads come up, one of them even phones me voluntarily after receiving a Professor Letter, but I have to swallow a hot, hard lump of fear before I answer the phone, not knowing if I'm going to get another one. Turns out to be a bit of a scalp, one of the people named as a director of a cull company. The call goes fine, he sounds – adult. Mature.

First, though, I'm going out on a limb. I've been scanning the Internet for farming contacts in the cull areas. There's not much, and what there is, I can't get them to pick up the phone or answer an email. I 'm beginning to think I'll have to organise a mass mail-out of Professor Letters to all, or nearly all, farmers in the cull areas, which is going to be a lot of work, extracting contact details, cleaning it up, merging it with a letter and making sure there aren't any mess-ups. But I have found one guy who seems willing to talk. He's got his own blog, says he farms in one of the cull areas, and looks like he would be quite happy to talk. I organise a car and, under orders not to use GPS, drive up to see him.

I'd been wondering why he hadn't given me directions. Maybe he didn't want to meet me at his house, or at least not at first. Or maybe he was planning to take me on a walk, a tour or something, around his farm. In the end, it was nothing, he just didn't believe in directions or GPS. I call him from a lay-by and he explains the way to his house. It's probably just outside the cull zone. The furniture in the living room is arranged oddly, and we conduct the interview side-on. He's started before I can even set up the voice recorder.

---

[11] Yes.

Seems like he might have done this before. Seems like he might quite like it. Why wouldn't he? He has a lifetime of experience to talk about before getting down to it. He ended his career in the farm recovery business, fixing sick farms and turning them into businesses again.

The first thing you have to do when you go on a farm is totally eliminate lameness in the dairy cow. All the lameness has to go, no lameness at all, not even 1%, not even 0.5% and by the way, the lameness in our national herd in this country is 22% ... once a cow becomes lame, she gets more mastitis because she lays down more, so then you get more mastitis problems, that's a big problem and that is increasingly getting worse because of antibiotic resistance, you can't treat some mastitis cases with antibiotics anymore because the bacteria, they're just resistant to it. And this impacts on fertility as well because lame cows rarely very show oestrus and they lose condition, so they just become dormant, so you can't get them back in calf and that is the main reason why we're losing a lot of our cows, is we can't get them back in calf. But the underlying cause in my opinion, is lameness ...

So anyway, I would take on these farms and they could be problem farms, so you would sit down with the farmer and I wasn't interested in the spreadsheet of how much milk, how much money he's making on his milk, I just wanted to know the veterinary reports and what the problems were that were causing this, the underlying causes.

Generally it was lameness, it was usually lack of foot trimming, it could have been a disease which was rampant at the time called dermatitis, which takes two forms, inter-digital dermatitis, it gets in between the claws of the cow's foot and heel dermatitis, both of them very debilitating for cows. That was rampant and it still is today funnily enough but it's very, very preventable, very preventable.

So you would see what problems they had with that, what problems they had with mastitis and you would sort them all out and everyone needed a different strategy. It could be walk-ways, it could be foot bathing, it could be bedding wasn't changed regularly enough or maybe the bedding was too acid and there was bacterial ..., could be a whole range of things.

But with all those problems, lameness, mastitis, you always had other multiple problems on those farms, which was generally it was either bovine respiratory disease, pneumonia, bovine TB or a bo-vine viral diarrhoea, veptosclorosis, they all had other diseases impacting upon them which became entrenched. ... But once you'd sorted out the core problems, all those other diseases became manageable and in the case of bovine TB, with bovine TB testing, it just cleared up. ... I took on an underperforming herd ... that had got problems with bovine TB, the whole area had problems with bovine TB, it was a hot spot area and through management over a period of six months, I managed to clear that herd of bovine TB ...

Now, back to bovine TB. In this country, since the 1980s, we've been pushing hard for milk production at the expense of other traits, with the breeding of the dairy cow. We started off in the 50s and 60s with the Dairy Short Horn, which was a good disease resis-tance cow, it never gave a great deal of milk but she was a subsis-tence type farming, subsistence type cow that could give a good income. But then we moved to the British Friesian and she was bred out, we bred the British Friesian into Dairy Short Horn, then the British Friesian, the wild British Friesian is a really successful disease resistant animal that has got longevity, but with our push for milk, to increase productivity and the economics of the dairy income, of the entire system, we bred a different type of cow, the Holstein.

Now the Holstein is a different animal altogether ... they're much bigger, they put on a lot of bone, a lot of frame, they're very highly productive, they eat more, they digest more food, give more milk and this is what the sort of cow that they have in mega dairies be-cause you can push a lot of food into them and if you look after them, they will be very productive, they're like the Ferraris of the dairy world if you like, that they need high octane care and high octane fuel.

So 95% of our national dairy herd is Holstein now. Now properly looked after, they're fine, they're fantastic, you won't have any ma-jor disease problems with the Holstein. But looking at the statistics that we have in this country and these are DEFRA statistics, they're not my statistics, we've got 22% lameness, we've got rampant masti-tis causing phenomenal rates of culling through not being able to get the cows back in calf and all that, all that is generated by stress because once you stress an animal, you decrease its longevity, you increase its disease susceptibility – with humans too – we know this, it's a fact. They understand these concepts in abattoirs, you mustn't stress animals before you kill them because you increase the lactic acid in the meat and the meat doesn't keep so long, it's all down to stress.

...if we look at the national herd statistics, which are yields of 7600, yeah, that's a reasonable yield, it is but for a whole scheme, I would say that's under-performing because a Holstein cow, 95% herd cows in this country are Holstein, you should be attaining yields of 10,000 litres in this country, with really no great problem at all.

Now the best farms are, they are, a lot of those are attaining those sort of yields but there are a lot that are very, very underperforming and in Holsteins, that's well within their remit, to make lots of milk and to have a longevity of eight years. Now the longevity of the dairy herd, the national herd in this country, in 2009 was five and a half years, five and a half years, they didn't get longer than that.

And that was just the beginning. While Gary (I'm calling him 'Gary') is warming up, it might be a good idea to take a closer look at some of these stats he's chucking out. Holsteins, 95%. Ch -

Oh, come on, this can't be that difficult. Some government or industry source must have published something somewhere that says 'this many Holsteins'. Some increasingly aggravated clicking later and I decide I can let Gary have this one. It's not exactly new data, but a DEFRA report in 2005 recorded 92% of the national herd as Holstein, and it doesn't seem unreasonable to think the figure has changed a little in eight years. Check. Lameness, 22%. That one again. Ok, there's something that looks like it might once have been a DEFRA report (DEFRA 2007), although it might have been written by someone at ADAS, a rural consultancy, and there's something in the *Veterinary Record* (Whitaker, Macrae and Burrough 2004). Oldish references, but at least there are two of them. Check. Yields, 7600. Good, this one I can bring relatively up to date, using annual DEFRA dairy statistics (DEFRA 2016b), although even this is not helpful and consistent, asking us to compare 2014 figure and 2015 figures. Assuming, fairly enough, that nothing much wildly different happened between 2013 (when Gary's speaking) and January 2016, the 2014 yield was 14.6 billion litres of milk, and the 2015 figure for the number of dairy cows was 1.9 million, call it 2 – average yield, 7300 per cow. I think we can let that one pass. What about longevity? I think we might want to ask a little bit more of Gary here. The way he puts it, it sounds like all dairy cows hit a wall at five-

and-a-half years old and then just blip out. We know that's not what he means. He's talking about an average. The thing is, there's more than one kind of average. If he's talking about the *average* average, the 'mean', the one most people are talking about when they say 'average' (the total age of all the cows put together, divided by the number of cows), then there might be a problem, because it would hide whether there are cows being culled very early which are balanced out by cows which are culled much later in life. As a 'measure of central tendency', then, the mean can be useful and statisticians and scientists have made very great use of it, but sometimes it's the wrong simple summary of the data. In this case the more helpful stat is – yes, there it is, in a report about agriculture and climate change, oddly, but it will do (DEFRA 2011, p. 32) – the median, the age where half of the herd is older and half younger. The report focuses only on breeding cattle (aged somewhere between two and three years) and only goes up to 2011. The median is fairly stable, at just above 5 years, possibly dipping towards 2011. Check-ish.[12]

When a calf is born, she is reared up to the age of approximately two years or sometimes three years and then she has her first calf, so she's two years old or three years old. She has her first calf. The first lactation is usually quite low because she's a young cow, she's not even fully grown, she's 70% size of an adult cow at the age of two years, that's why some farms rear them to three years when they're a bit bigger, which is actually on some farms, it's a better idea but it costs, you're rearing them for another year.

Now she has a first calf that's usually a very mediocre lactation, the lactation is the period they give milk and it's not usually a very high yielding lactation. The second one is better, the third one they start taking off, the third lactation, remember she's five now, they really start going and generating profit and at six, seven and eight years, they're at their peak.

---

[12] For in-plain-English introductions to statistics see Clegg (1982) and Wood (2003).

Now in 2009, we were losing them at five and a half and the then Animal Welfare Authority – because in those days we had the Animal Welfare Authority and the Veterinary Licensing Agency, there are two different organisations and the Animal Health Authority, they flagged it, they said "look, we're losing cows at the age of five and a half, there's something wrong, this isn't good for the industry, there's something fundamentally wrong to lose them at five and a half".

Now we're in 2013. The average age now is five, we dropped six months ... since 2009 to 2013.

Cows not living very long, lameness, percentage of lameness in the national herd, all those things point to the fact that there's something fundamentally wrong with the way that we're producing milk and we're producing meat, there's something wrong because otherwise the statistics would be differently and so would the bovine TB statistics, they would be totally different, we wouldn't be struggling with it like we are at the moment.

Many farms struggle with that ... many farms have been shut down for years, I know farms that have been shut down for years and I can go on a farm and you can see the problems plainly. I first voiced my opinion on this in 2011 ... one of the main reasons why a lot of farms struggle with bovine TB – one of the main reasons, it's water management. Whenever I took on a farm, I would always make sure that all the troughs first of all were all scrubbed out and not necessarily disinfected but scrubbed out. You can't actually line the troughs, you rinse them out because that's what they do in New Zealand because the equine industry, the possum gives horses a disease, so the equine industry took that on board, that it's water management but they're also culling possums in New Zealand.

But the reasons that they've lowered their TB rates is mainly because they've taken on biosecurity and water trough management and feed management and all the rest of it, we're not doing that in this country.

... during the winter time when cows are in the sheds ... those troughs out in the fields, usually one in every field, they're left open which is fine, they become drinking fonts for wildlife, for the eco system, you get birds drinking out of them, you get birds diving in them, you get rodents drinking in them and you get rodents dying in them. They all carry TB, Avian TB in the form of birds.

*And if those troughs aren't washed out, when those cows go back
out into the pastures about March, April time, they're petrie dishes
of infection. Now it's pretty obvious to me and it always has been,
that you wash those out, certainly before you turn the cows out
because remember, if you've got a bovine TB problem, your cow's
drinking out of those troughs, salivating into those troughs and
cows make 60 litres of saliva a day, incredible statistic but they do,
they drool and they salivate and they cough and they're big mucus-
making machines, cows are, it's what they are, that they infect that
water trough but in the autumn and that stays open to the wildlife
all winter and at the end of that winter, you could well have contaminated the wildlife with bovine TB, as in the rats, as in the
birds, as in the badgers and in the deer, you've done it, you've contaminated that wildlife. When your cows are turned out, if those
troughs aren't washed out, then you've got a huge amount of bovine
bacteria in those troughs.*

Basically, Gary has three lines. The general health crisis in dairy
cattle is the result of stress caused by the trajectory of agricultural
policy and economics over the last thirty years. Good basic husbandry is at the root of healthy herds of cattle. And small scale, but
widely implemented, biosecurity measures can help limit the risk of
infection from badgers. He goes on later to doubt the level of infection present in badgers, and the likelihood of their passing bovine
TB on to cattle – which either mildly contradicts his suggestions
about biosecurity, or explains why he thinks bovine TB can be
solved with such small measures. I take two things away from this
interview, apart from a delicious lunch and a warm feeling of easy
friendship with Gary. First, much more of an idea of what it means
when people say 'it's a problem with cattle', and more of an idea
what people are getting at when they talk about the other health
problems that are more prevalent in cattle: infertility, mastitis,
lameness. No-one so far has been able to make more than a rhetorical link between these more serious issues. I've been wondering
what they've been getting at. Checking the transcripts, it's only the
people I interviewed at Camp Badger who have caught onto these
statistics, so it seems likely it's come from one source and then been
passed around in conversation at the Camp. But where is it from?
It's helping them suggest that more effort should be exerted trying
to solve these more serious problems. Going for this expensive cull
is overkill. Gary is able to go further than that and turn a line of
rhetoric into a line of reasoning. It's not just that the effort should

be proportional to the problem, but that the prevalence of bovine TB is dependent on the prevalence of a number of other basic health issues – so obviously, treatment should address the causes, not just the symptoms. I start hunting around on the Internet, trying to find the source of this statistic. I've seen a chart somewhere, summarising all this. Where?

Can't find it. What I do find, in a number of reports and press releases, is a reference to an article in *Farmers Weekly* back in 2003. Lucky I've got a British Library reader's card. In London, I discover that the article is reporting a speech made by Dick Sibley, a Devon vet. He thinks that the right strategy for TB is tolerance, not eradication. This is what he said:

"While 18,000 sounds like a large number, it must be remembered that 90,000 cows/year are lost to mastitis, a further 31,000 are culled due to lameness and more than 125,000 have shortened productive lives due to infertility. In addition to this, 120,000 calves/year lose their lives from neo-natal conditions before six months old.

"Perhaps we should look to control these conditions before we try to tackle something like TB. We should develop a health and welfare strategy which includes these economically significant conditions, as well as those, such as TB, which are governed by legislative requirements" (Farmers Weekly 2003, p. 40).

So Gary has wider professional support for what he's saying. But the problem is, Sibley was speaking in 2003, too long ago. But haven't I just allowed myself to use some statistics from 2004, 2005, and 2007? Yes, but while I was open about the dates, reasoned out why I could still use them and only used them to do some loose background checking, in the press releases and reports I've seen in the Internet soup, the date of these stats is often hidden in a footnote,[13] or worse, an endnote.[14] The bovine TB statistics have got consider-

---

[13] Like this one.
[14] Which I'm not allowed to use.

ably worse since 2003,[15] and that might change the balance of con-
siderations for some people. I can hardly believe that some of the
charities and groups opposed to the cull are relying on this old reference to support a numbers-based argument in such an unquali-
fied way. To any intelligent eye, referring to a newspaper article
written more than a few years ago to support an argument about
the present amounts to an admission of weakness. Is that all you've
got to back your argument up? But still, I haven't found that chart I
was looking for, so maybe there's a better source out there.

I've got a couple of other problems, though. Now I've met him, I
know that Gary isn't really farming, and he isn't in the cull zone. I've
got interviews with three more farmers lined up, and not one of
them farms inside the cull zone. To make matters worse, next up is
Angry Voice.

*

I park at the end of a long drive, walk into the farmyard, trying to
work out where I should go. I find what looks to me like the front
door, and knock. It turns out not to be, or at least, not the door I am
supposed to use. A tall man has appeared out of the side. Hello? It's
him. He leaves me standing on the flag-stones while he goes into
the kitchen and boils the kettle for some tea. I'll need it after waiting
out here for him, on a typical day in November. Eventually, he leads
me over to his office.

I've decided to play this interview absolutely dead-pan. I've been
pretty angry and upset about this in the couple of weeks since that
nightmare call; I've felt something dark lodge itself inside me, and I
haven't got rid of it. Violence. The only way I can get through this
interview is simply detach, do the questions and get out. I've been
terrified he's going to have another go at me, and I mustn't react.

---

[15] The officially accepted statistic is 'new herd incidents per 100 herd years
at risk', or "the number of new incidents ... [divided] by the total
amount of time the herds tested during the period in question were un-
restricted and at risk of infection since the end of their last TB incident
or negative herd test" (DEFRA 2016c, p. 2). This figure more than
doubled between 2003 and 2013 (DEFRA 2016d).

Probably best if I don't even respond. Usually at an interview, you try and develop a rapport with a person, make them feel at ease, more open. But in these circumstances, it feels dangerous. I also don't want to let him brush off his aggressive behaviour, let him develop any rapport with me, take advantage of my inferior position.

So. Dead-pan. No rising to provocation, no banter.[16]

We get through the legal bits without any major bumps, and I start the interview. He switches mode once the voice recorder is on, going from curt, testy, to more expansive. Not much more expansive, though. Not at first.

Can you tell me a bit about what your perspective on what's happening?

I think where we've been ... pleasantly surprised I suppose is it's proven, we were given three things to achieve, safety, humaneness and efficiency and I think the safety has, touch wood, been proven, the humaneness has been proven, the wounded badger patrols have not, as far as anyone knows, found any injured badgers and the efficiency, it's a process that worked and what we've found is obviously there's an enormous amount of disturbance by protestor activity and that has made it less efficient than otherwise it might.

Can you tell me a bit more then about what you've been doing, what actions you've taken in the debate on bovine TB?

I suppose my strongest role has been as a media presence in order to explain the need for controlling TB in both wildlife and cattle. Obviously we've had increasing restrictive measures on the industry, cattle testing, slaughter, movement restrictions, trading restrictions, biosecurity, all that side of it has increased progressively over the last 20 years and we have always said, going back I suppose about 15 years ago, we said "it's fine, we're prepared to accept increasing controls on our businesses, in order to mitigate the disease but at the same time, it's crazy unless you have some measure

---

[16] For more on 'rapport', see Goudy and Potter (1975) and DePaulo and Bell (1990).

of control of the disease in the wildlife which is spreading as well".

That's what I've been trying to achieve, a public understanding of the need for it.

So you would say that work you've been doing has had an effect?

I think so. It's incredibly dangerous to disregard a huge electronic petition, 300,000 signatures across the country but technically, that leaves about 59,700,000 people who haven't signed it, so democracy is always rather a challenge, not comparing like with like but Tony Blair when he came to power in '97 with a landslide victory, a massive majority in the House of Commons, he never had as much as 25% of the population voting for him, so 75% never supported him and that's the same, it's a vocal element who speak, on both sides, it doesn't matter which side you're talking about and farming is a very small minority issue and you're looking at 1% of the population, so we don't have that enormous database of willing email petition responders. So that's why it happens.

I think that on a one to one, when you talk about it, when you have meetings and discuss it, people relate to the fact that if it was them who had the same sort of problem with their pets or their businesses, they would have to take action and therefore they understand.

So what would count as success then for this sort of communication problem?

I suppose ongoing invitations to continue to be involved and I think that we have deliberately, as a policy, because the protestors have wanted to raise the profile all the time and it's an extraordinarily easy thing to yell, "it's cruel to kill badgers" and when you're arguing the case in support of the cull, it takes a long process, much longer than a journalist is prepared to give and so we felt, right at the beginning, it was unwise to continually be proactively looking for media coverage because the media has to be even-handed and so if the protestors were jumping up and down saying what they wanted to say and we as a policy restricted ourselves to simply talking about the reason for the need for the cull, it would reduce the interest that it has.

I mean obviously there's local interest, there's bound to be but nationally it's lost its profile.

Tell me a bit about how you found out about the arguments and the debate?

By being part of it.

Have there been particular sources that you prefer to use, to get information?

No, we've obviously used, we've accessed an enormous amount of data, whether it's veterinary, the DEFRA, our own vets, the veterinary world themselves, the Bourne Report[17], the knowledge that the NFU brings to it and experience and in Gloucestershire, it just happens that we had the Thornbury Trials going back 30/40 years ago[18] and yeah, we aren't allowed to use them as a peer reviewed scientific study because they were never peer reviewed, they were a one off and therefore there's no base category to compare them to, which is really difficult to appreciate because they categorically demonstrated that the removal of the badger population considerably stopped TB in its tracked for 10/12 years, then the badgers came back in and TB came back in, there's absolutely no question about it. But that sort of evidence is there but it's not part of the public discussion.

Just talking about evidence, there's a second set of trials, I can't remember the acronym now, a decade ago, the Krebs ...

RBCT, yes.

Do you use those as well? What's your response to their findings?

Yes, that's where it becomes confusing because it depends who you are as to how you interpret them. It was a very frustrating trial, it was completely ... we were say because I know some of the people involved in it, that it was so badly executed that it's almost invalidated as a scientific trial and the level of trap destruction and

---

[17] On the results of the RBCT (ISG 2007)
[18] See the interview with 'Henry', later, for a more on the Thornbury Trial.

*damage by protestors was colossal, over 50% of the traps were dam-
aged and destroyed, so it wasn't realistic.*

*... the protestors who theoretically claim animal welfare is their
sort of motivation, are actually defeating themselves because they
are preventing an experiment, it is an experiment, it's a pilot but if
the pilot has been allowed to be carried out successfully and we had
reduced the badger population by 70% in the six week period, then
we would immediately be seeing the gains and we're not about
exterminating the badger population, there are hundreds of thousands of badgers in the country so there's no threat to their population and if we could improve their level of density of the county, you
have healthy badgers and healthy cattle, end of story.*

**What about sources of information you might avoid or that you
dislike?**

*Give me some ideas. I don't think I've got any ideas of ones I
would ... there are ones that I would suspect were less valid but*

Which ones come to mind?

*I'm trying to think ... you try and read them all or take heed of
them all. And the vaccination studies are interesting, our argument
within the NFU is that for back to badgers, I personally have a
moral concern that I'm not entirely certain if you require a vaccine
for a wild animal, it's the right way of going, that's a slightly different issue. But if you are going to vaccinate them, what I think I
would recommend is that you reduce the population and then
vaccinate and you use vaccinations to ring fence protection at the
frontline of the spread of TB. You've obviously seen the maps of the
TB explosion from South West outwards and if you could reduce
that, if you took a, is it Portugal, The Lines of Torres Vedras where
they blitzed an entire area of the peninsular walls and burnt it, so
there was no food for humans at that stage or animals, so you
couldn't basically campaign in that area, what we would like to do
is to reduce that badger population from Cheshire to Hampshire, a
swathe like that and then vaccinate everything that remained in
that area because then at least you have made a real start at stopping it spreading, you've got that barrier up there as a sort of cor-
don sanitaire, that prevents anything exploding and then you work
backwards into that area, reducing the population progressively
and ... whether you vaccinate at that stage, I don't know.*

Tell me about the argument that the right biosecurity measures would be helpful, maybe even sufficient, as an alternative to culling?

What, for cattle?

Yes.

You've come to the wrong farm because ... our animals, they never come indoors, they're always outdoors, they're always grazing. What do you do?

Would it be appropriate for the more intensive dairy farms?

So you're saying intensive dairying is housed 24 hours a day, 365 days a year is a solution to TB?

No, I'm saying are there farms for which biosecurity measures might be more appropriate?

Yes, if you were the Knockton Dairy and you had your 1000 or 3000 cows ring-fenced in a housed environment and you could guarantee that the fencing around that was badger protected, that would be brilliant, that would be a real end game.

There's a video of badger spending two and a half hours trying to get through a gateway and it failed and went to another area and got through a gap that was 100mm wide. So the problem is if you've got a modern farmyard with purpose-built buildings in a block which you can ring-fence and shut one gate that leaves nothing bigger than 100mm gap all round it, you can get away with it.

If you've got anything like a traditional farm ... that 90% of farms have got, where they've got out-buildings ... to ring-fence that is incredibly difficult to any meaningful extent. You can do it but the problems is it's rather like when a fox is on patrol, if you don't shut your chickens up one night, the fox is around and zaps it.

If you do all your fencing and one evening you leave a gate half open and a badger goes in, your defence is broken down and so biosecurity is an add-on, it's a benefit once the problem has been resolved but in order to get to the situation where biosecurity is relevant, you've got to reduce the pressure on both the badgers and the cattle.

What do you know about the process for deciding whether the trials have been a success?

The three criteria on which they're based is safety, humaneness and efficiency, so that's what they'll be judged on, bearing in mind the conditions that we have been subjected to. That's up to presumably DEFRA to resolve.

My personal belief, observation would be to see what happens in three years' time, to bring back the level of TB in that area, that will be really exciting.

Because the consequences are long term, you've got to wait a long time to see ...?

Yes.

If the trials are deemed a success, do you think that will lead to a consensus on the need to cull badgers?

If they're deemed a success on the criteria on which they have been established, no, it won't because it's DEFRA policy to cull, they're not altering their policy, that's what they want to achieve, the cull that we've got at the moment is to establish, I said those three criteria.

Now that doesn't alter public opinion, what will alter public opinion is in three years' time.

So there's a long term way out. Is there a way out of the conflict over culling badgers in the near term?

Well, the conflict is only between the protestors and the cull, an awful lot of people are not involved in it. I don't think it's necessarily top of anyone else's priority other that the couple of hundred animal rights activists, I don't think anyone else would notice. I mean who sees a badger? Is it relevant?

I think that we cull rats, we cull pigeons, what's the big deal?

So you're saying it doesn't really matter if the conflict continues because it's a sideshow?

I think it's really sad, I think it's a huge – waste of energy is the wrong way of putting it – but it's a hugely challenging climate for farmers and those involved in the cull, to live under, if they're perceived by some to be brutal, unpleasant murderers because nobody wants to be thought of as that. It would be much nicer to be seen as protecting your livestock, protecting the industry, providing beef and milk for the country.

Have you met people who hold a different view to you?

Regularly!

Is that face to face or ...?

Yeah.

What happened? What was the circumstance?

I suppose there were two, ... County Council, where there was a debate, ... District Council, the Green Party discussion group in ... where, I suppose about 20 people who held the same view and me and it's not a problem, we're all civilised human beings who can have a discussion.

Where it becomes very different is in the dark of night when you've got animal rights protestors who we have, on a regular basis, we're not talking about the wounded badger patrol, we're talking about the SHAC and Huntingdon Life Sciences and the people in Oxford Laboratories, those sort of people with balaclavas outside your house night after night, camping in your fields without permission, without right, defending the badgers they will say. They are pretty unpleasant.

I could take you to half a dozen farms where their children haven't been out at night for two months because there's a fear of leaving the house and that's in this country.

Have you met some of those people?

The protestors or the farmers?

The protestors.

No.

So all those events where you have met people, what's your reaction to that, to them?

Discussion like this.

What's your reaction to what they think about the cull?

I fully understand and appreciate that if you have no responsibility, then you can have a view and the people that I've met have a view, have an opinion but they have no responsibility for the impact of their views or opinions on the management of the countryside, that's the difficulty. I've been to the Wildlife Trust where they're adamant that they'll support vaccination, in fact they haven't, through discussion, they haven't opposed, they're against the cull, the ... Wildlife Trust but they haven't opposed it, which is a slightly different positioning because they understand the need to do something and they understand that vaccination of badgers is staggeringly expensive.

I think you can ignore the cost of the cull because without the protestors, it would be a very cheap policy, it's entirely farmer-funded other than the policing of it and the policing of it is only necessary because of the protestors, not because of the cull ...

I click the voice recorder off. "All right?" he says, without it being a question, and turns away. I am dismissed. At the door, he sends me off with another 'Well done', which I realise as soon as he says it is just his stock way of patronising people. When I first heard it, over the phone, I had thought it was some sarcastic comment, but he probably hadn't even noticed he'd said it. Relieved I'd got through the interview without another scrape, I rolled the car down the long drive, trying to work out what I made of it. For a man who obviously prides himself on grasping harsh realities, on realism, on responsibility, he does a lot of wishful thinking. Wishing his opponents away. We can ignore the biggest petition in the history of the Downing Street website so far (Team Badger 2013). We can ignore the cost of policing the cull, ignore the effect the protestors are having on the effectiveness of the cull, and ignore public opinion when it comes to the results. I tried to imagine what it would take to shake his belief that badgers are equivalent to vermin, and failed.

On the other hand, he had the most detailed knowledge of the evidence and practical problems related to the cull and its alternatives of anyone I had spoken to yet. Just because scientists say one thing, doesn't make it right, or relevant to the current case. No one until now has been able to give me an assessment of the validity of the claims being made by the anti-cull, RBCT scientists. This farmer can. If you're going to take him on, it's not going to be on the basis that he doesn't know what he's talking about. I wonder though, about the subtlety of the perspective he's bringing to the debate. When I asked him about biosecurity, trying out Gary's ideas, he stayed fixed on the Fort Knox version of 'bio security' – as if it's still two words. He just dismissed any idea that there was anything that could be done in the field. But still, he is prepared to consider alternatives, like vaccination – but he doesn't like the cost.

There's something else bugging me as I reach the end of the drive. Something he said about the debate. That's it – he'd said the NFU were playing down the issue, trying to make it seem less interesting. That seems worrying and strange at the same time. Worrying, because it matches with exactly what the Wounded Badger Patrollers had been telling me about the coverage of the cull on the BBC. Is it too simplistic to believe someone might have had a word in an editor's ear? I find it hard to believe that's happened, but even if it hasn't, the idea that news editors can create bias just as a result of how much coverage they give, and the idea that the NFU know it – that's worrying. But it's also strange, because it seems so counter-intuitive. If you believed you were right, wouldn't you be happy for more chances to explain why? It's now obvious to me that broad arguments are not going to make a difference here – it's the details – so why wouldn't you want to move the debate on from useless and entrenched generalisations to specifics, about, say, how hard *and* expensive vaccination would be? Wouldn't that help – if you are as right as you think you are – reduce the level of conflict? But then, if you discount public opinion from the outset, you're not going to bother, are you?

At the bottom of the drive I turn into the lane and start the journey home – and stop, after only a few hundred metres. A fox. Loping along the lane from verge to verge. Dark, amber, slim fox. The fox stops and looks at me for a minute. I look at the fox. I've never been so close. Instead of running off, the fox carries on, trotting along the lane going from hedge to hedge, as if looking for something – food, or a way out. Amazed, wanting this to last, I glide the car behind the fox with the engine off, trying to keep up, trying not to get too close. I think of what Angry Voice would say if he saw us now, just on the edge of his land. Researcher and fox, not hunter and prey, just two individuals passing on this corner; wary, complicit.

Just over a week later, and I'm turning up the drive of another farm, wondering what treatment I'm going to get. I needn't have worried. This farmer, a strong advocate for the cull, but *still* not based in the cull zone itself, seems like his voice – comes from deep.

He ushers me through his cluttered office into the house and we set up at one end of a long, light oak dining table. Almost as soon as he starts speaking, I realise that this is going to be something different. He's reflective, nuanced, deeply involved, knowledgeable, passionate. He – and his family – have also been on the receiving end of some pretty unpleasant treatment.

It's been an interesting experience, they are pilot culls. As far as we can see, obviously it's down to the independent panel to make the judgement in the end, the safety and the humaneness seem to be evidentially fine. There is obviously the debate about badger numbers and the targets in the cull. But the licence was made up around various assumptions and arbitrary guesses of this and that and trying to extrapolate data from RBCT which I don't think anybody in the farming world actually thought was a particularly well run culling trial anyway and came to some very equivocal conclusions at the end, that can be interpreted either way, so it didn't really help too much.

I think the one thing we learned is a six-week period in the cull is not long enough. We had a significant amount of highly targeted protestor activity … [our] Police Force were peculiarly unhelpful, all they wanted to do was stop the battle, they weren't in the slightest bit interested in allowing us to carry on and do what was legally something government had asked us to do. That made life quite complicated for us and undoubtedly affected our efficiency at doing what we were asked to do, which was to test out free shooting of badgers.

In the end, we did resort to some trapping, a lot of those traps were totally illegally, criminally damaged or removed, the police took virtually no action whatsoever about that, which wasn't particularly helpful and neither did they stop them being targeted. So it is very difficult for anybody to interpret the numbers and say if it was rolled out on a wider basis, where I think naturally you would get a huge dilution of protestor activity and therefore probably much more success with both trapping and free shooting, just what numbers you could expect to get.

The other thing was we took an arbitrary guess at the best time of year to start. It turned out this season and because it was a pilot cull and all sorts of people had to be involved, we did have to stick to some dates, we couldn't be very flexible because the independent panel were overseeing, we had to accommodate a huge amount of overviewing on what was going on, so we weren't terribly flexible on when we could stop and start and that sort of thing.

So the season turned out to be a slightly awkward one, we'd had a very late winter, late spring, the cropping season was quite good but it was all about two weeks delayed, that meant there was a lot of maize in our culling area, came off late, so there was tons of food around for the badgers, a lot of natural wild food around for the badgers, they were in very fit condition, they weren't terribly hungry and therefore not terribly easy to bait. In a drier summer or earlier in the season, it might have been easier to get them and I think the timing of whenever one does this sort of culling needs to be fairly flexible and based on what the season is developing into.

So it's been an interesting experience, quite a challenging one but I believe we've been surprisingly effective, given the restraints we've had. I think we've proven the safety, we obviously had to put that as absolute paramount because we knew right from the beginning that there were some nutters out there who were just going to get in the way, whatever we did, so safety was absolutely paramount and you know, the wounded badger patrols haven't found a single wounded badger, the stories about screaming badgers and wounded animals all over the place turned out to be utterly false, which we always believed it was going to be anyway; I think we proved that point.

There was a lot of the harassment of the farmers down there, it is quite difficult when you've got this somewhat uncontrolled and really extreme protest element involved in this, to actually get farmers comfortable with and certainly some of the behaviour of the protestors was utterly obscene, you wouldn't have put up with it for two seconds, nor would I, the families were targeted, their children were targeted, grossly unfair but I guess that's part of the thing you're looking into, in terms of the social aspect of this policy.

Can you tell me a bit more, be a bit more specific about what sort of harassment you mean?

I'm only picking up anecdotal evidence so I don't really know, I didn't experience it but people were having torches shone in their windows late at night, into the early hours of the morning they had people shouting abuse over the garden fences, if they happened to be by a footpath or private road, kids were terrified, it was just utterly ridiculous behaviour which the police were very slow at responding to and obviously, the awareness of some of the problems that I'd been through last year when my name became public ... and the threats and emails and nasty letters that we got, got out and people get put off by that, so the farmers themselves were rather ... they want the cull to take place, they're absolutely desperate for something more sensible about TB to be done and particularly about TB in the badger population because it is a huge, huge problem, it's a massive natural reservoir of TB that's constantly spilling back into the cattle population.

Until we do something about it, all farmers know we're just on a hiding to nothing in terms of being able to run our businesses and forever more pay for increased cattle-based measures, which just do not work, they patently don't work. That's the worry, the farmers were wanting the cull to take place but they didn't want to be terribly public in being shown to be taking part in it.

So what would farmers be telling you, if you were trying to encourage them to take part? What were the things they were talking to you about?

The vast majority of farmers want something sensible done. There wasn't much disagreement about whether a cull was the right way to proceed, the difficulty was that they wanted to remain anonymous and to ask farmers for four years money upfront for anything, is bloody challenging and those were the two main obstacles, were really trying to maintain their anonymity and this involved many farmers who weren't even – because an awful lot of farmers who signed up weren't cattle farmers, they were just land owners – but they just all wanted to see something more sensible happening, a lot of the big arable people don't like too many badgers because they cause all sorts of other ecological problems, ground nesting birds and hedgehogs and bumble bees and God knows what, quite apart from the physical damage everywhere, so they were quite keen to have control over badger numbers anyway.

So the problem wasn't getting the idea across to people about the necessity for a cull, it was really just getting them to sign on the dotted line, pay up four years in front and this potential of being exposed because there were only two areas running, to protestor harassment. They were the biggest obstacles by a long way.

Funnily enough, hasn't he just corroborated some of the conspiracy theorising going on in Camp Badger (different county, I know.

Sort of corroborated, then)? Fran had wondered aloud about the purpose of the culls, had looked at the type of land involved and seen that it wasn't all, or even mostly, cattle pasture. But then, what does it matter? The culls are taking place over huge areas, and it's never all going to be pasture, is it? An operation of that size might need to build a coalition of participants with different intents, but it doesn't change the overall intended purpose, does it? That problem of reading intentions off consequences, again. But there's another problem, one that possibly explains why conspiracy theory has so much room to grow, and that's the lack of transparency as a result of, from the farmers' point of view, fear. I ask about his own troubles and he gives me a short version of the story. I'm a little unsure of this, but I'm not going to repeat the details, as the last thing I want to do is let his aggressors identify him through what they've done. It involved threats and defamation, a lot of worry and stress, and a long and probably expensive struggle to get things put right.

It was just a load of harassment, it was just trying to intimidate you into publicly changing your view on things which I wasn't going to do because my views have come round from many years of practical experience and it's all about fighting TB, it's not about fighting badgers, it's just bloody unfortunate that badgers are the reservoir.

If it was rats, we wouldn't have had any of this problem at all, it's just that people cannot understand that huge reservoirs of badgers are holding bovine TB and it's a dangerous and nasty disease but it's TB that I've been fighting for years. It's just something sensible being done about the wildlife reservoirs.

Was there ever anyone, any speaker or a paper that particularly struck you?

No, there's probably hundreds of papers, there's so much, it goes on and on and on. There's no one particular thing changed my mind on this whatsoever, you just became aware of the nature of the problem. What I find really frustrating is when we're told that this is a cattle based problem, badgers are just catching TB from cattle and you can deal with it, it's patently and utterly untrue that you can do that, it just will not happen and that is something I'm utterly convinced of.

Can you tell me why that won't happen?

It's a long and complicated story but in essence the disease in cattle is a spill-back, our classic picture here is that most of the time when we get reactors, we'll get one or two in amongst maybe, up till last year, we've got less animals now but up until last year we had 350 animals on the farm, it would only take one or two animals to shut you down, it wasn't that we had a raving problem amongst our animals. But those one or two were enough to keep your whole herd shut up, all your trading pattern locked into control measures, severe interpretation on anything you'd got and endless testing to try and get rid of it.

While you had cattle outside, we've got cattle ranging 550 odd acres of grazing around the place, you were just constantly picking up the odd little bit of TB, we've never had any picture of expansion within our herd or particular groups of animals, we've had some quite big hits on groups of animals but I think that's all from a common wildlife source or a contamination source that we've noticed. So you just get this picture and thousands of farmers picture exactly the same thing, there's just about nothing you can do to stop your cattle getting it and yet if I farm my cattle in exactly the same way as I do in the Eastern counties, I wouldn't have any problem at all, it's just purely you pick up that picture of when cattle are living alongside diseased badgers, you cannot ever truly long term get rid of it in the cattle, it will keep coming back. You may get periods when it doesn't come back in, three or four years but I've spoken to many farmers who say "my badgers are clean, I haven't got it", the next year you see them, "oh Christ, we're back down again". This topic, you can't deal with in half an hour.

What in your view is the point of contact or transmission, the way in which bovine TB is transmitted?

I think it's various and I don't think at any one time you'd ever know quite what it was. It's environmental contamination, urine, waymarking is probably the No. 1 method because badgers tend to be quite territorial but they also, when they go through hedges, just way mark and dribble out into the field and contaminate grazing and if they've got kidney TB, which a lot do have, they can contaminate grazing that way, some of it, probably a very small amount is aerosol, classic TB transmission routes, badger close to cattle, that might happen inside, I think it can happen outside, it's probably quite rare.

I think dead TB, deaths of badgers in fields where cattle go and sniff, our picture is that the latrines don't seem to be much of a problem because the area where we've always had a lot of badger latrines, we've probably had a picture of some of the least level of TB coming off that area from cattle grazing that we've ever seen.

You occasionally get contaminated food, if you've got a sick animal and sick badgers particularly, when they're getting close to death with TB, behave very abhorrently, they'll fight their way into buildings, they just want an easy food source to see the end of their life out, they're thrown out by the other badgers in the social group, they're probably quite dangerous, they're a relatively small number but I think there's more of them than the conservationists would necessarily say exist.

I think it's just general level of contaminations out there and it may take very many forms. I heard of a dog the other day that caught bovine TB because it had a puncture wound in its chest, that was just probably TB that somehow was on a bramble or something in a wood, I think it's a bacillus that can hang around for a long time in the right conditions, okay you've got to get quite a load of it if you're not breathing it in but that load is out there on occasions.

Exactly what transmission route exists for any particular case, you will never find out because you never find the case out quite some time after the initial infection has taken place but my suspicion is the majority of it is from way marked urine, grazing contamination, possibly latrines in certain areas and maybe direct aerosol and occasionally contaminated food sources, that sort of thing.

I'm going to try and talk a bit more about the cycle of TB or ways in which it's passed around. How would cattle pass it to each other and do you have any sense of whether the rest of the cycle of cattle passing it to badgers or into the environment, where other wildlife live?

The risk of cattle passing it to each other, with the amount of testing we do in what we call the hot spot areas or the endemic areas, where we're on annual testing and a lot of the bigger herds are on 60 day testing, is very limited because you're constantly removing

TB at a very early stage. The chances of coming across a vet who's ever seen a pathological case of TB are pretty rare I should think, there's probably about three vets in the whole of the country that have ever seen pathological TB because it never gets to that stage.

There is some indication in cattle that there's a period, about 28-30 days after initial infection, where they may just be slightly more infectious than at other times but cattle are like humans, they tend to wall off the disease and they don't spread it very readily amongst themselves, we never had a picture of the disease spreading amongst cattle, even when we've had quite long periods when we haven't been able to test foot and mouth, the vets say they don't ever really see it.

The classic case with animals was that it's an aerosol-transmitted disease and when animals are shut up in buildings together in winter time, if you're not removing it, you will tend to get a spread of it. But even in the days when there was just no TB testing and TB was endemic in cattle herds, most vets said when they came to do TB testing and remove animals, it was somewhere between about 15-30% of animals seemed to have TB despite absolutely nothing being done to stop it spreading. A lot just are naturally resistant, never got the disease at all.

So I think in cattle, there is very little picture of the disease build-ing up to any extent, where cattle are particularly infectious, it can happen on occasions and it's more of a worry in the four-year test-ing areas, where you might not pick up an animal that has moved there or just picked up infection somehow and has a much longer chance of developing it and becoming infectious before it's discov-ered, but I think in the one-year test areas, providing the testing's done accurately, the chances of animal multiplication and cattle multiplication of the disease are very small.

In terms of its – and again the picture you get in pretty well every vet is because of the nature of handling animals, particularly larger herds, you tend to do the majority of TB testing in the winter, you probably start in October, November when you're housing your herd, if something's discovered, you test every 60 days, you've prob-ably got a chance to get two or three tests in before you turn out in the spring, you'll clear it up in the herd, there will be no sign of it there according to the skin test, hey presto, you come back in the autumn, just when you think you've turned them out into a nice healthy environment, no closed, there's this impression of a 400 cow herd, that you've got 400 cows crammed into one building all huffing and breathing all over each other, it's just absolute ..., you don't have anything like that, modern buildings are well ventilated, yes cattle are pushed in but the maximum we ever had was 150 cattle together in the dairy unit in a very large, well-ventilated building. All the other groups of cattle were quite autonomous, they were in their own buildings, they were separate from each other, they weren't just spreading it willy nilly amongst themselves and when we did get infections, it nearly always was animals, well sometimes you get one animal in a young stock group and one dairy cow got it and you think ... what sense can you make of that? And the young one wouldn't have ever seen the other one at all, the picture of it spreading amongst cattle is absolutely a red herring, with the current testing regime, it doesn't happen in the annual testing area.

In terms of the indicated spread back to badgers, if you look at all the work that's been done around, I mean the Irish have done as much as we have, if not more in terms of pragmatic research into this, their evidence is that your badger to badger link is very strong, your badger to cattle link is very strong, your cattle to cattle link is medium, potentially there but when you're testing annually, it's really quite small, your cattle to badger link is almost nonexistent, we just don't ... you cannot deny that at some stage or other, badgers picked up bovine TB from cattle, I think that's why it's called bovine TB in badgers, I think what we have now is badger adapted TB that's spreading back to cattle all the time.[19]

It's essentially the same but when you look at the spoligotypes, each badger group seems to develop its own and again, the spoligotype evidence is another one that actually very strongly refutes that cattle are a significant source of both infection and movement of it

---

[19] This is not the place to try exhaustively to review the literature he's referring to. The point is, this is his view, and he's involved. If you're not sure how to start, get onto 'Google Scholar' (https://scholar.google.com) and search for something appropriate, like 'badger cattle transmission bovine TB'. There's quite a bit that's publically available now, and if there's only an abstract, it should give away the findings.

because the spoligotype map, I don't know if you've ever seen it but it's amazingly discrete. I can show it to you when we've finished if you want but when you spoligotype and a lot of the data was collected sort of 1990s, the early 2000s where they were testing badgers and cattle, when they were culling badgers, it shows that each area has its own spoligotype and that if cattle were the main culprits in expanding the disease and moving it about, you would end up with this amorphous mess of spoligotypes and it would get back into the badgers and the badgers would pick up a different type from the cattle all the time and you would end up with an absolute mess.

But you don't, you get this classic very discrete picture of a locally cycling disease the whole time, that isn't getting spread, isn't getting muddled up, it strongly indicates that badgers are the primary source, yes you can track disease that's gone from Cornwall to East Anglia, you can tell exactly where it came from by looking at the spoligotype but it never develops anything in East Anglia and that's another part of the story, that East Anglia, the North of England, people in the West Midlands before they developed significant badger populations were constantly importing TB from cattle in the West and even while they were on four year testing, it never developed into this endemic, persistent TB that just wouldn't go away. It's only when you've got cattle living alongside diseased badgers, you get this problem where you just cannot get rid of it.

It's a mass of little bits that just, you begin to get a picture of what's actually happening. But I honestly don't think cattle are really any significant danger to badgers at all, you've got to be careful because you don't know that but I don't ever see quite how, apart from a very heavily infected dung pat where TB might have potentially got into a worm that's under the dung pat that the badger's after, I cannot see quite, other than the aerosol transmission route and that's probably how it got into badgers in the first place, was probably the odd aerosol transmission and when you look at the situation, when badger numbers were less and when they had, I mean we virtually eliminated TB, this is when the conservationists keep going back to, "you used cattle testing, you got rid of TB", we did except for three or four tiny areas in the West Country, where they couldn't get rid of it and they couldn't understand why and it was then that they discovered TB in badgers.

Then they started culling badgers and they got TB down to what now would be classified as eradication but they eased up on that.

The point was while we'd had a hugely diseased cattle herd living alongside probably a lower badger population but a very extensive badger population, for hundreds of years, there was still only tiny pockets of badgers that indicated they'd managed to pick up TB.

I think the passage of TB from cattle to badgers is extraordinarily difficult but it can happen.

But the passage of TB within the badger population, once it gets established in them, is very rapid, they are probably the perfect hosts for it and that's the problem we have, they live underground, they can transmit it, they're young, they're territorial, they fight, they move from one group to another and off it goes and I think that's exactly what's happening now.

What's your response to the idea that if you take the right kind of biosecurity measures and husbandry measures together, you can protect your cattle against the TB that might be present?

You can't. There isn't a biosecurity measure short of not having cattle, it's just a joke, pretend that biosecurity is ... it might lower your level of disease risk but it's never going to eliminate it, not ever, there are numbers of closed herds I've seen going down with TB that in all essence have very good biosecurity, particularly in terms of defending themselves from other cattle and lock up their feed stores, fence off latrines and badger setts as much as they can but still go down with TB, you know, those guys are desperate, they think "what the hell else can we do?".

Have you tried these kinds of things yourselves?

We've tried excluding badgers from buildings but with a range of buildings like we've got, that cover nearly two acres, it's unbelievably difficult. Badgers are very, very difficult animals to keep out of anything, if they're really determined but the big problem is when you turn your cattle out, trying to keep badgers and cattle apart in a field situation is impossible, I would say it's not difficult, I would say it's impossible.

There's just nothing you can do about it, it's just going to be there, you can spend hours trying to fence off latrines but actually what happens in the summer, you fence off a latrine, the cattle can't get at it, the grass grows, you get a dry period, the cattle think "a bit of grass under there, I'll lean under and get it", but of course what

you've created is like another hedge barrier, the badgers are proba-
bly thinking "we'll just way mark this and make sure nobody ..."
and you're probably adding to the problem by doing it.

What do you think of the idea of washing out water troughs be-
fore taking the cattle out?

We do that every year, we do that anyway, we do that regardless of
TB, you just do it to give cattle clean water, in our buildings we
clean out the troughs regularly, in the cow shed we had tip over
troughs, we were constantly cleaning those out, it's an utter red
herring, it makes just about sod all difference at all, it's not the No.
1 problem, we've hung mineral bins in the air, we've fenced off
latrines, you can't fence off the... that's just ludicrous, it just doesn't
work but none of our were out in the middle of the fields.

There's just a limit to what you can actually do. Protecting your
feed store is probably the No. 1 thing you can do and we did that
right away, in fact we did have one obvious feed store contamina-
tion incident and it was a badger getting under a gap about that
high. You wouldn't believe that it could do but it must have been
getting in there because the only, we literally went down, nearly a
quarter of a herd gone and we just thought we were going to go
clear one test and then we had it in three week old calves, we had it
in young stock, we had it in the dairy cows and we couldn't under-
stand what was going on and it was only when we sat down and
thought about it, we thought the only thing that was common to all
those animals was maize gluten feed and we'd obviously had a
badger getting in the maize gluten feed store, most of the time you
just would not have thought it was possible but it just happened to
be getting in there, we adjusted that door but you wouldn't have ...
you'd walk round the farm and not thought twice about it, if you'd
looked at it.

If you can tell me a biosecurity measure or measures that are
going to work, I would have done them years ago, I did not want to
lose half a million quid fighting TB. But there's a limit to how
much resource you've got, people talk about fencing off your silage
and you can put up elaborate fencing but we've only got two blokes
working on 500 acres, looking after 400 cattle, they're busy, they're
flat out doing all sorts of other things, we just don't have the re-
sources to put in place all ... we've got five roadways coming into
this farm building, if we tried to exclude badgers from our set of

buildings, we'd probably have to spend £40-50,000 on fencing, we'd have to maintain it, how we'd do it on the roads I don't know because I've never come across any way that can stop badgers, short of having some weird electric matting and even that doesn't seem to stop them. The moment you turn all your cattle out on the field, you're back to a hiding to nothing.

The only units that probably can be relatively bio-secure are completely new zero grazed dairy units but you are bringing in food from outside, the zero grazing, there's always a potential of contamination there or maybe a fattening beef unit, where you can make the building secure like some of the approved fattening units that are being put up now, to enable farmers to trade properly without forever testing.

The reality is that biosecurity measures, you can reduce risk but you will never, ever stop it, there just isn't enough measures out there, the only bio-secure route you can take is to either not have badgers or not have cattle, simple as that.

One of the things that people have been challenging is they've looked at the chart of the increasing rate of testing and the increasing rate of discovery of bovine TB and they appear to go up together, is there an issue of well there is TB in cattle and the more you test, the more TB you find? What was the situation before ...?

I think that's in essence, for about 25 years, we've been using cattle as sentinels of where TB has got to in badgers and we never quite know where that edge in the badgers is, so you're always playing catch-up with it and so we keep expanding the testing area... I'm hoping in the edge area, we may be getting to a situation under the

*new three area system[20], where we can get some handle on where
the disease is in badgers and where it is in cattle.*

*But there is no doubt in cattle that the harder you look, the more
you will uncover but the indications are it doesn't solve the problem, that if that is just a spillback from badgers, all you're doing is
just working out slightly more defined ways of where you've got
infection in the badgers, that the picture is that you remove these
animals and that's why I go back to the Downie era in Cornwall[21],
it made no, you can keep relentlessly moving any animal so at the
slightest hint of bovine TB, but it makes no difference to the overall
problem, you don't solve the background problem.*

*The moment you relax it and it happened in foot and mouth as
well, there were plenty of completely clean herds from the East of
England, the example you always get from foot and mouth is that
you guys moved TB to Cumbria and it caused all sorts of problems
because they came out of the South West.*

*What you forget is that that TB has gone, we've used the skin test,
we've cleared it up, it's disappeared.*

*What people forget about is the clean herds that were actually
moved, sometimes whole herds at a time from the Eastern counties
and the clean areas into the South West, that within six months of
being there started going down with TB. Those cattle were clean*

---

[20] As we are speaking in late 2013, the government is setting out its intentions for
the testing and regulation of farming in different areas of the country,
zoned according to the risk of bovine TB within them. The High risk area
consists of: Cornwall, Devon, Dorset, Somerset, 'Avon' (the zombie county,
as it isn't alive, but refuses to die), Wiltshire, Gloucestershire, Herefordshire,
Worcestershire, Shropshire, Staffordshire and part of Cheshire, Derbyshire,
Warwickshire, Oxfordshire and East Sussex.The Edge area consists of Nottinghamshire, Leicestershire, Northamptonshire, Buckinghamshire, Berk-
shire and Hampshire, and the other parts of the counties mentioned above
(see DEFRA 2013b; and DEFRA 2014a for the full strategy).

[21] Looks to me like he means 'the Downie era in Ireland', but I might be wrong
(*Bovine TB Blog*, 2005). A period between 1988 and 1992 in which very
strict cattle measures were introduced, to apparently no avail.

when they came in but they just came into an environment where TB was existing and hey presto, they started getting that.

You never get that quoted at you, it's always "you put TB all over the place", you can move TB all over the place, we've been constantly doing it to the Eastern Counties but we've never had this picture of persistent, recurrent TB developing there, you just clear it up with the skin test, it goes away, it's only when you've got wildlife that have got it alongside the cattle that you can't get rid of it.

What's your response to this kind of statistic that's been given a lot of profile, that came out of the Krebs trial, that culling would only result in a 16% reduction of the rate of increase of TB?

It's reduction compared with non-cull areas. I view the whole RBCT with some scepticism because it was an interestingly conceived programme, when John Krebs thought of it, he had a proactive, completely removed the badger area, reactive culling area and a control area replicated 10 times.

What happened was that the Conservative government was going to get on and do that but the Labour government came in and took over and decided to carry on with the RBCT, but Jack Cunningham, the then Minister of Agriculture, took John Bourne who was running the experiment to one side and said, "look, I'm not ... removal of badgers completely in any one area at all, you're not allowed to do that", so immediately the whole idea was completely compromised because the plan was if you'd had an area where you totally removed the badgers in a 100 square kilometre area, you could then once and for all, actually ascertain the level of TB that came from badgers and that didn't come from badgers.

But because he was stopped from doing that, it would have been challengingly difficult I do admit, he was stopped from doing it completely and therefore the whole essence of being able to at last define what level of TB came from badgers and what came from cattle, just went out the window.

Then the reactive area got dumped very quickly because it appeared to be causing this perturbation and an increased level of TB, rather than carry on doing it which is what most farmers wanted to see would happen if you carried on doing it long enough, would you have made any difference, because politically it was a much easier way into culling rather than mass cull, you just did it where you had problems and gradually expanded that area ... but that was dumped so at that point, the scientific credibility of it for most farmers just went out the window and that was only two years into it.

We then got foot and mouth which stopped it dead in its tracks, the whole thing was very slow to get going anyway, they decided to use cage trapping which was very open and they were hugely public about where they were going to do it, so they got a mass of protests, so there was huge problems with protestors and traps smashed up and then they gradually got acquired to that and didn't announce the areas anyway, so they got better at it and there was probably only about two years of it where they were doing the job properly.

They never, ever, in the first years, caught as many badgers as we've managed to get, even in Gloucestershire and Somerset is way ahead of anything that was caught in the first years of the Krebs trials, which was supposed to go on for five years, some had five years, some didn't but anyway, we then ended up with this sort of result at the end where, because they picked relatively small areas and they hadn't had huge cooperation from the farmers involved in them, that they got this perturbation effect around the outside where there was an increasing level of TB, where there was upset badgers but a significant decrease in the middle and the decrease in the middle was quite significant.

But we felt, most people that were in those trial areas didn't feel the culling was done particularly well, although John Bourne reckoned he removed 70% of badgers, I don't think they removed anything like 70%. They averaged about 2.5 badgers per square kilometre removed per year, the reality is if you remove 70% of badgers, it doesn't take long to do a quick bit of maths and say at the end of five years, you would have no badgers left at all because they just cannot breed the level to replace them.

The reality is he caught about 2½ badgers per year, virtually every year, some few places he caught slightly more in the first year, some places he caught more in three and four years than he did in the first year, so he never removed 70% of the badgers, certainly at the beginning, he might have got slightly closer to it in the end.

So it was a reduction in badgers but it wasn't anything like the 70% target we were given to do and despite that, there was a significant reduction in TB within those areas, even – and it's still going on even now – it's still there, that reduction, so his conclusion was based on his costs of trapping which were done under government conditions and it was purely an economic decision, he didn't say "culling won't work", he said "I cannot see how culling can take place if the government are going to do it", there were various bits that get left out of his statement. "Culling in the way we did it and at the cost we did it, could play no part in the future TB control" and that's very different from just saying "culling cannot …" and he called his work, "the science", I mean John Bourne was known for his arrogance but that is the ultimate in arrogance, "the science on TB and badger culling". Load of bollocks. It's the other bit of evidence you take and it was all … in Thornbury, between the River Severn and the M5, they removed in the late 70s, early 80s, they just removed badgers, within four years there was no cattle TB at all, absolutely none, for 10 years they had no cattle TB there whatsoever, it just disappeared. It cost them a lot of money to do, they were doing it by gassing, it took two years to get rid of them and another four years to make sure they hadn't come back, but no cattle TB observed. But it wasn't a replicated trial, there was no control area, it was just an empirical experiment and that was done in …, it was done in Steeple Lees, back before then, smaller areas but exactly the same result. Remove the badgers, cattle TB disappears. There's just so much evidence about it.

In Ireland, East Offaly [at the] start, [and] within the four counties[22], exactly the same, significantly reduced the badger population, cattle TB almost collapses. The evidence is overwhelming but it just, it's the difficulty that you have to be very thorough with culling and it's this social nature of badgers and the fact we've allowed the badger population to build up to such enormously high levels.

We have culling on this farm, I tell you this out of interest but we were catching, when it was legal and they had cage trapping, between us and our neighbours, 700 odd acres, probably three square

---

[22] For a paper dicussing the implications of the East Offaly Badger Research Project that ran between 1988 and 1995, see Máirtín et al. (1998); for a discussion of the Four Counties that took place between 1997 and 2002, see Griffin et al. (2005).

kilometres, they caught 120 badgers in that area, it was one badger to every four cattle we had at the time and probably 25% of those were showing growth pathology of TB which probably means 60-70% of them were infected with it. Frightening. Just the sheer numbers and level of disease in them.

Tell me about the last issue then that I think a lot of protestors and opponents have raised and talked about, which is what you mentioned with perturbation. You mentioned that in the trial, that there were issues around the outside of a core where the reduction had taken place, what's your view on that?

I think that that appears to be a genuine issue and it's exactly why we have chosen much bigger culling areas because the bigger the area you get, the less the perimeter is in relation to the area in the middle that you're trying to protect. The harder the boundaries – because John Bourne never had any particularly hard boundaries – he just used parish maps and small roads, whereas the licence condition we're operating in is trying to use A road motorways, rivers and much bigger areas, so mathematically we should be significantly reducing the potential perturbation.

It seems to be tied up with this social nature of badgers but the interesting thing is it happens so rapidly, that it actually I think reinforces this whole indication that there is a pretty massive level of disease in the badgers, which actually doesn't take very much disturbing, when they come under stress, the disease will develop in them, that stress may be disturbance in their social communities, whatever, in this situation it can be weather as well, a combination of both could be pretty lethal. But you know, the whole reason is to try and get a persistently good cull which you've got to do over a number of years, obviously as quickly as you reasonably can do it but that depends on the method you choose to do it and the level of protest you get while you're doing it.

The interesting thing with the cull we've just done, that if there is any indication of perturbation down there in terms of manifesting itself in increased cattle TB, I would lay significant percentage of it at the door of the protestors who are at times, just camped out on top of badger sets for the best part of three months.

What those badgers made of it all I don't know because their whole behaviour pattern would have been shot to bits, either they'd have scarpered or I would think there's an element of them died underground, certainly probably started urinating and defecating underground which is utterly unnatural for a badger, so I would think ironically, they may have caused a lot of perturbation or even in fact caused a very welfare unfriendly death of badgers by the nature of what they were doing all the time and of course, because they were stopping us going in and cleanly shooting a lot of the badgers because we just couldn't get access to the areas, it was probably creating the potential for perturbation that might well happen but this is year one of a four-year cull and we've just got to take it as we see it.

Are the badgers that are caught and killed, are they going to be tested in any way to find out if they had TB?

No, because the assumption, (a) it's very, very costly, testing badgers for TB, firstly you've got to use a Category 3 lab these days because TB is a dangerous pathogen and there aren't many of those around and (b) a lot of the time, badgers, because it doesn't manifest itself in lesions like it does in cattle and human beings, it is quite difficult to see TB so that salami slicing a badger and then culturing that which takes anything from 6-12 weeks, very complicated and it's a difficult bug to transport about.

There's really no point. We're in an area where we know from past culling and the nature of TB and cattle, that there is endemic TB in the badgers and that is just accepted. That was accepted by all government parties who set this up. I think they did examine a few badgers up there but it was really very few and they were absolutely riddled with it because I think they were just a bit worried about handling them. But the vast majority of badgers will look quite healthy but it doesn't mean to say they aren't carrying TB.

It's purely a cost issue, I know politically it would have been nice to have persuaded the government to do it but it would have taken months to do and cost an enormous amount of money and of course, the government just doesn't have any money at the moment, that's why they asked us to do the culling.

Would it be cheaper to test a random selection sample of those?

*It was deemed to be unnecessary by AHVLA[23], by Natural Eng-
land, by DEFRA, by anybody who's set up these things, yes the general public thought this was being set up to test the badgers whether they had TB or not, to see whether it made any difference on
cattle, it wasn't even designed to do that, it was just designed to test
the effectiveness of free shooting badgers, that was all the pilot cull
was designed for, to check that it was safe, to check that it was humane and to check that you could remove a significant amount in
a short period of time. It wasn't designed to do all these other
things.*

**You've mentioned a couple of times, it would seem that there is
a certain amount of conflict between people who think like you,
you need to go ahead with the cull to try and deal with it and
protestors and others who don't agree ...**

As an interim policy.

**... who have been there and to some extent disrupted what has
been going on. Do you think there's a way out of that conflict?**

*I don't think there is. I think the views on it are so polarised and
it's partly because the science is, the science that John Bourne put
forward, the RBCT is so equivocal in the way it can be interpreted,
that we've got this problem today, that there is no doubt when you
look at all the evidence from Ireland, from previous culls done in
this country, from when we were ... trapping from even the RBCT,
that culling is the only thing that has shown any significant effect
on reducing the level of TB in cattle in those endemic areas.*

*In the Eastern Counties you don't have the problem but you bloo-
dy well will in 10 years' time, if you don't stop it somewhere and at
the moment, we can see it in the edge areas beginning to pick that
up and hopefully will show us, I think, that TB in badgers is ahead*

---

[23] What do these acronyms mean, Humphrey? Forgive me, minister. The
   AHVLA stands for the Animal Health and Veterinary Laboratories
   Agency, and the APHA stands for the Animal and Plant Health Agency.

of TB in cattle and that somehow you've got to stop it and it's not cattle giving it to badgers, it's badgers giving it to cattle but it's spreading in badgers giving it to badgers across the country.

So you could rid the South West of every single cow in it for 10 years and you'd come back and put them down and within three years, you'd have exactly the same problem, it's sod all to do with the cattle, it's to do with the frigging badgers.

It's how you deal with that and I don't have any easy answers, vacination may be the longer term most useful tool we have but it's just not ready to use yet and the only other tool we've got is culling of badgers, just reducing the whole disease load.

Biosecurity, you've got to try but it will really, there's no single experiment, people say "you've got to be bio secure", there's no experimental evidence anywhere that it's ever made any difference.

How would you try and manage the sort of conflict that has resulted?

I think probably one of the most effective ways forward is if we could find some way of identifying the worst TB infected sets in any area because there is no doubt, the disease pressures, Woodchester Park[24] is an example of that, within the badger community, vary from social group to social group at any one time but if you can find a way of testing the level of severity of TB in any one badger sett or population, at any one time and cull out those worst areas all the time, now that might be a PCR[25] technique using latrines or ideally air sampling, if you could do it because it needs something that's relatively quick and easy and therefore not just an indication that you've got embolus there but the level of embolus relative to the next set, which is really what you're trying to look at.

---

[24] Since 1975 DEFRA have funded studies of the badger population in this well-protected site in Gloucestershire.

[25] A polymerase chain reaction test, which is a way of analysing or testing for the DNA of an organism.

I think there should be some mileage in training dogs to do it but nobody's ever done that yet because they're pretty good at that sort of thing. If you could do that and then you could use gassing as a technique to remove a sett at a time, when you found the most dangerous setts, you might find you could have a much more targeted culling which I think would be probably more acceptable to farmers and the general public, particularly if you've got a reliable method of doing it and the trouble is we don't have that reliable method of doing it, we've got a government that's refused to investigate gassing of setts, which has to be the most effective and probably humane way of dealing with animals, if you have got to cull, far, far more safe and effective than free shooting but for 20 years I've been imploring governments to get on and do that work but they just haven't, politically they've fought shy of doing it.

I think we need in-sett culling and some way of finding out the worst affected setts in any one area, at any one time and dealing with those. That I think would be a big step forward and then the use of vaccination, if you could couple all that together, I think you might have quite an effective tool.

Spoligotypes. Now, there's a word. I am, during this interview, out of my depth a number of times, but spoligotypes drag me farthest from shore. Back in the office, I look them up. Spoligotyping is a kind of genotyping, a way to identify genetic differences, that was developed for tuberculosis. My interviewee talked about maps of spoligotypes data, so that's what I look for. There's a website, called 'mbovis.org' run by Noel Smith and Rainer Hilscher that has them. It's a site for scientists by scientists, aiming at 'giving authoritative names to spoligotype patterns'. The site shows two maps, showing, it says, "the location of 50 isolates randomly selected from each of the eleven most common spoligotypes [except SB0140 (VLA type 9)] found in Great Britain. Genotypes are labelled by International type followed by VLA type in brackets. Twelve spoligotypes (those shown here and VLA type 9) account for over 99% of all isolates of bovine tuberculosis in GB." The blurb carries on with a bit of technical stuff, and finishes with: "We do not like being referred to as 'ferrets'." (Smith and Hilscher 2006).

Odd. Underneath, there's a reference to an academic paper written by Noel Smith and four others, and I decide to see if Exeter has paid for access to this one (Smith et al. 2006). Oh good, it has.

Well, that was an eye-opener. The paper has three maps, the first two on the website (maps a and b), and a third (map c) – it shows the distribution of different subtypes of the missing SB0140 spoligo-type. Here they are...

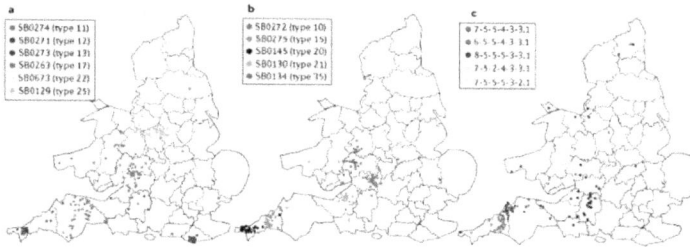

Figure 4.1. The geographical localisation of Mycobacterium bovis geno-types in Great Britain.

Source: Figure 3, Smith et al. 2006, p. 676. The authors explain that maps a and b "Show the location of 50 isolates randomly selected from each of the 11 most common spoligotypes (except SB0140 (VLA type 9)) found in Great Britain. Genotypes are labelled by international type followed by VLA type in brackets." Map c "The geographical localisation of five of the most common VNTR types of spoligotype SB0140 (VLA type 9) representing 87% of all type 9 isolates." These 12 spoligotypes account for over 99% of all isolates of bovine tuberculosis in Great Britain.

In fact, the authors of the paper are using spoligotyping and another method of genotyping called variable nucleotide tandem repeat typing, or VNTR. VNTR gives the authors something like, but not exactly, subtypes of the main spoligotypes. But the spoligotypes that have been identified are not just different, some of them are closely related. This is where the details start to get confusing, but I'll try to explain as I go along. Two overall points are more or less clear. First, most of the bovine TB in the country is part of or de-rived from the SB0140 spoligotype. Second, there is much less var-iation in the types than in France, so that in the *British Isles*, 60% of bovine TB cases are associated with spoligotype SB0140, but in France it takes 11 different spoligotypes to make up two-thirds of the cases (they seem to say that when you take Northern Ireland out, this figure rises to 85%, but they use the term 'clonal complex', and it's not clear they mean the same group of spoligotypes as be-fore. Probably) (Smith et al. 2006, p.677). What's even more surprising is that France is nearly TB free – logically you would expect less diversity in France and more diversity in Britain, because Britain has many more cases, but in fact, it's the other way around. What's going on?

Noel Smith and his colleagues think there are two possibilities. The first is that it has always been like this – SB0140 just does better in Britain. The authors point to evidence from human cases of bovine TB that suggests this is not true. These cases tend to emerge in older patients who were exposed to bovine TB when younger, for example, drinking unpasteurised milk. These cases suggest that there was, in fact, a wider variety of different bovine TB spoligotypes around in the past. The second is that, for some reason, SB0140 has some kind of genetic advantage that allowed it to keeping going during a period of population decline when other types failed – the 'bottleneck theory'. What sort of advantage? Again, two possibilities come up. It could be a genetic alteration which makes bovine TB easier to maintain and be transmitted in the badger population. That's what my knowledgeable farmer – I've just christened him 'Henry' – that's what Henry thinks. The alternative is that the genetic alteration means that cattle with this strain of bovine TB are less likely to be detected by the test. Funny how Henry didn't mention this. It's their story, so I'll let them tell it:

"One possible selective advantage that the SB0140 clonal complex might have is an ability to escape or evade the test and slaughter protocol. In the British Isles, an extract of M. tuberculosis was used in an immunological test to identify cattle infected with M. bovis until 1975 ... In an attempt to improve the specificity of the test, this strain was subsequently replaced by an M. bovis strain called AN5, which was isolated from an English cow in the 1940s. The AN5 strain has been shown to be phylogenetically distinct from strains of the spoligotype SB0140 clonal complex... It is reasonable to suggest that a clone marked by spoligotype pattern SB0140 was distributed throughout the British Isles before the introduction of the bovine tuberculosis control strategies, and that this clone had some small advantage to evade these protocols and rose to a high frequency as other clones were eliminated" (Smith et al. 2006, p. 678).

But, somewhere in the middle of there, they also say:

"Among the 30,000 strains from Great Britain that have been spoligotyped, no strain bearing the AN5 spoligotype pattern (SB0268) has been identified"

So it's a bit difficult to see why SB0140 should be less likely to be detected by the test than any other strain – unless what is important is not just the absence of the AN5 spoligotype pattern, but full phylogenetic distinctiveness. So, maybe the test works well, maybe it doesn't – research is ongoing, trying to find better bovine TB extracts to use in the test. But what about the badgers? Does research into spoligotypes show any geographical link between the strain of bovine TB found in cattle and the strain found in badgers?

I look at one of the articles about this that Noel Smith and his colleagues refer to. That's interesting, it's by members of the Independent Scientific Group that was involved in the Randomised Badger Culling Trials. Anyway, this is what Rosie Woodroffe and her many colleagues have to say:

"We show, for the first time, that M. bovis infections in badgers and cattle are spatially associated at a scale of 1–2 km. Badgers and cattle infected with the same strain type of M. bovis are particularly closely correlated. These observational data support the hypothesis that transmission occurs between the two host species; however, they cannot be used to evaluate the relative importance of badger-to-cattle and cattle-to-badger transmission" (Woodroffe et al. 2005, p. 852).

So, maybe it's badgers, maybe it isn't. With all of that still going down, I dunk my brain back in the Internet soup. There's an article in *Farmers Guardian* (2007) that shows the farming community is onto this – although it seems to have been picked up in a different way from the academic papers – something that was echoed by Henry. The argument is that the overlap of infections involving the same strain of bovine TB in cattle and badgers, and their local clustering, implicates badgers in maintaining and transmitting the disease back to cattle, because not only are they a reservoir, they also tend to stay in the same place. The claim is that if cattle-to-cattle transmission is the most important reason for the spread of bovine TB, different spoligotypes would be mixed all around the country, without any sign of clustering. I'm getting deeper in the soup when I find this – it's a response to a page about spoligotypes on a blog called 'Bovine TB Blog' which was published in 2006 – before even the *Farmers' Guardian* caught on. The page starts with:

"The map of GB bTB outbreaks, as determined by the spoligotyping ferrets at VLA, is not - as one would expect if cattle to cattle transmission and cattle movements were the primary cause of the disease, - like a kaleidoscope of scattered strains" (Bovine TB Blog 2006).

I think I've found the cause of that very strange comment about ferrets earlier. Why ferrets? Anyway, the response is written by Trevor Lawson, of The Badger Trust. He says that the 'scattering' theory only works if cattle are moved relatively evenly across the country, but they're not. Most cattle movements are local. The owner of the blog, 'Matthew', replies. He sounds cross. Cross, but knowledgeable. The source of information about cattle movements is probably rubbish, and anyway, each county has two or three different strains of bovine TB in distinct geographical areas (local movements would create local mixing); any infected cattle that are moved are picked up by the test and there's no reason to doubt the test as it's the same one that has been used in successful bovine TB reduction programmes in other countries (but maybe they didn't have SB0140); the VLA's (Smith et al.!) calls for more research into the test stinks of opportunism (maybe that's why they're 'ferrets'), especially when few cases of bovine TB are identified at the slaughterhouse (in other words, the cow passed the test, even though it was infected). Matthew's passion grows. He is very critical of the RBCT – in his mind they were not 'culling trials' but 'dispersal teams':

"No bought in cattle, and a healthy respect for 'our badgers'. Unfortunately that comfort blanket disappeared when 'our' badgers became infected and Bourne's badger dispersal teams stirred the whole lot up, leaving social groups shattered and the area heaving with sick, stressed and very infectious badgers.

400 head of cattle on five farms down this valley paid the ultimate price of this prevarication. As did the hundreds of dead badgers found on roads and in fields in various states of emaciation.

Mr. Lawson, when herds like those belonging to the contributors to [this] site, go under continued bTb restriction, and 'No bought in Cattle' appear on their TB 99's,[26] it is up to those denying the role of the badger to hypothesise an alternative source of infection (Bovine TB Blog 2006)".

---

[26] This was a questionnaire used during the RBCT to gather data on the types of farms and herds that were suffering bovine TB breakdowns.

Dispersal. In Matthew's mind, the lack of hard boundaries around the culling areas in the RBCT wasn't just a design fault, it was an outrage. I pick up the subject with the next farmer I interview, Jonathan, a smart professional man, a good, clear communicator, although incidentally, he also doesn't farm within the cull zone. He is Somerset-based, though, which is handy because when I look at the map of west Gloucestershire, I can spot hard boundaries quite easily, but in Somerset, I can't. Well, I say 'look at the maps'. There aren't any, not official ones. From what I've been hearing, not even the police have them. Only the 'Badger Killers' website is confident enough to publish maps of the zones. There's the M5 and the River Severn to the east, the M50 to the north, and – well, not much to the west, but there is, eventually, and well outside the suspected cull zone, the River Wye. In the Somerset zone there's – not a lot. The Bristol Channel to the north. So, Jonathan, hard boundaries?

The hard boundaries in Gloucestershire are pretty obvious. Can you tell me what are the hard boundaries for the West Somerset area?

There's coastal, there was a hill lying, some main roads and yes two hills were the main thing because there's a lower density of badger populations in those areas, so therefore spread out isn't going to be there. Conurbations can be used, rivers, motorways, there are all sorts of things that could potentially equal hard boundary.

Hills. Roads. Because a badger has never crossed a road successfully. Or gone uphill. Perturbation and hard boundaries is now something I'm going to ask about more often. It's the reason why a cull could make things worse, but solve the problem of hard boundaries and the benefits of culling become more obvious. The cull's supporters claim they've nailed it. Really?

Chapter 5

Vaccinators

So, everyone – hard boundaries. A quick survey of the interview material, then, of those I speak to in the coming weeks, people who support using a badger vaccine, vets (who don't), and a mystery star guest. In this order, they are Harriet, Ingrid, Julia, Larry, Katherine, Richard. This is what Harriet thinks.

The view of some of those I've spoken to who are supporting the cull, is that that trial failed in many respects, that there was foot and mouth in the middle of it and all of these kinds of things, but one of the key problems of design and not just event that arose was that there were not hard boundaries to the sites that were chosen and where the culling took place, so that it almost built in a perturbation problem, whereas in these trial areas, they've been selected for having hard boundaries.

What hard boundaries did they have?

In Gloucestershire, it's quite clear, there's the River Severn, the River Wye and two motorways, it's an area within hard boundaries ...

So they don't cross motorways ...

And in Somerset, I think it's less clear but it's highlands, large roads, the sea. What's your response to that?

Having released one badger one side of a river and watched it swim over the river, find out it should be on the other side and swim back again and then run off in the opposite direction, kind of makes me feel that maybe rivers aren't particularly a hard boundary.

Motorways, have they got fencing to stop the badgers coming through? Because they can go through a ditch quite easily and unless it's actually fenced in a way that it's going to stop badgers from going on there, there's no such thing as a hard boundary. And even if you have got something that has got a hard boundary and you can prove that you can kill badgers in an area where there's a hard boundary, you cannot move that to somewhere else where there's a TB problem that has no hard boundaries.

So you can't transfer it anywhere else, so what is the point of looking for something that isn't going to be available, when you have TB problems? If you can't transpose that research, it's useless, it just shows it happened and it worked but actually we can't copy this because where we want to go, there is no hard boundaries.

That's a 'no', then. Next, Ingrid's view.

What would be your response to the idea of these hard boundaries?

The only hard boundary around here is the [Severn/Bristol Channel], end of story.

So you wouldn't be convinced by the use of roads or the use of rivers...?

No, badgers can swim, they're very good swimmers, the River ... which was the river that comes down... badgers would have no difficulty in crossing that. The only hard boundary within [this] cull area from as far as I can tell, is the [Severn/Bristol Channel]. There are no other hard boundaries within it.

Now at one point they were talking about a 2-kilometre ring around the cull areas, a vaccination ring, I don't think that ever took place, there's no evidence that any badgers were vaccinated within a 2-kilometre ring. The randomised badger cull trial recommended that there needed to be hard boundaries, they recommended that you needed to cull badgers over a very large area. Well the cull area itself was a large area but the actual shooting within that was centred around some very key areas, it didn't take place across all of them and I don't know how it was organised but it was more random I think than perhaps people would have guessed.

But the hard boundaries thing, they weren't able to – as I say the [Severn/Bristol Channel] is the only hard boundary.

Would a motorway count as a hard boundary in your view?

It would depend how well fenced off it was, you do see road traffic casualties on motorways, in fact there was a dead badger on the road this week, on the M5 and one on the flyover of Junction ..., so badgers do get on motorways, it's true that when big motorways go through, probably in a lot of new roads, the big major roads, they do put in underpasses these days for badgers...So you can get movement from one side to the other, even under the underpasses ...

How broad does a river have to be before it becomes a boundary? Do you have a sense of that?

I don't but I do know that badgers can swim in quite large rivers. I know someone who had a badger that used to visit them and it used to swim across the river, so they're quite capable of it.

Alright. Next: Julia.

One of the arguments that were made by supporters of the cull is that in fact what they're doing is improving on what happened during the RBCT by choosing areas that have hard boundaries in order to limit perturbation. Choosing quite a large area and choosing those areas with hard boundaries and culling within them to minimise the problem of perturbation. What's your view of that?

Well they haven't have they? That's their story, but they haven't done that, there are no hard boundaries apart from the [Severn/Bristol Channel] that's the only hard boundary. And we know some of the boundaries and they're actually very minor country lanes. But like I say, Chris Cheeseman held a meeting on this very subject and they put this to him that they would do it better than the RBCT. And he said, "You haven't, the RBCT was chosen to have as many hard boundaries are possible in the trial areas, but there are no hard boundaries apart from the sea to a badger."

This isn't going very well, is it? Next! (Larry)

So I don't know how you view how successful hard boundaries may have been in ...[this area], and how that might help with that issue?

Well having knowledge of the boundaries pretty much... I mean the sea is one boundary, so that's pretty effective. There's a busy road at the other side of it, which is I think had limited effect really. In the middle of the night, there's not many cars on it, so a road, although it's a hard boundary, it's not like a motorway where noth-ing can really cross it, unless it's very quiet. I think the boundaries used were useful, but some farms have been dissected down the middle. One side is someone's farm in the cull, and one side isn't. Whether that surely stopped them I don't know. I think if there were fewer protestors around people would have culled in areas that weren't in the cull. It is going on now, for sure. It's illegal ob-viously, but if I was a farmer, I would have a long time ago decided to deal with it myself.

So the boundaries, yes the perturbation effect, I think the idea was that the area was so large that you get perturbation around the boundaries perhaps, that it would be very unlikely for badgers to travel the distance right into the cull area. So you may see a wor-sening on the boundaries, I don't know.

A 'hard' boundary cutting a farm in two. Hmm. Next! (Katherine)

One of the claims being made about these trial culls and pre-sumably any others that would follow them, is that they're de-signed as improvements upon the previous set of badger culling trials because they have hard boundaries, the idea being that the issue of perturbation will be dealt with better than it was pre-viously.

What's your response to that argument?

The first thing is we don't actually know how these trials have been designed because DEFRA hasn't released that information, even though they've had legal petitions to try and get them to do that, we don't have the information. Obviously hard boundaries are meant to be there but if you actually look at a map of where they shot ..., okay there's sea on one side and there's hill on the other but there's some huge gaps either end where there could quite, I mean obviously badgers weren't going to swim the [Severn/Bristol Channel] but they could certainly move out of the other end, so I was quite surprised the first somebody being on the ground actually put a map of it because I really did expect it to have, I don't know why except probably not thought out the areas but I was thinking M5, ...[hills], [Severn/Bristol Channel] - absolutely barricaded in but it's really not, there were open ends there and one would expect the perturbation, it will be interesting to see what happens to TB in cattle on those edges. But there are some significant edges there and I would expect us to have perturbation.

I agree that trying to have hard boundaries is probably a good way of overcoming that aspect to some extent and I guess people would argue that Thornbury was the example of the trial where we had hard boundaries, repeatedly culled badgers and cattle TB went down. But we're not going to be able to roll that policy out and I think even though they tend to do it in [the nearest cull area], it's not very convincing when you map it.

It's quite clear in West Gloucestershire, there's two rivers and a motorway ...

Yes, badgers can swim, I know Chris Cheeseman would immediately come back to you and say but badgers can swim but yes, certainly creating some sort of geographical limitations is likely to limit perturbation outside of the area.

Hard boundaries, they work and they don't. Next! (Richard)

One of the arguments that's made by the supporting of the cull is, well actually we're taking on board some of what was said about what was done in these Krebs's trials, by the scientists that did them in their report. Specifically that future culls needed to be done over a large area, and with hard boundaries in order to reduce the effect of perturbation, which was one of the consequences?

Well that's part of the reason why they've chosen this area round here, because it has hard boundaries.

So to come back to the issue of perturbation on the cull then, what are you saying? Are you saying you're not sure it's an issue?

I'm saying that I think it probably is an issue, and it's a particularly worrying one for us because we're on the very edge of the culling area. But it's something that we're prepared to put up with and hope that it won't be too serious, in order to help the cull to be a success. But I wouldn't say that it's not an issue at all.

Spot the cull supporter at the end – a farmer, participating in the cull, in the cull zone (got one, finally!). Yes, we've got hard boundaries, but it might not do us any good. Having been to the farm, I couldn't say I spotted what the hard boundary was. A particularly steep slope?

There's something else in those answers that bothers me. There we go. No maps. The only way you could know what the boundaries were was if you were involved with the cull, or believed what you saw on 'Badger Killers' (and even their maps aren't very precise). The police, as far as I have heard, don't even know. Isn't there a problem with that? It's not just that without knowing what the boundaries are (supposed to be), it's impossible to say, in three, four or nine years' time, whether the culls were a success or whether they just caused more bovine TB through perturbation. It's not just that without knowing the boundary, it's impossible to keep tabs on whether night-time activity involving 4x4s and guns is illegal or not. It's impossible to make any clear judgment now on whether the claims made by the cull operators stand up. We don't live in a world where people are prepared to take your word for it, not the word of government, not anyone else masquerading as an authority figure, not anymore. The cull operators have a good reason, though. They can't give too many details because of the threat of intimidation and interference by protestors. But I'm beginning to wonder whether this isn't just a convenient bogeyman. There is, after all, quite a big difference between defamation, or being frightened by a bunch of people in balaclavas, and being run over, burnt, or shot by someone in a balaclava.

Yes, but – going round again – so far, haven't the cull supporters had, by a margin, the better arguments, the better information? Can't I accept that they are genuinely concerned about the threat from animal rights protestors who have, in the past, crossed a line? And aren't I, by taking a series of quotes from cull opponents, being a bit unfair? I don't know, but in the next couple of interviews, talking to people involved in vaccinating badgers, the question of boundaries of different kinds comes up again and again.

It's getting towards Christmas, and the next place I visit is ready for it. It feels comfortable – there's something familiar about the part utility, part beat, tea, biscuits, and a couple of dogs atmosphere. As we get going, I discover I'm in the company of a tough-, critical-minded, intellectually decisive woman, well-connected and articulate. I'm relieved. Here, at last, is a cull opponent I can stand up against Farmer Spoligotype. This is Harriet.

I think the press and media have a huge bad effect because they love it, it's an absolutely wonderful story, it doesn't matter where you can go, if you talk to someone about badgers, immediately it's bovine TB and those nasty farmers. So from their point of view of photographs and all the rest of it, it's fantastic and I think this side, that side, press have been so busy looking at each other that they've failed to notice that the one person that is to blame for all of this, is DEFRA because why are we implementing now, things that they suggested at the end of the Randomised Badger Culling Trial in 2007? Why has it taken six years to bring in those things that they suggested should have been done?

Can you tell me a bit about what those range of things are and how they might count as alternatives to culling?

One of the things that they were slow at bringing in was calf passports, which we now have. I defy you to go to any market and see the biosecurity of people walking in and out with wellingtons and cleaning their cars and their lorries. We have now only just decided that cattle going to a show ought to be tested because the farmers say 'well that's my best cows who surely doesn't need to be tested' and why would you want to take your best cow to a show and have the general public walking up and down behind your cows, going from one cow to the other?

They're now thinking of zoning the country so that people will be asked not to buy cattle from certain areas. Why is it you can choose, why isn't it actually compulsory? We have a TB problem, we could have a non-TB area of Britain and a TB area of Britain and it should be totally down the line and you know, if it means instead of killing badgers, we can give more compensation to these people that have got TB outbreaks, so be it. Why should TB animals still be on a farm three months after it's been tested positive? Why aren't we saying to them, give you a grant, you can put in the biosecurity that you need to metal line your gates, to actually do all the things to stop contact between badger and cattle?

There's just so many things that are there but they're not really hammering it home.

One of the counter arguments against too much concern about cattle movements is an argument which says there's a relationship between the type of TB in the wildlife in an area and the type of TB contracted by cattle, so if you move cattle outside of that area, they might take TB with them but it goes out of the area, it's discovered in that area but it doesn't stick, it dies away because the TB in some way can't continue in the ...

Why is it increasing then? Why is the area increasing? Why is the ...?

The argument is that there's a front where there's a kind of relationship between badgers and cattle, badgers with TB are moving north-eastwards ...

Badgers are moving? [laughs]

So the TB is moving through the badger population north-eastwards and developing relationship with, creating a cycle of infection with the cattle in that area so the TB hotspots in cattle are catching up with where TB is in the badger population and then you might get spots of infection in cattle, where cattle have moved out of that area to different parts of the country but it doesn't sustain because there's no wildlife reservoir in that area of the country, to help it sustain.

The first argument is and there's someone who does a very good talk, he's absolutely sure that he got TB from badgers on his land and every slide, everything he talks about is you can't argue, it's got to be badgers on your land.

The one question that makes it fall down is you say, "have your neighbours got TB?" because badgers don't live on farms. If they haven't then your problem isn't badgers. A farm will probably have, depending on its size, anything from one to two to six different social groups, those social groups don't just live on that farm, they're moving between farms, so if they haven't got TB, it can't be your badgers. It doesn't make sense and to talk about it moving, you've got different strains, there's 58 different strains of bovine TB so there's different areas where different strains can be found.

The biggest problem you've got is the test for cattle and the fact that it's only 80% specific, so 8 out of 10 cows are correctly diagnosed and 2 aren't [Robbie points out later she means 'sensitive', not 'specific': but that's ok, this is a chat, not a treatise]. When you multiply that by the fact that since the 1990s, I think we've lost a third of our milk herds or our farms but the number of cattle within the trade has remained the same, it just means you have bigger herds and if you have bigger herds, you multiply the number of animals that are false negatives that remain within a herd when they're testing, and it's known that when a cow is pregnant, early stages of pregnancy, it won't react to the test if it's a positive animal and if it's in the final stages of the disease, because the test picks up antibodies, it doesn't pick up the disease, once it's succumbed to disease and it's not creating antibodies anymore, it won't get picked up.

So a very high percentage and I think it's almost 25% of our cattle are now being picked up at abattoir stage, even though those animals have gone through a testing regime. And what's really interesting is the first badger with TB was found in the 1970s and speak to any scientist and they will tell you that the transmission between badger and cattle is overwhelming but they still don't know how it happens.

If you can't find that out in 40 years, I don't think it's quite so much of a problem as you seem to think it is. And the next question is, we can't deal with a problem in our cattle if we don't look at the wildlife reservoir. Look at Australia, look at Canada with the white-tailed deer, look at all those things that have only been controlled by us doing something to them. Then you say "but we've got a vaccine for cows, we've got a DIVA test that tells us the difference between an infected animal and an infectious animal" and it's been tested in, is it Mexico and Ethiopia? And the argument is we can't count those tests because it hasn't been carried out in the EU and it's not the same when you do things in other countries, as it would be if you did it in the EU. But we can still talk about possums in Australia [she means New Zealand, they're indigenous in Australia, but that doesn't affect the point she's making] and we can still talk about white-tailed deer in Canada, totally different countries, animals that aren't indigenous and suggest that we've got to follow that but actually, where we've tested, we can't count that because that's not the EU.

We either do listen or we don't and in both of the situations, with the possums and with the white-tailed deer, particular with the possums where they just put poison down everywhere, they have reduced the population dramatically but it's actually increased the amount of TB in the population left and they're now going down the vaccination route.

No slight imprecision of phrasing allowed. I'm not sure I'm entirely convinced, though, by her reasoning about badgers and farms. Badgers' territories are not as big as most farms – at least not now, so whether neighbouring farms are at risk of suffering from bovine TB depends on the size of the farm, the contiguity of its land, the position of the main badger sett in relation to the edges of the farm and what the neighbours are farming. So I'm not convinced by her dismissal of spoligotypes, her conviction that it's to do with movements of cattle, because there might be 58 different types, but there's basically one that matters. There's a hint of starting with a conclusion and arguing towards it, but then as far as I can tell, that's no different from what Farmer Spoligotype or anyone else is doing.

I count six references on a theme of boundaries - passports, biosecurity, zoning, farm boundaries, tests, other countries. Maybe there's a seventh, too: vaccination. After Christmas, I find myself talking to a vaccinator. We talk in her living room, at the back of the house, looking out over the garden, a few damp birds, and the rain coming in over the hillside. Like Harriet, Ingrid is a serious, decisive speaker, well-informed and, like a farmer, expert in a practical way.

I'm a trained lay vaccinator, volunteer ... I decided to go down that route ... because I wanted to have a positive thing to be able to do, to offer farmers and landowners, as an alternative to the cull and you know, scientifically, badger vaccination has been proved to work, there is scientific evidence to say that there's a big percentage reduction of badgers, some 74% who don't show a positive test to bovine TB and that recent research also, which was published last year, suggests that cubs that are born into vaccinated groups, have an 80% less chance of catching TB as well. That all adds up to significantly reducing the risks of badgers passing on bovine TB to cattle and so if you believe from that perspective, that vaccination works and the Welsh government have gone down that route, then it might make you realise that it was devastating to realise, despite huge public outcry against it, that this government decided to go ahead with two pilot culls. It was a really, really bad thing from my perspective. ...

As a licensed lay vaccinator, I have to stick to extremely strict protocols that are laid down by the AHVLA [APHA, now] and also Natural England, who licence me to vaccinate badgers and those protocols centre around badger welfare, they centre around biosecurity on farms, they centre around safety. I have to stick to those, that means that I have to make sure that the vehicles that I use and the other volunteers use are properly sprayed with the right consistency of disinfectant, so that we're not carrying disease from one farm holding to another. I have to make sure that the badger welfare is absolute so that where I deploy traps, how long badgers are likely to be in a trap, all of that has to be taken into account and done properly.

During the cull, people found evidence that badgers, they were supposed to be properly bagged up, they were found just slung in the back of pick-ups, there was no evidence at all that vehicles travelling from one land holding to another sprayed their vehicles with the proper disinfectant. There were traps found with badgers that, I think the traps had been put in a, I haven't seen this myself but I've got no reason to believe it wasn't true, in a ditch that because of the very heavy rain, the ditch was filling up and the badgers were absolutely panicked.

We had a 200-metre protection zone agreed by Natural England, around a very, very large area that we vaccinated, within the ... cull area and Natural England said that no culling operations should take place within that 200-metre zone. We found traps on two occasions placed within that 200 metre zone, we also had an incident one night when a cull operative was found, unfortunately he managed to drive off before the landowners could catch up with him but there was an empty gun case in the back of his vehicle which was parked on their land one night and that was protected vaccinated land and when this person was interviewed by the police, apparently this person said they'd miscounted the gates and they should have been two gates further down. Well even two gates further down, that person would have been within a 200-metre protection zone which they should never have been on.

So it all adds up to a total lack of integrity about the way in which it was carried out.

And so these things all add up to a situation where there is a total lack of trust in the way it was carried out, it will have probably made the situation worse for farmers rather than helped them at all and instead of wasting all that money, and a big percentage of it will be taxpayers' money, that should have been spent on progressing cattle vaccination and carrying on badger vaccination in hot spots, until cattle vaccine becomes a reality because that's realistically the only thing that's going to help the farming community get rid of bovine TB.

Let's talk about vaccination, tell me about what you do and how that works.

... we offer farmers and landowners badger vaccination at a cost of £25 per badger. The vaccine costs £14.50 or it has done the last two years, the rest of that £25 goes towards paying some of the other consumables costs that we have.

Everybody in the team ... give their time for free and it means that we can offer farmers within the cull areas, a really good viable alternative ... there is a growing interest. The process is about a fortnight and you start off with surveying the area to get an indication of badger numbers, we set up night cameras at strategic places ... to check out badger activity and to get a bit more accurate idea of numbers. Then we put bait marks out in key areas like main setts, sometimes subsidiary setts, big latrining sites and if those peanuts disappear – and we do that for 2-3 days – then we can be fairly certain that if we put a trap there, then we should be successful in catching the badger. Our trapping success rate is very good. The traps are secured in the open position and baited over the next 6-7 days, then set to capture for 2 nights and captured badgers are then vaccinated. In all, the process takes about 2 weeks. ...

What are you trying to achieve through the vaccination?

We're trying to achieve a number of things, (1) give farmers and landowners an alternative to culling, which we believe is more cost effective and works. We're trying to reduce the risk to cattle from badgers potentially passing on bovine TB, although I believe that is a lot less of an issue, it's a very small part of the equation and Lord Krebs said some time ago that if you assume that culling badgers reduces the incidence of bTB in cattle by 16%, then you've still got 84% of the problem and that you have to continue tackling that. Badger vaccination, I see that as a short term thing, what I want to be able to do is to try and continue doing that whilst cattle vaccination is progressed -

Little does she – or you – know it, but Ingrid is debating head-on with Henry (Farmer Spoligotype) over the effectiveness of the vaccine. Henry's interview was so long and detailed I had to edit a lot of it out, even though my intention is to keep a lot of the interview material in. He gave me a great, detailed response about vaccination, and rather than let it get tangled up with spoligotypes, I've saved it for now. Here we go, then, back to Henry.

One thing we haven't talked at all about yet is the idea of vaccination of badgers and of cattle, can you tell me a bit about what your views of that is?

First of all and this is know I've gleaned over the years and even goes back to my own experience as a child, is that there is no good vaccine for TB in the world, we've only got BCG.[27] BCG is not a very effective vaccine, half the world's population it has no effect on, in this country we only use it in a city/urban areas where there's some TB coming in from Third World countries.

It's trying to understand the nature of TB and that it's probably one of the hardest diseases in the world to find an effective vaccine for, so you've got that as a starting point and there is only one vaccine that the world has known, despite pharmaceutical labs the world over, looking for a better TB vaccine because they'd make a fortune out of it and they haven't yet found one.

So we're starting with an inefficient vaccine that will not work at all in a diseased animal so you then have with cattle, to develop the DIVA test because the big problem with BCG is it triggers the reaction to the skin test, at least for six or nine months after you've given the vaccination. All indications are that it won't last very long in an animal, particularly if you're trying to protect them from disease, it shows that it might diminish the level of disease but in very few animals can it totally protect them from it. You're probably in a number of animals, totally protected from BCG, you're down to maybe 30% or 40% of those injected.

Of the other animals, you might get another 20% that get some level of protection, probably for 40% or so, human beings or animals, you get absolutely no protection, it doesn't do anything, if they're diseased it won't do anything in the first place.

In the badger population, you've got two problems, (a) a very inefficient vaccine being used on a quite highly diseased population. There's a big debate over the level of disease but they did the vaccination trials ..., they used three different blood tests on the badgers

---

[27] Stands for 'Bacillus Calmette-Guérin'.

they caught, they had to discard 68% of the badgers, as those blood tests indicated that they probably carried TB.

Most of the conservationists will tell you that you only get 10-15% of badgers have got TB, it's absolute bollocks. Most badger populations are carrying a TB infection level that's about 45-60%, so it will have absolutely no effect on that 45-60%, however many it is, depending on the particular badger population you're in. You've then got to catch them to give it to them. You're probably only ever going to catch 50% of them and that's going to be relatively random in any one trapping season. Very well done trapping might catch 60-70% but the reality is that it's very difficult, so you've got a random 50% being caught, you've got a vaccine that's probably only 40% effective or less than that in terms of imparting true resistance to TB, so you sit down and the Irish gave a very good paper at the London Zoo the other day, the Zoological Society, saying if you wanted to use injectable vaccine alone and even if you wanted to use oral vaccine on badgers to try and reduce TB to a point where you'd eliminate it, you'd have to do it for 20-25 years.

The cost of doing that, because it is phenomenally expensive, dealing with a live vaccine on trapped animals, on a random basis, the costing coming out of Wales show £660 a badger caught and that's probably only 60% of the badgers they caught anyway and there's absolutely no experimental work anywhere, that shows that vaccinating badgers has had any effect on reducing TB transmission levels to cattle. There's some laboratory work that indicates that yes, you can reduce the disease level and therefore have some effect on badgers in a lab situation but the field situation was ... clouded in so much as it said yes, we get this 74% reduction in TB or 74% protection which is a load of bollocks, what they showed was that the most extreme levels of TB, yes you did show after vaccination on those few animals they found were clear of TB in the first place, some reduction in the severity of the TB but it wasn't an absolute protection.

If you go back to looking at the Gamma Interferon tests they did on those badgers, it actually had no significant effect at all, the only thing it had on fact was on the STAT PAK test which really only tests for animals about to die of the disease. So it is meaningless, this claptrap that you get 70% protection by vaccination badgers, you don't and to get herd immunity in badgers through injected vaccine would cost so much money and take so long, that it's not even worth thinking about starting out, it's a complete red herring, absolute farce to think it can work.

It would take years and years and years and cost phenomenal amounts of money and there's just no work anywhere that shows it actually makes any difference to cattle levels of TB, which is really what you're doing it for in the first place.

It doesn't mean to say that I'm against vaccination. What you need and I think I believe and I think NFU do, that vaccination in the long term will be a useful tool but you need to be vaccinating badgers with oral bait vaccine, that's effective and cheap to administer and we're a long way from that yet because it's getting the dose rate right and enough badgers and doing it consistently enough over a number of years so it has any effect, plus alongside that, in the same areas you need to be vaccinating cattle.

That's currently totally illegal, we know we're entering a phase where we're going to field trial some vaccines and more particularly the DIVA test but if you looked at trying to bring in cattle vaccination into this area, I don't know quite how you'd do it because the majority of herds in this country are on the 60 day testing, that means you've probably got to use your DIVA test on every single animal, it's a hugely expensive test, nobody knows quite what sort of indication it's going to give you. If I was in East Anglia, I wouldn't buy a DIVA tested animal, you wouldn't know what the bloody hell you were getting.

So you think how do you actually bring it in and probably you would start because I mean there is indication that that's ... older cattle, it's just a waste of time, its effect is lessened over the age of the animal so the most effective use of it is with neonates but they've got to be vaccinated every year. So you probably start introducing it, so it would take quite a long time to build up in a cattle herd to the level it was beginning to give you some significant herd immunity and you've got to run that alongside badgers and you've firstly got to have it legal to have it used in cattle and you've got to work out the programme of who's going to pay for it and how you're going to use it because the majority of farmers couldn't afford to pay for it initially because they couldn't afford the DIVA testing, it would be colossal.

Skin tests at the moment government pays for and they're now asking us to pay for some of that, that's about £5/6 an animal, DIVA test is £20/25 an animal, that may come down a bit but it's quite a complicated test, it has all sorts of logistical problems because you've got to get blood to the lab within 24 hours at the right temperature, then you have to interpret the results along various scales, so vaccination I think will be quite useful but it will never be an utter panacea, it's not like vaccinating for a virus where you vaccinate 9% of animals and it just dies out, it will never happen like that with TB. You may get it down to quite low levels after a long time but it will take some time to build up.

So I would see vaccines as being something that may be useful in about 8 or 10 years' time but the effect of using them will take a long time to build up because you've got to start using them in neonates in generation after generation, gradually building it up and that's once you've decided who's going to pay for it. Not a simple answer to the problem but probably a very useful tool when we get there and that's why we see culling as an interim policy, I think we only ever see it as an interim policy because it will reduce that disease load in badgers which then reduces the spillback into cattle and reduces the disease load in cattle, before you start introducing vaccines which hopefully will protect both populations even further still.

It's time to find out about this for myself, as it seems important – the only way, in fact, of arbitrating between the rival claims being made by Ingrid and Henry, especially given they're making claims of fact about what the research says. Ingrid is saying that vaccination reduces bovine TB in badgers by 74%. Henry is saying that you can't rely on that result because the test it's based on, a blood test called STAT PAK, only picks up very ill animals. Instead, when you look the results of a different test, the gamma interferon test, there's no benefit at all. It sounds like they're even talking about the same article, so off I go, hunting for something solid in the Internet Soup.

There it is. 'Bacillus Calmette-Guérin vaccination reduces the severity and progression of tuberculosis in badgers' written by written by Mark Chambers of the VLA (which became the AHVLA and then the APHA) and about 30 others, including Robbie, and published in 2011 (Chambers et al. 2011). It's publically available online, so I won't bore you with the build-up. It takes me a couple of hours, and, I have to admit, some sleep, to unpick this one.

The authors admit that the blood test isn't very good unless the badger is very ill. The percentage of badgers that the test will suggest are healthy when they are not goes up to about 65% when the badgers are only at the early stages of the disease. This falls, though, to about 20%, when the badgers are at an advanced stage of the disease, and TB lesions become visible. At first, Henry seems to be doing rather well, but then after thinking about it for a bit (thinking, sleeping, what's the difference?), I'm not so sure. I'm not sure that scientific method is about making sure that everything is perfect – it's more about making sure that everything is consistent. So yes, the blood test might not be so good with less sick badgers, but it's the same test. The scientists are comparing two groups of wild badgers, one that has been vaccinated and one that hasn't. Both groups get tested with both the blood test and the gamma interferon test. 74% fewer badgers tested positive for bovine TB using the blood test when they had been vaccinated than when they had not. It doesn't mean they don't have TB, it means they don't have it badly. But then, that's what the authors are talking about, reducing the 'severity and progression' of the disease. There's a question about the point at which a badger becomes sufficiently ill to infect cattle, but that's not covered here.

But then, what about Henry's second problem? The other test showed no significant difference between vaccinated and unvaccinated badgers at all, although vaccinated badgers did test positive slightly less frequently than unvaccinated badgers. The authors discuss this problem too. They suggest that it's either because "of the relatively low power of the field study to detect a significant difference or because of false-positive test results associated with the vaccine itself" (Chambers et al. 2011, p.1918). In English, this means that there are two possible reasons why the gamma interferon test showed no significant difference. One reason could be that there weren't enough badgers included in the study for this to be so. Any statistical study involving very large numbers is almost certain to find a statistically significant difference, no matter how small the difference in the results between two categories – it's just a statistical fact of life. That's why some statisticians don't like tests for significant differences at all, and prefer tests of 'effect size'. The other reason is that the vaccine delivers a much higher dose of bovine TB than animals are likely to come across in the wild (it's just a very weak, or 'attenuated', version of it), so it's quite likely a vaccinated animal is going to test positive after it's received a vaccine. There isn't a 'DIVA' (Differentiating between vaccinated and infected animals) test for badgers, so the authors have to use their brains to assess the evidence presented by the two contrasting tests. They conclude that the lack of a significant difference on the gamma interferon test is because the test is responding as much to the vaccination as to the infection. So, they think they were probably underestimating the positive effect of the vaccination – in fact, they were probably underestimating its effect both on the gamma interferon and the blood test, as neither can differentiate between a vaccinated and an infected animal.

Henry's conclusion is that the vaccine isn't really having very much effect at all. To think that, he's not reading the positives given by the gamma interferon test as 'false-positives', caused by the vaccination. Instead, he's concerned that they really are infected and that they are also infectious to cattle – he's dismissing the blood test because, in his view, it picks up on the disease too late. The first part of his conclusion looks to me like it's a case of 'don't know' – at least, not until there's a 'DIVA' test for badgers. The second part – that looks like a real problem doesn't it? You wouldn't want to be using a test on badgers that meant you would return infectious animals back into the wild, not if they were on your farm and you believed they were passing bovine TB to your cows. Not unless you had a great way of protecting your cows – a vaccine perhaps. And that's where my next interviewees come in – or at least, that's where they end up.

How to describe Henry's thinking?

A lot of academic work, even when it's not trying to be scientific in a narrow sense, is very systematic, even when it comes to something like reading. You follow up lists of references, identify your target readings and chunk through them, trying to judge how deeply to go into each one, how much time to spend, and record your notes, sometimes even using a table. So, now and again, it can be a good idea to do the complete opposite and pull something off a library shelf not-quite-at-random, or follow up a vague background hunch that such-and-such might be good to read. There's a danger of wasting your time, of course, and there's a danger of coming across something really powerful that makes you think you have to change your ideas, leaving you with a new mountain of reading that you're not going to get through by the deadline. With this book in mind and the aim of making Thinking Through Badgers interesting, rather than dutiful, I've been shelf-surfing. One name has been going round in the back of my mind for a while, something I picked up from a seminar once that made it sound interesting. I've not had the chance find out about it yet, and, spotting an unintimidatingly short tome on the shelves, I take it out (Mansfield 2010). Alexis de Tocqueville, a scion of French aristocrats who was an involved observer of French politics during the reign of Louis Phillipe (1830-48) and then during the Second Republic (until 1851), has become known not only as one of the best contemporary interpreters of nascent (and abortive) democracy in America and France in the late eighteenth and early nineteenth centuries, but as the author of key texts for understanding democracy now. Top Chinese politicians have read him (*Financial Times* 2012), fearful that if they are not careful, they could recreate conditions similar to those that preceded the French Revolution. De Tocqueville is seen as the founder of political science; he talked about how politics was done, not how he thought it ought to be. Coming well before the twentieth century, when political science sought to mimic natural sciences, de Tocqueville talked about elements of the political economy that we're not used to thinking about anymore; for example, pride. Pride was, for de Tocqueville, an important part of national, or cultural, character that had a huge influence on the behaviour and fate of individuals as well as whole societies. He didn't use the term in the simplistic, only-positive way we tend to use it now, but in a way influenced by how it used to be understood, as a sin. For de Tocqueville, too little pride led to personal or cultural weakness and left you open to being exploited or oppressed, too much pride created delusions about one's own strength and led to destruction. Pride was a factor through all aspects of politics because it influenced the operation of that element most vital in a democracy: opinion. This is what de Tocqueville wrote about the freedom of the press that he discovered when he visited America:

"The nations amongst which this liberty exists are as apt to cling to their opinions from pride as from conviction. They cherish them because they hold them to be just, and because they exercised their own free will in choosing them; and they maintain them not only because they are true, but because they are their own" (de Tocqueville 1862 p. 213).

Pride might have dropped out of the way we explain politics, but opinion hasn't. In fact, opinion has become more important as democracies have developed. There is now more at stake in trying to work out why people think as they do, because from that, we might try to predict how they vote, which might help us work out what messages we need to promote to whom in our attempts to get them to vote for us (and, reflecting on how there are two or even three kinds of 'we' in that sentence, we the people, we the analysts, we the politicians, it occurs to me to point out that political science is intricately involved in hierarchies around the running of a democracy). One of the developments of contemporary political science on the start made by de Tocqueville is to differentiate between those whose opinions are formed as a result of paying a lot of attention to issues (perhaps through reading the 'free press', or, these days, going online and reading a website, Facebook page, or even a publically available academic paper), and those whose opinions are based on less engagement. The problem that bothers political scientists, and especially those interested in political opinion polling, is that as those who are less informed are perfectly capable of holding contradictory views, their voting behaviour can be very difficult to predict.[28] The interesting thing for us, though, in a conflict like this, is that the opposite also tends to happen, that the more informed people are about an issue (which is not the same as saying 'the better informed'), the more rigid they tend to be in their views. Political scientist John Bartle writes

"- the more aware are more likely to both screen out information that contradicts their predispositions and accept information that supports those predispositions" (Bartle, 2000, p. 471)

- which sounds amazingly like pride to me. The slightly worrying thing is that, even as we're trying to do the right thing, and become more informed about important issues, we could, if we're not very alert in really quite a subtle way, make things worse. It's not just Henry and Ingrid, although picking through my interviews with them provides the opportunity to say this, but all of us, if we're not careful. What predispositions, assumptions, values, unexamined patterns of thinking do we bring to bear on political issues so that no matter how much science we consume, we are proud to be right?

---

[28]   The irony is that this variability is exactly what is likely to make them the focus of political parties' campaigning efforts, involving messaging designed for people with very little political background and very short attention spans, meaning that political messaging is less informative, resulting in a larger number of less informed people, meaning there are more people with unpredictable voting behaviours, which...

My next interviewees show just how important boundaries and the ways they are applied are for the different conclusions people have come to about how to manage bTB. But maybe even the most natural ways of thinking about things have a big effect on the conclusions we draw.

It's January 2014 and it's been raining a bit. On the hillside, every road's a river – not because it's raining right now, it isn't, but because it's been raining so much the soil and the stone have soaked up all they can take, weeks of it, and now they've burst. It's not just the banks of rivers, it's every bank, ditch, slope, every last pore in the soil. Round here it runs red.

I drive at a crawl around blind corners along a deep-set, single-track lane, looking for a farm. I pull up beside a stable, and try to imagine a tractor squeezing past on the drive. Maybe. At the house I knock and see a dog fetch its owner. We settle down in the kitchen to talk, wrapping hands around cups of tea and patting the dogs. Eventually, Julia and Kevin decide they'll both do the interview. It's about time for a break. They've spent the morning doing the animals' bedding. They don't just seem tired. They're beat. And something else too, something that seems to come from it and through it. Tender.

Julia does most of the talking.

Well we were in the cull area here, we chose not to participate in the cull. Our badgers are vaccinated but had been previous to the cull starting here, we'd started off a four year plan with them before we even knew this would be in the cull area. That's the basic background to us really.

So tell me a bit about the decision to vaccinate and how that led to not taking part in the cull?

Well it's based entirely on the science, the science didn't support a cull, and we've suffered with TB here since 2008. We've been shut down for most of that time, although we did have 12 months when we were free. We felt we had to try and do something to improve the situation really. We have more than just badgers as a disease factor in this area, the deer are an issue as well which has just been completely ignored in the badger cull.

So you're still shut down now as a result?

We are shut down again yes.

Tell me about your views then before you started looking into the science? Would you say you were minded to try and avoid...? What was your attitude to badgers and wildlife in the area before then?

Wildlife is important to us, we have a lot of wildlife on the farm, and it does enrich your life. But disease control is also very important to us, because we just suffer terrible heartache, never mind the financial situation. Losing cows is just devastating. So an effective disease control is very important to us. But we were relieved when we saw the results of the RBCT, which indicated that killing badgers wasn't going to be an effective route to go down. Given the other wildlife that it clearly isn't, what's required is a vaccine, and this is just a red herring really, it's just a diversion. Just now we're seriously looking at cattle vaccines, they've just recently put out to tender to research into the cattle vaccines which we know they're using in other countries.

The BCG vaccine isn't a brilliant vaccine which is unfortunate, it's worse than most. No vaccines are 100% but that one is worse than most. But it's still probably enough that it would damp it down. You know we're relying on that on the badger vaccine. The results are looking quite good too, the research into the badger vaccine, it is showing encouraging results. So something is happening with that vaccine.

Are you able to assess whether vaccinating badgers has made a difference on your farm? I know you're still shut down, but are you sensing that...?

Well we're never going to know, especially now we've been a cull area, we're going to have perturbation of other badgers onto our land, so we're never going to know that. But a badger from one of our setts was killed, well it was hit on the road, and managed to haul its way down the lane, and it died. We sent that off for testing and that was completely clear of TB, but obviously not all badgers have got TB anyway. So we're never going to know, especially not with the high deer population we've got on the farm as well

How are you managing it then when you're shut down when there are control measures?

We've had to alter our system. Previously we would have sold store cattle at about a year old. With the traditional way of hill *farming you have suckler cows and then you sell their calves at a relatively young age. Well we've had to keep them right through to finishing now. So in the first year, that's devastating, you haven't made enough forage for them, you haven't got anything, everything has to be brought in for them, which is financially awful. So we did have to change the system a lot, and of course on a hill farm you're not set up with buildings either for huge numbers of cattle. So it's still ongoing very difficult with our building situation.*

But we've learned to live with it, but you never know what's round the corner. You can't plan, you don't know how many reactors you're going to get next time. In terms of losing cows, they're not replaceable, you can't just buy another cow to replace her because you're shut down you can't buy anything in. So it does knock the middle out of your herd really, you end up with either very old cows or very young cows, but not an even age to a herd at all. When you lose youngsters, although you're compensated, you've lost the business that they would grow into, you haven't got those going on, producing an income for you really.

So it sounds like there's a lot of change to a different pattern of farming, created a lot of upfront costs ahead?

Yes it does, it did. The first year we were shut down it was financially very serious really. Even now, although we know we're highly likely to get reactors, it's still a shock every time, you never quite stop that feeling of shock. And not knowing, you may have three reactors this time, you just don't know the next time, you're just anticipating the worst really, how may you'll lose or what it will be.

But the test is very erratic, if there was a logic to it and you felt, "right if we did this, this and this, we could stop it," but you don't get that with the test. Although we're actually shut down now, our previous test was completely clear, the test 60 days later we've had another three reactors. That makes no sense, even if they were incubating it at that time, you still would have expected to have seen a little reaction, even if there wasn't enough for it to be a total reaction, you'd have expected it to come back as an inconclusive or to show something on the neck. But it's very frustrating the test, where it's missing.

These cattle are indoors, they're not picking it up from wildlife, so they cannot have picked it up from anywhere else ... we use night vision cameras to check there's nothing going in, so we can be abso-

lutely definite. People say, "badgers aren't getting in here," that sort of thing, but unless you put up cameras you really don't know. Because they can climb up almost anywhere, they're phenomenally good at accessing buildings.

How do they work? Presumably you don't sit down and watch hours and hours of footage?

Well they only operate if something comes into vision, so it's not hours and hours. It's always surprising what you do pick up too. If it's not badgers it's, "oh I didn't know the cats were going over there," or something. But we used it too around the badgers' setts, so we know roughly how many we've got to vaccine and that sort of thing. So we've gone about it in the best way we can to try and free ourselves of TB really.

So what's your view about the badgers then? You were saying how it's very difficult to stop badgers getting in, so do you think that badgers are hosts for TB, are they a possible vector towards your cattle?

Well they definitely carry TB, there's no two ways about that, we know that for certain. What isn't so well known is how they pass it on or if they pass it on or which way it goes. I suspect it goes both ways, it's logical to assume that really. I don't think it's well enough known really, the link between the two. I really don't know how it's spread between the two, because as regards airborne infection, I think they count sort of close contact to be 1.4 metres, well it's unlikely that badgers are sneezing all over the cattle outdoors at 1.4 metres. The other source of infection is from urine and latrine sites.

How can you judge? You can't say, can you? We just don't know how much of an issue that is really. It would seem sensible to keep your latrine sites fenced off, but the problem is, which nobody seems to mention in their research is that badgers will follow cattle around and latrine where the cattle are, because that's their food source. They'll go in turning over the dung pats for the beetles. So we noticed, if we're moving our cattle up and down the lane, the badgers will latrine outside the gate where the cattle are. And as the cattle move, the latrine site will move.

- we have learned a tremendous amount about badger activities since we've been vaccinating our badgers. They are very interesting really, and I think in some instances I think they have the larger

setts and then they have the smaller setts, that they don't always occupy. But I think if you move cattle a long way away from their major sett, and they've got a smaller sett near where the cattle have gone to, I think it's in all probability they very often move to that smaller sett so they're closer to the cows, so that they can feed from the insects under the dung pats. They are very interesting if you follow them closely.

So how long have you been vaccinating?

We've done two years of vaccine, and this will be our third year now.

So you're looking forward to two or three years time in theory, for most of the badgers in the setts...?

Should be vaccinated.

[Over talking – I ask something like: is it a risk that you miss one or two badgers] *consistently.*

Well there's always that possibility, because you do get ones which are trap shy, but they're not long lived. Four or five years is about the lifespan of a badger, so either way they should die. In any case it's more a herd immunity we're looking for rather than every single one ...

So tell me a bit more about what you think might be going on about how your cattle are contracting or appear to be contracting TB? You mentioned deer a couple of times?

I certainly think the deer are an issue. We'd been clear for 12 months up until this summer, and we had to have a contiguous test [carried out when a neighbouring farm goes down], we weren't due for a test until this March, and were ordered to have a contiguous test because a neighbour had gone down. We don't border, we don't have any direct contact with neighbours ... so there's no nose to nose contact of other neighbour's cattle. So we had to have a contiguous test in the summer, and we had six reactors and one inconclusive, which was quite a serious breakdown really. It made no sense with what we know about our badgers' social groups. It was across the board in every group of cattle where there'd been no mixing of the cattle groups since the previous clear test. And across all the age groups, and across all the social groups of badgers. But deer are much more likely to cover that whole area than badgers were. And we were very suspicious of one deer in particular that wasn't in good condition. And people don't appreciate the time that deer spend with cattle, they say, "oh they're up on the moor," or something.

But throughout the entire summer we had approximately 20 red and 20 fallow grazing with the cattle day and night. They never went away from them. If any one of those is carrying TB in the same way that if you accept that cattle can pass it to cattle, then you've got to accept that deer can pass it to cattle. But that's not being accepted generally, they're saying, "no it's not relevant," but I'm sure it is.

So what would you do about the risk of deer passing TB to cattle?

Well there's nothing you can do, the cull of deer I'm sure would be even more unpopular with the general public than the cull of badgers. Plus the fact that they travel such long distances, that if you culled all the deer on this farm, there would just be more move in from other farms. Culling in my mind is just an old fashioned way of trying to deal with disease, and we've never got rid of disease in that way, it just doesn't work. It's always been vaccines in humans, and we use vaccines constantly in our animals, like farm animals. And that's got to be the way to go with TB, there just can't be any other way in my opinion.

[Kevin] That's right, you can cull as many badgers and deer as you like, but they just come back again, there's no end to it. You can shoot 20 deer or 20 badgers on your farm and in no time at all, you've got just as many again. So it's an endless process really, which gains you nothing at all.

[back to Julia] We're not getting very far with it in cattle either whilst the test isn't accurate enough. There's always going to be animals harbouring it, as you can see from areas where there is no badgers, they still have TB. So it's not a disease of badgers, it's a disease of cattle that's the relevant bit. Not a disease of deer, it's irrelevant to us whether deer have got TB or whether the badgers have got TB, it's what's happening to our cattle.

Because it's not a welfare situation for badgers at all, even in the severest hot spots, there's only 1.5% or 1.6% of badgers showing serious problems with TB. So Mr Paterson's saying that there were many diseased badgers removed from this area, is absolutely nonsense because he doesn't know, they weren't tested, and so few show visible signs. And even the visible signs are easily confused with rump wounds from normal fighting of badgers.

[Kevin] I've lived [around here] for 60 years and farmed all that time really, even as a boy you know helping all the family farms. I can honestly sit here and say I've never ever seen a diseased badger, never. It's ridiculous.

[Julia again] Well not since we've been vaccinating either, all these badgers we trap, they've all been normal body weight. I think we just had one, and that wasn't emaciated or anything, it was just an old badger whose teeth were going, so just normal wildlife stuff. But over their two years we haven't seen anything that's concerned us at all. Not even rump wounds actually, obviously their territories are well able to sustain them, because they're not fighting amongst themselves.

Tell me about this cull this year or last year, how have you found out about that? What have you used for your source of information?

Well not very much really, we made a mistake in that we should have gone to the initial cull meetings, but we didn't because we already decided we'd vaccinate. We'd decided that was the scientific route to go down. But initially we had been intending to claim grant to do it. Then we found out that you couldn't have grant unless you claim through the NFU... were handling the whole grant, which was an absolute shock to us, because we'd just assumed it would be like our normal farm grants.

You just apply to DEFRA and you get it. So that was devastating to us because not only did we not want to be involved with the cull, we believed the cull to be totally wrong. So we then didn't want our farm included in the area, they needed 70% of the area signed up, and we didn't want our farm to be included in their management... so called management, re killing badgers scheme.

So just to clarify, because that sounds both confusing and amazing at the same time. There's a grant available for vaccinating badgers or for controlling badgers in some way?

For vaccinating badgers.

**But to get that grant, you have to go the NFU and become part
of the NFU's whole...?**

*Management which includes the cull. We were never clear
whether that meant our acreage would be then attached to the 70%.
But we were actually shocked, because the first we heard of this, we
were in the middle of lambing last year, terrible wet lambing, it was
awful. Anyway we had a phone call about half-past seven in the
morning. "If you want a grant, come to a meeting today," we said,
"we can't possibly, it's chucking it down with rain, we've got baby
lambs everywhere," you know when we're lambing we're working
20 hours a day.*

*You cannot take even five minutes out of that day without some-
thing going wrong. So we then tried to get in touch with Natural
England, I emailed them, but you email Natural England and you
don't get a reply until 10 working days. So that was no good, so you
rang DEFRA, you rang Natural England and nobody knew. So then
I emailed the Badger Trust, because I thought perhaps they would
know. They didn't know either, but through them we were then put
in touch with somebody who would help us voluntarily. So we just
abandoned all hope of grant and went down this route of using
volunteer vaccinators. We still paid towards the cost of it, but nothing like what it would have been.*

*It's allowed us to do a lot of the work ourselves, we do all the pre-
baiting ourselves, we place the traps with help from the volunteers,
so it keeps the costs way down. But it also means that we have a lot
more control, if I feel that we've missed a badger or haven't had the
number we expected in one place, then we can go back again, and
have another go there. Like I say, with the night vision cameras,
we're fairly certain what we've got in each place. If we know we've
got a badger we haven't trapped, then we will go back again to try
and get it vaccinated.*

*- we've had a neighbour come to see us, so he was very disap-
pointed we weren't culling, I think he was one of these people they
call the parish coordinators of the cull, that sort of thing, the supposed official. But for an official he knew very little about it really.
So that's what we found generally, that people don't understand
the entire issue really.*

So this was a sort of recruitment visit, or simply a visit to express collective disappointment?

Well you'd already told them we wouldn't join didn't you, on the phone. I think it was pressure really, he said, "how are you going to feel when your badgers are infecting everybody else's land when they're clear?" Which wasn't very scientific really, because there's much more risk of their badgers infecting ours through perturbation. Plus our badger population should stay stable.

Was he aware that you were vaccinating?

Yes he was, but people were initially told that the vaccine was expensive, but compared to the cull, the vaccine looks incredibly cheap now.

So how did you react to that particular view?

I wasn't surprised really, because people had been given a lot of misinformation I think. Like I say the meeting I went to ... was completely biased. The Animal Health were there, and they had a PowerPoint demonstration, which they showed many so-called diseased badgers, you know nasty looking photographs, that would upset anybody really. But no explanation to them, no whether this was captive badgers that had been inoculated and kept alive, because badgers in the wild would be unlikely to survive in those sort of states. They'd be unlikely to reach that stage, and also they could have easily been infected rump wounds, there's no explanation to the source of the photos or anything.

They were just trying to make a drama of it really. And then of course people lapped it up, they said, "show this to the general public and they'll all be behind the cull." Well the general public we've come into contact with, well the protestors since the cull, are actually very well informed about the numbers of badgers that would likely to be in that state. I think if you don't delve very deeply, if you believe what you're being told, you would probably have gone along with the cull. And of course the farmers expect the NFU and the government to tell them the truth, not tell them a cherry-picked version of the truth.

So what do you know about the process for deciding whether the trials have been a success or not?

I'm sure that they will be a success, they won't be allowed not to be. I have no faith in whether they deem to be a success. I notice now all the politicians have dropped the word effectiveness from it. They say the humaneness was all right and the safety was okay. But they're not saying anything about it being effective because clearly it wasn't effective.... I don't know what to make of it, I don't have too much faith in any of it to be honest. We had three breaches of licence, we had armed trespass on our land, trying to shoot badgers.

We also have a 200 metre no cull zone to protect our vaccinated badgers and that was breached twice, there were traps found in that area. We notified Natural England and it was a total whitewash. They took no action at all. In fact the armed trespass had suddenly become unarmed, although we'd informed the police and the police had told me it was a cull operator and he was armed. But by the time Natural England had investigated it...

That's extraordinary.

Well it is extraordinary because if he wasn't armed, that explains why the cull wasn't very successful. We're running around after badgers unarmed. It was ludicrous, such a white-wash.

I didn't realise Natural England had a role in policing crime anyway?

Well it was even worse than that, because I expected the police to take action, but they said no you have to bring your own action against them. We weren't happy that Natural England didn't take that more seriously. The one trap that was found, was so close to our boundary, and no badgers in the area of that neighbour. They were clearly just trying to catch our vaccinated badgers.

It was very upsetting really. We expected that would have been the end of it, but not at all, there was another one found a week later. We had expected Natural England to investigate it properly and take serious action against the cull company. But they didn't, and that's when we realised that no matter what happened, this cull was going to be deemed as a success.

Is there a way out of the conflict?

Vaccinate the cattle. No I don't think there is with the cull, I don't think it will ever be acceptable to people. They feel, this has been the two pilot culls, so obviously you've had the protestors mainly concentrated in this area. But I think that protest base is building, and I think each area they go to will build its own base.

So you're saying in terms of the solution ... vaccinating cattle and vaccinating badgers?

Oh vaccinating cattle alone, I'm sure in 10 years' time when we look back on this we will think, "what on earth were we doing vaccinating a wild animal?" And we're very dedicated to it, but unless you're very dedicated to it, I don't think it will be successful. It's not that easy, even with the trapping to cull they didn't find it easy. They're quite wiley sort of animals aren't they, you've got to outwit them a bit.

I don't think the disease in wildlife is relevant at all. I would imagine that as it went down in cattle, then it would decrease in badgers. It's a lovely idea that you would have lovely happy healthy badgers, I'm not sure it's necessary. They have to cope with other diseases too, we can't interfere.

We had to think long and hard about this, whether it was right to interfere with a wild animal, to vaccinate it. It was really quite a difficult decision, to decide whether that was ethical to interfere with an animal to that extent. I mean the decision really was taken because obviously culling is a worse option for wildlife, that's the final interference really.

So what about the issue that a cattle vaccine is in maybe 10 years away, and something needs to be done?

Well the cattle vaccination is available now ... you know they say they have to go through all the safety procedures. It's the same as the human BCG, and [we] have both been vaccinated with it, all the population was years ago. So it's really unlikely to have any safety issues, and I think those have already been covered in other countries in trials. So why we can't use their trial information I don't know. But I think the real thing that's slowing this thing us is with the EU, the not allowing vaccinated cattle.

But we don't export huge numbers of cattle, and to short-cut this, it could be offered to farms who would then undertake not to sell their cattle for export. Which would apply to us, our cattle would go direct to an abattoir in this country, and they're going to [a UK supermarket]. So they're not being exported anyway, and I'm sure there are many cattle farms in that situation who could undertake that those animals wouldn't be exported without it affecting the market price drastically I would have thought.

You mentioned an occasion when someone came here, and you've mentioned a few meetings. Are there any other specific times where you've met people who hold a different view to you?

Well it's very interesting that a lot of them are... I mean that one neighbour I mentioned coming here, obviously had strong views, but many of our neighbours had no strong views at all. The reason they gave predominantly was because they didn't want to let other farmers down, that was why they joined the cull.

I'm truly flabbergasted that they managed to get as many farmers to sign up as they did, because it wasn't cheap, there is a cost involved.

We've had several bad financial years generally in hill farming, I'm surprised that anybody felt they could spare the money. What's really curious, is that when you speak to farmers just outside the cull area, their view generally is, "you're absolutely crazy you lot in the cull area, whatever made you sign up to that?" So it doesn't just make you wonder what was going on. Many farmers reported coming under a lot of pressure from the cull company to sign up, you know being phoned constantly.

[Kevin] Well we had pressure as well didn't we?

[Julia] Yes you were told you wouldn't be popular.

[Kevin] I can't tell you what my reply was.

Well we can edit it.

[Kevin] It's roughly I couldn't give a damn really, you just stand up for what you think is right, and no amount of pressure is going to push me one way or the other.

[Julia] In fact quite the opposite really, I don't understand why people cave in to pressure.

[Kevin] It's our farm, it's our business, it's our money, we will do just as we wish. If we think that culling badgers is wrong, which we very strongly believe that it is wrong...

[Julia] Well wrong for TB control.

[Kevin] Yes wrong for TB control, then why go down that route? If you're being pressurised into something which makes you go down that route, then you've done something that's against your belief, which is even worse. But we did have pressure, but we tried to stamp it out from the onset.

[Julia] Well, we weren't going to change our mind. But this is a problem where you have weak science supporting something. You know you were saying what can you do to reduce the conflict, you can't where there is such weak science. When you've got the authors of the RBCT telling you don't do this, this is wrong, then it's hard to see why anybody would think it was the right thing to do.

I think a lot of cull supporters are very critical of that trial, they see it as a failure. It was disrupted by foot and mouth and all kinds of things and didn't get going properly until the last couple of years. There were problems with design and that kind of thing...

[Julia] Yes there were problems with it, but there will always be problems with any cull too. As you know we've just seen what an issue protestors can be. They can be a serious issue, and they're learning all the time too, they're learning how to be there and how to be in the way, and how to make their voices heard. That was despite really quite strong measures taken by the NFU to try, in the form of the injunction to try and stop them.

And a huge police presence too, the police presence was not comfortable all the time.

[Kevin] It's certainly something that the population of [this area] has never seen anything of the like. This is a quiet peaceful area, and all of a sudden we're swamped with police, and it's just not what we're used to.

[Julia] We were speaking to some friends at one of our gateways one evening, it was dark. We had four separate lots of police stop.

Stopping asking you?

What are you doing? Are you all right? Do we look like we're not all right? And then I was stopped going out at the top of the lane one evening. You know, "what are you doing?" Well you know, "I live here, I'm coming out of the lane, what do you think I'm doing?"

[Kevin] We did have four policeman stop and ask us the way.

[Julia] Yes they'd come from Bristol.

Well I sympathise with that.

No very strange times indeed, everybody was so suspicious of everybody else, it was not pleasant at all after dark, very unpleasant.

Yes there's a lot of mistrust, this is what's so uncomfortable about the whole thing, it's very mistrustful. I just wish it hadn't come here, I just don't like that it sets neighbour against neighbour and it's nothing like we've experienced here in this area before. It's very sad really.

As I wind the car back up the lane, rain smacks into the windscreen. Surrounded by a storm, safe from it; a comforting feeling, a feeling Julia and Kevin are reaching for, a feeling they are denied. Maybe the cull operator who came onto their land wasn't aware that the badgers there were being vaccinated – let's be generous. Following the advice from a meeting of expert convened by the government's Chief Scientific Advisor, Professor David King, in 2007 (King 2007), it was the policy of the culls to cull right up to the edge of any land not participating, to try to shoot badgers from those areas if they strayed onto participating cull land. But shouldn't vaccinated badgers have been viewed differently? The cull operator should have known that, right? It should have mattered to the people running the show that mistakenly culling badgers on Kevin and Julia's farm risked completely undermining their own genuine efforts to deal with bovine TB. They might not have agreed, but they could have made sure that didn't happen, as a matter of respect, no? No – not if I believe what I've heard about the way people connected with the cull company are prepared to behave. What Kevin and Julia said is 'putting it mildly', there's been pressure, but there's also been abuse, a sense of coercion.

I'm struck by the way Kevin and Julia are absolutely clear about what the important boundary is, and where it should lie. Between cattle and tuberculosis. If the badgers are sick with it – they're wild, we shouldn't interfere. I'm not sure though.

The wild is the totem of romantic political ecology, the place where nature is free and things are as they should be. Where is the wild? For many Americans, the wild was in the west, before it was subdued by the expansion of the railroads. For Europeans, it was Africa. Wilderness was the opposite of civilisation, devoid of civilised people – so the people who inconveniently turned out to live in these wildernesses Europeans had first invented and then discovered couldn't possibly be counted as proper people because they were wild, savage. They were pushed aside, traded, or killed, and their histories ignored or erased, including the history of how they had influenced the 'wilderness' they lived in. In recent decades, human and cultural geographers such as William Cronon (1996) have been trying to unpick this colonial history, as well as trying to work out and correct the pattern of thinking that lead to it. Talking about wilderness in Britain has always been a bit hopeful, as it suggests vast landscapes that don't exist. But still, a category of wild things still persists, living in the countryside, somehow bound together by the idea that all that is 'nature', even though it has been obvious that people have been working and transforming the landscape in Britain for a very long time – but of course those people were labourers and peasants and didn't count, at least not to those recording our language. Our whole thinking and speaking is woven with these kinds of distinctions – boundaries. Humans and animals (even though humans are animals). Civilisation and wilderness (even though the wilderness is cultivated and civilisation is savage). Male and female (despite wide-ranging anatomical variations). Man and woman (despite frequent cultural confusion about how these two – only two! – categories should be performed). White and black.

What's going on here? There's a discussion in a book that Steve got me on to, by a British geographer called Doreen Massey, arguing for the importance of space for thinking (Massey 2005). Well, she would, wouldn't she, being a geographer – but then the book, reading it, is so intensely engaged in unpicking how various lines of thinking got tangled up that there's absolutely nothing that can be taken for granted about it. The discussion has to do with the way we think about difference, and highlights for me just how difficult it is to think about difference differently. It's about an exchange between two French thinkers, Jacques Derrida and Jean-Louis Houdebine. Derrida was notorious as being one of those specifically targeted for criticism during the Science Wars, for being the architect of a practice called deconstruction, which aimed deliberately to destabilize the relative certainties of meaning that scientists – almost all of us – take for granted most of the time (so, 'facts' and 'knowledge' were a bit of a problem). One of the places Derrida's thinking starts from is the idea that the meaning of words is not based on a connection between a word and the object it refers to, but on the relationship between the meaning of one word and another, different word, that might represent its opposite. One of the things Derrida thought about most, then, was difference. The point of the discussion the two Frenchmen were having was whether, in the background of the way in which they were thinking about difference, in the terms they used, there was an assumption that everything started as the same because things only become different through 'negative' processes of "displacement and exteriorisation (...abjection, repression, etc.)" (Massey 2005, p. 52), or whether they were allowing for there also to be 'positive' difference in which different entities – savages, women, animals – have not been forced out, down, or away from some pre-existing unity, so that we understand that some things are just, or started out as, or perhaps even wanted to be, different. Now, Derrida's reputation and influence on the humanities and social thinking are as big and controversial as Maradona in football. Regardless of what anyone thinks of how he used his mental capacities, they were obviously immense. The thing is, Derrida didn't get it. Massey, who calls the exchange 'hilarious', reflecting just how deep into these debates she went, tells us that Houdebine had to try and try again to get Derrida to see that rather than difference being all about some act of violence or denial, some things are just different.

Now I'm worried I've made this sound too easy. Of course, some things are just different, stands to reason. Well, try this. Think of someone you really dislike, someone you think is morally reprehensible, whom you accuse in silent or not-so-silent ranting condemnations when you get worked up. Oh, politics is always a good place to start. Think, depending on your personal proclivities, of either Arthur Scargill or Margaret Thatcher. If not, your boss. Ready?

So why can't you just accept them for who they are? Some people are just different, right?

It seems as though, in a much more galling way, Julia and Kevin are stuck thinking with negative difference. They have nothing other than, in this case 'exteriorisation' to express themselves with. 'Badgers are wild animals' draws a line between us humans and them. They are outside our sphere. It's galling because they care about badgers, they don't hate them, the way you hate [enter name here]. Their care is subverted by that negative pattern of thinking. They express concern for wildlife at first, but because wildlife is nature, an aspect of something we often deny in ourselves, therefore different, not human, it's separate and shouldn't be interfered with – should be left, when sick, to die. The category – the human category, the *socially constructed* category – of wilderness has somehow won out over the real thing.

Chapter 6

Vets

- my view is that we need to eliminate infected badgers, partly for the benefit of the badger and partly for the benefit of cattle and my grandchildren and to as part of eliminating the disease from badgers, I would ring vaccinate around the current infected area, so I'd vaccinate healthy badgers where you have a chance of the vaccine working, having some effect and that will slow down the rate of spread of TB into other badgers.

And the reason for not vaccinating cattle, why would you want to? I can see no logic in it whatsoever, why don't we eliminate TB as we've eliminated smallpox and rinderpest all the other diseases?

Mark holds completely the opposite view to Julia and Kevin – he believes that vaccinating badgers is the most important thing to do, and vaccinating cattle is ridiculous. That's not all – he also supports the cull. He's the first vet I manage to speak to. They always promised to be an interesting lot; on the one hand, they're probably more informed about the scientific studies on the nature of bovine TB and the effectiveness of the different treatments, on the other, they're deeply involved with the practical concerns of looking after animals.

They are also, it turns out, deeply divided. When you become a vet, you have to make some choices about what you're going to specialise in. Some vets specialise more than others, but even those proclaiming general skills will tend to know more about, or do more of one thing. After all, if your business depends on the expertise of your vet, you're going to choose an expert. So they tend to know about either large animals, such as those you find on a farm or at a stable, or small animals – pets. A few get involved with exotic species or wild animals, but there's not so much demand. So if you're a suburban vet, you may not have much experience or understanding of bovine TB. On the other hand, if you're a rural, farm vet, you may not know much about the disease in badgers, and, because they're wild animals, there aren't very many people around who can put you right. Of the three vets I interview, two are (mostly) farm vets, and one is a badger specialist. And that combination reveals to me a funny thing about veterinary knowledge on bovine TB.

First though, I get interested in the practical details of testing cattle, and the farm vets I speak to are happy to share the nitty-gritty of the job. Most of the time, it turns out, it's just gritty. Mark, in his large office, every surface piled with books, reports and papers, like one or two university professors I know, describes what it's like, testing a dairy herd, in summer:

- he's got 200 cows and if he's got 200 cows, those cows will give birth to roughly 200 calves each year and those calves come into milk when they're 2 years old and onwards. It means if he's got 200 cows, he's going to have 400 other animals on the farm coming through until they calm down to start producing milk when they're 2-2½ years old.

In the summer ... quite a lot of the animals are out grazing in different age groups, so the day before the TB test, he has to bring all those animals back in and they could be ... off-lying land so he has to hire transport to bring them back to the main area, then they have to be housed and then when they're being housed, they have to be given more expensive feed because during the summer, grazing is the cheapest feed. So that's what happens the day before the test.

The day of the test ... each animal has to come through a cattle crush, you have to take its ear number, clip on the side of the skin, two areas of hair, measure the skin, inject the ... tuberculin and then the animal goes and you have to bring them in one at a time, restrain them, ear number, clip clip, measure skin and so on.

Quite often and it depends on the layout, it's impractical to send the animals back to grazing again, all of them, because you don't want to do the transport, so you keep them in for three days, so if you inject them on Monday, on Thursday you then go through the whole lot again, bringing each one into a cattle crush, that's a chute that restrains the animal and then on the Thursday, check its ear number, measure the skin where you injected your tuberculin to see if you get an increase in thickness of the skin. And the labour involved in just bringing each animal in because they don't come in voluntarily, into the crush, they have to be pushed or shoved or cajoled, you have to bring them around in groups, you've got large numbers of different groups of animals within a farm because you don't want to mix the cows and the calves and the heifers and the

bulls and the steers and so on, so you have to find some way of jug-
gling these groups around and just in the moving of the groups
around, there's quite a bit of effort involved on a farm like that.

On some farms it's relatively easy because for example on the one
I did two weeks ago, they're all dairy cows and so I get there at
about half 4 in the morning and as the cows are coming out from
milking, he employs extra staff –extra cost – to make sure as they
come out from the milking parlour, they go through the handling
system and then from the handling system, back into where they
came from and they're all dairy cows and they go through much
easier.

Mark shows me some estimates he's put together of how much
each test costs a farmer with a herd like the one he's described. The
extra labour is the most expensive, coming to over a thousand
pounds. But for a while the cows won't produce as much milk, so
there won't be as much to sell. On the other hand, the price of milk
is so low, the loss doesn't add up to much – fifty or sixty pounds. But
that's if there isn't a reactor – if there is no hint of bovine TB in the
herd. If there is, the costs start mounting: compensation that
doesn't match the value of the cow, having to sell cattle at reduced
value, increased risks of other diseases, loss of output and income
as reactor cows are culled, and more money spent on trying to deal
with the problem. For many, that means trying to do something
about the badgers.

Mark is adamant that the problem is badgers and culling is the
answer. One of the reasons is what he knows about how a cow's
immune system deals with a disease like bovine TB:

- when you have some idea of the pathology of the disease within
cattle, whereby within an animal, the infection goes into a cow and
it's walled off in a nodule and the animal is shown to be a low
excreter, isn't it 1040 samples of reactor cattle were taken from the
Krebs trial? Not one of them was positive ... I accept there's one
experiment where you put the animals in very close confinement,
then it did transmit but there's lots of data to show that if animals
are running out in a field or in cattle housing, you put reactors in
with them, then the disease doesn't spread.

Mark is another very knowledgeable, intelligent and articulate cull
supporter. There aren't many cull opponents I could compare evenly to him. Part of the reason for his concentration on badgers is his

confidence in the test. I suppose he would be, he's the one adminis-tering it. But some farmers have been raising questions about the test – not how effective it is, but how well it's administered: whether needles get reused too much and whether the tuberculin is put in correctly. I need to know more about how the test is done and what it involves. Speaking to the next vet, that's exactly what I get.

A short while off the motorway and I meet the weather front. One minute, sallying along at fifty or so, the next bursting through walls of water and half-foot lakes on the road. Still, though, I'm early, and after aquaplaning around a few roundabouts to make sure of my destination, I park by the water for a bit and watch the weather coming in. The water's dirty brown and choppy. The wind shoves the car around and makes waves in puddles. I spend a comforting half-hour with the radio and then head back to the surgery. I'm shown into a battered-looking common room behind reception by a rushed-looking vet. He's got a few things to do. Twenty minutes?

"Excuse me, is that your car outside? Peugeot."

"Yes, probably." (Hire cars. I'm never too sure.)

"It's got a flat tyre."

It's about 3pm, early January. I've got an interview in a few mi-nutes, one that's taken months to set up. It can't wait, because there's no way I'm doing this in the dark. Especially as I wouldn't know what I was doing. If I had time I could call someone and they could talk me through it. Dad, probably. Instead, I call the AA (no, the other one) and leave the keys at reception, passing up the op-portunity of learning one skill to learn about another

- have you seen the TB testing being done?

No.

You clip two areas of hair off from the neck above each other, you measure the thickness of the two bits of skin, so you pick it up like that, you measure the thickness in millimetres with a pair of calli-pers, and you inject intradermally within the skin ... We use two different proteins, one from avian tuberculin ... avian TB's in a lot of the birds, and it's a kind of control if like, that's the red one. And the bovine Tuberculin, you stick in the blue one, you clip two areas of hair from the neck, one at the top and one at the bottom. You measure the thickness of two double folds of skin, so you pick up a bit like that and read it off in millimetres on both sites. Then you inject intradermally, so within the skin, you're not trying to going to go through the skin. Cow's skin is quite thick, so if you've got a reading of eight, it's obviously a piece of skin that's four millimetres thick, which is quite a bit.

You've got to go in obliquely, top and bottom, and you feel for a bleb, to check the stuff's injected. It's only point one of a mil, so it's not very much. You go back at 72 hours approximately, and you re-measure, you check the skin for the increase in thickness. For the most part, you just rub your hand across it, and you can feel, like if you've got a mosquito bite, you get that nodule in the skin. I think the mean mechanism is very similar, it's the body reacting against the foreign protein, the mosquito saliva. So it is an accumulation of inflammatory cells in the skin.

So you go back and measure, and if there's a significant swelling there, you measure the thicknesses, and you compare the measurement at both sites. Where I see it goes a bit wrong, is if you measure a cow's neck and it's got an eight at the top, and a 10 at the bottom, then during the preceding 72 hours, if each millimetre of skin increases in thickness by 50 percent, an eight becomes a 12, 50 percent increase. And the 10 becomes a 15, so that's gone up by four millimetres and five millimetres.

Each millimetre of skin has undergone the same amount of cellular infiltration, but because they measure on an absolute basis, a number basis, that would be an inconclusive animal. But really because the thicker bit of skin is thicker to start with - So the TB tests are a little bit flawed in the way that it's interpreted. It's a bit biased, because often the two sites are different thicknesses. The bottom one is often a bit bigger, eights and tens is very common, or seven and eight.

So is there 50 percent increase, that's what you...?

Well you have your little chart, which I haven't got here, but you measure an increase of avian. Basically if they increase in the thickness by the same at each site, each one gets two, three, four, five, six millimetres thickness, it's fine. If you get a bigger lump at the bottom, sometimes you get like 30's, you can't even pick the skin up it's so huge, like a big fried egg. They're fairly obvious, but sometimes you'll measure it and it will be a couple of millimetres.

So it's very fine, there's a bit of room for error I guess, or room for interpretation.

So if the two sites are different thicknesses, what happens?

Well we've got a chart, obviously we have a reading for the first visit, we know that on day zero if you like it was eight at the top and 10 at the bottom. You go back and if there's nothing there, you don't bother measuring it. Initially you just pick up the skin and just feel for any increase in thickness, like a mosquito bite. Sometimes they're very small nodules, like the size of your little thumb nail, sometimes they're huge great things and the whole neck swells up. So you measure those two sites, and compare the increase in measurements, you are comparing numbers really. It doesn't really account for a percentage increase will be more accurate. The TB test is quite reliable on picking up the immune response, people say, "oh the TB test is rubbish," I think it's actually probably oversensitive if anything. But there's this situation with the animals that are not producing the immune response, or the disease is hidden away that you don't pick them up.

So just to make it clear, so when you say a reactor, a reactor is then and an animal whoes skin has thickened, by enough on the chart to say , yes that's a...?

Yes, there's a whole table... I think the protocol's available somewhere on the AHVLA [APHA] website, which I tried to find the other week, but there's a protocol that you must follow. There's a table and numbers you can follow this chart. Anything that has only increased by two millimetres is a negative reaction, and if it's three or more, it's a positive reaction. And if the bovine injection site is more positive than the avian one, it's an inconclusive or a reactor.

That seems strange that there seems to be some kind of processing to be working with some kind of link between the bovine and avian flu?

Yes, the reason for that is it's a comparative test, so if you inject a foreign protein into any animal or person, you might react against it. Like the mosquito analogy, some people don't get big swellings, other people do. So I guess you're using the nondescript foreign protein to see what the background level of reaction is, when you're using the bovine one. If you just injected one injection into the bovine one, it could be the response you're getting is an allergic reaction to the foreign protein if you like.

So sometimes you'll get swellings at both sides of equal magnitude, and say, "well, that's just a background level of reactivity against a foreign invader." Like a snake bite produces a swelling or an insect bite produces a swelling. So you're measuring the background reaction and comparing the two.

I'm getting much more than I expected here. This vet – Larry – has doubts of his own about the test process, although they're not the same as the concerns going around online. I'm wondering quite how I ask him about human error without sounding like I'm accusing him of being a rubbish vet – but then he lets me off the hook.

- it's pretty repetitive. Some days it can be lovely, you've got 10 cows, a nice sunny farm, it's outdoors in the fresh air, it's joyous. But imagine spending eight hours, with things trying to bash your hands in while you reach through the bars, and the crush, in the rain, freezing to death. It's not why you became a vet really. Even the farmer would say it's not necessarily got a useful end point. You think, "Well I'm in this awful job state, but I know after I've done it, I'll make a real difference." It's like calving a cow can be difficult sometimes, but at the end of the day you've got either an alive or dead calf if you're unlucky, but you can see kind of a reward point.

It you're doing TB testing, there's not really improving the TB situation in the country, even locally. You might condemn a few animals to death, but you're not dealing with the source. You get quite demoralised about it if you over think it. They're not even my cows but you start feeling a bit depressed about the whole thing. Not in a medically depressed way, but just... But a lot of practices rely on TB testing to supplement their income. We're not just a farm vets, we do horses and small animals, so if one goes out, there's variation. If small animals go quiet, we've got plenty of farm work, and vice versa. So practices that just do large animals probably are a bit worried about losing TB testing.

But the positive I mentioned earlier, it does get you on the farm, but I can be quite a nice easy day out sometimes. If the cattle are quiet, if there's nice handler facilities, it is quite pleasant. Cup of tea, coffee, biscuits, but wild cattle, poor handling systems, bad weather, it's not so nice. That's the welfare from the vet's point of view. And it's not a very fulfilling profession either. It's why a lot of vets stop doing large animal work actually I think. You go through university thinking I want to be a cow vet, and then you go to your first job and they just send you TB testing all the time.

I don't need to ask, do I? In these conditions, it'll happen – not through negligence, maybe – exhaustion, rain, struggling and muck would probably cover most mistakes, but if on top of that you're sick to death of doing it, wondering where your life is going.

Larry tells me change is coming anyway. The contracts for testing work are being re-tendered by the government in an effort to save money. No-one's too sure what difference it's going to make: there's a chance it'll just be the same people, but just a different system, and less money. In the end, who else is going to do the testing, except vets? Some vets rely on the work, and although it's a chore, some will prefer to keep it as an opportunity, as Larry said, to get on the farm.

But others might have a different point of view. One veterinary surgery I called who didn't agree to an interview mentioned that they'd contracted the testing work out to a Spanish vet who flew in every few weeks for the testing and then flew back again. Weird. But it reminds me of something Harriet had said to me, that I hadn't really understood at the time.

- one of the things that I also think is the problem with the testing regime is why on earth are you testing your own customers? Your own clients? If I've got an inconclusive and it's one of my best customers, I know which way I'd jump, even though we know that most inconclusive cattle do eventually become conclusive animals. It should be totally independent, it should be done by ministry vets who are trained to the same standard, going to a farm that they have no knowledge of and it should be done properly.

Testing could be a double-edged sword – it gets the vets on the farm to discuss a range of health matters that could help the farmer, but at the same time those visits builds a relationship that could be an obstacle when an awkward moment comes and you've got to make a decision about a borderline case. From what I've heard, though, that's not the half of it.

It's when I'm speaking to Katherine that that funny thing about vets comes up. She's a badger specialist, and she's telling me about how badgers deal with the disease, biologically.

*There's been some published work that you get a latent infection
in badgers, you get the equivalent of ... in badger lungs and Woodchester's work would say that they had badgers and they were infected but they're not culturing any evidence of shedding from. So
we certainly seem to get that.*

Cull supporters and badgers supporters both claim 'their' species,
cows or badgers, carry the disease without becoming infectious.
Farm vets know this about cows, small mammal vets know this
about badgers (if they know anything about badgers at all), and that
knowledge is used to back up a position that says "it's not the badgers'/cows' fault" (delete as appropriate).

This seems silly, and these people aren't silly, so I'd better to look
into it some more. Deep breathe – it's time to get my head around
immune systems. Cue the sound of throat clearing.

(Which, it turns out, is a good place to start.) Biologists talk about
two main systems of immunity – the innate system and the adaptive
system. The innate system is a standard set of defences the body
possesses that repels possible infections in the same ways. The first
line of defence is the skin, saliva, and even tears that keep infection
out by blocking it or washing it away. Once in, the blood takes over,
with white blood cells there to ingest and kill infectious agents
(white blood cells that do this are called 'macrophages'; there are
number of different types, and there are also white blood cells with
different jobs – in other words, they are not 'phagocytic'). If that's
not enough, the white blood cells send out chemical calls for back-
up. The first result is inflammation – the blood flow to the infected
area increases and it swells, feeling hot and looking red. It that's not
enough, the next stage is fever – the whole body heats up, the raised
temperature killing off persistent infection. If that doesn't work,
there's a problem, because inflammation and fever cannot be sustained for long without harming the sufferer.

The adaptive system is the part which provides specific responses
to specific infections. It's not entirely separate from the innate system. White blood cells issue messages with chemicals called cytokines that call up the agents of the adaptive system, and then deliver the infectious agents to these specialist cells. There are two kinds
of responses in the adaptive system – the antibody response, and
the cell-mediated response. Antibodies are the truly bespoke immune response. They are special proteins that are made to bind
with a specific antigen – an infectious agent. When they bind with

an antigen they either block its function completely, or they flag the antigen for destruction by a different kind of white blood cell. B-cells produce antibodies, and they also produce 'memory' cells, which are the ones which keep the record of what kind of antibody to produce with this type of infection. Cell-mediated response involves white blood cells and another type of cell called a dendritic cell delivering antigens to specially-adapted T-cells for destruction, combined with the secretion of further cytokines to enhance the response to the infection.

Different kinds of infection receive different combinations of response from the immune system. Tuberculosis is dealt with mainly with a cell-mediated response. To put it another way, the body finds it hard to come up with an antibody to deal with tuberculosis. Tuberculosis cells have a tough cell wall, which makes it difficult for antibodies to bind to it. The other effect of this toughness is that swallowing a TB bacillus does not mean victory for the macrophage. TB can continue to multiply inside it and destroy it. That is what makes it such a tough disease for any organism, human, bovine, or badger, to beat.

There are differences though, in the way cattle and badgers respond to TB. Mark said that that cattle 'wall off' the disease, and that's a popular way of putting it. Mark called them 'nodules', the biologists call them 'granulomas', but it doesn't really matter. In humans and in cattle, white blood cells called monocytes surround the locus of infection with a fibrous wall, giving the body time to develop immunity – or succumb at a later date. In humans, it has been known for people to show symptoms of the disease as much as 60 years after the initial infection. In cattle, it's this walling-off which contributes to some of the difficulties with the test – a cow with a walled-off infection of bovine TB can pass through skin test as a negative, but she is unlikely to get the time, or the rest, she needs to develop effective antibodies.

Strangely, I can find scientific papers that state that badgers (along with other small mammals) can't perform this walling-off trick (Buddle and Young 2000), but I can also find work that does talk about a latency period for TB infection in badgers just like that in humans, a very slow progression of the disease in badgers, and the chance that a badger that has carried bovine TB for a long time may become immune – get better – if it's able to avoid any one of numerous possible stress factors (Corner, Murphy & Gormley 2011; Gallagher and Clifton-Hadley 2000). It's one of these papers that my badger vet is talking about, one by Gallagher and Clifton-Hadley (2000). It concludes that only slightly infectious badgers probably aren't the main problem for cattle, it's those animals in the advanced stages of the disease.

*

One of the ideal visions a student can have of university life is of the intellectual connection, or relationship. At a highly selective university, and probably one at which the students understand implicitly that they share comparatively good chances of greatness, students can probably expect to find that in each other: it would seem worth it, wouldn't it, to engage with ideas for their own sake with your peers, rather than simply because you've got an essay to write? Maybe only in some corners: student societies for philosophy, perhaps, or debating, or literature.

Another version is the connection with an academic. A tutor, maybe – if you're lucky enough to attend a university that offers tutorials. A less sinister *Miss Jean Brodie* of higher education, or *The History Boys II*, where the sex is less pestilential. Or just, maybe, an inspiring tutor. Or at the very least, one willing to choose protégés. That happens – I've watched with, I admit, some envy, as an academic cherry-picked a student with the right political and class credentials (in this case, radical and working, but I suppose too often it's conservative and middle) and kicked them into fast-forward. No otherwise-obligatory Masters in Research Methods for you, my son, go straight into a PhD of questionable intellectual worth followed by a lectureship at a university of my choice (mine). I'm not envious of the advancement, knowing now how hard it is to keep up in academia, especially at the beginning. If he survived, then who's to say the professor wasn't right to save talent the pain of a slow, bureaucratic, insecure struggle through the wastelands of post-doctoral teaching and research? But I always wanted the relationship it seems to imply, when someone you respect, with that much knowledge and experience, opens up sympathetically and draws you up to them, intellectually at least, helping you become the best of yourself. Surely, that's one of the things that draws quite a few students into doctoral research in the first place – the idea that they will become accepted, enter the circle of light.

There are good reasons why it doesn't happen. Perhaps an academic thinks favouritism is unfair, and that if someone has the talent and desire to become an academic like them, then they will emerge from their student cohort on their own – there are plenty of other students, struggling, disadvantaged, troubled, who could much better benefit from their attention – or at least, who must not suffer while staff play with their favourites. Or possibly an academic believes that kind of closeness is too risky – it creates personal, intellectual and professional dependency that can only harm the young people involved. It would be nice to think that there are academics around with such high pedagogic principles – it makes it easier to accept when your dreams don't happen. But those probably aren't the real reasons why. The real reason is workload.

Academic work (at least, in the social sciences) goes like this. Your time is divided up – so much for teaching, so much for research, and so much for admin. However, the only part that is used to judge whether you get promoted (or at the beginning, not fired), is research. But you are given very few resources to conduct research. Instead, you have to apply for funds from one of the Research Councils, or one of the other funding organisations. So the university pays you to write research proposals, so that you can be paid by someone else. Good system, isn't it? If you're lucky enough to get funding, your wages don't go up, it's just that now the research funder is paying part of your wages, not the university (although it all comes through the university), and you've got some money to spend on travel, or transcription, or a dogsbody – speaking! – or elaborate experiments. Getting funding, doing research – it takes time – probably more that you asked for in the funding bid because you were stupid and wanted to make your proposal look like value for money (or, more often, cheap). One is not enough – you need to be thinking ahead to the next project immediately – after all, you don't know how long it will be before you are successful again. So you carry on writing funding bids. It seems like you're doing more work with less time. Because you are. If one of the other bids comes along too, well, then you'll have to do that as well – and perhaps this time it involves working with a team of academics based at other universities, or in other countries, and suddenly you're haring around trying to build working relationships and communicate almost incommunicable ideas to people who have a completely different point of view, because interdisciplinary work is all the rage now, and it seemed like a good idea at the time, to get the money. Meanwhile your research assistant – at your service! – on the first project could really do with some guidance, and you really really have to write something, because otherwise you won't meet your targets in your annual review, which would mean delayed promotion. You start looking forward to the long train journeys you now make because they're such a great opportunity to write, uninterrupted. And then there's teaching. Two, maybe three courses, depending on the number of tutorials you also take, as well as the Master's dissertations, and possibly, PhD students you supervise. You're relieved to have got through the first three years of your job because you were having to write everything you taught from scratch, prepare for tutorials exhaustively and spend hours fielding emails from all of your students asking questions you had no idea how to answer as well as – nightmare of nightmares – to complete a PGCHE to prove you could teach, or more to the point, to learn how to. But far from being in the clear after three years, you started becoming the second supervisor for PhD students, and because the only other person in your department working in your field is a male professor nearing retirement whose answer to time-management is to absent himself for long periods from the department and claim incompetence with email, you are lumbered with three desperate students needing guidance who take up an hour every time you see them, which now means you're trying to think of ways of moving around the department without being seen. And then there's administration, where, to your amazement, you discover that despite existing since the beginning of the twentieth century, the university still hasn't settled on a straightforward system of administering exams, regularly changing one small element that requires a cascade of further alterations such that the entire system has to be practically reinvented every year, while administrative staff, once the grail of all knowledge about how the university is actually run are being moved, merged, cut, centralised, and generally demoralised by the latest management cult that promises better performance indicators on smaller budgets[29].

Then, some bright effing spark points out that the University of Somewhere Else is offering tutorials to first-year undergraduates which is proving a very popular selling point with potential recruits at UCAS open days, and perhaps we should emulate them, and you think of the paper you have to write by Friday for that conference in

---

[29] For an insight into the sort of culture emerging in some sections of academia, read Colquhoun (2014).

Switzerland, the marking you have to do, the *so*-not-a-PhD you have to read at the weekend (the bad ones always take up more time), and the stumbling marriage that you pretend is fine, but that is basically conducted in the five minutes between finishing work and falling asleep and   you think NOOOOOOOOOOOOOOO!!!!!!!! NOT *MORE* STUDENT CONTACT TIME!!!!

As time has gone on, you've picked up some tips about how to deal with your workload. Early on, you were advised by your mentor at your annual review that your teaching only needs to be 'good enough'. That didn't rub up very well against your feelings about how much students were now paying for their degrees, but as the time demands started biting, you saw sense. You cobbled together a set series of tutorials in which you first teach and then insinuate the values of independent learning in your undergraduate and post-graduate students, so at least they don't bother you so much over the email, or outside of scheduled times. If that fails you imperceptibly trim your behaviour so the student concludes that you are inadequate and decides to bother someone else. And final-ly, as much as possible, you 'stop feeding the email monster'. It starts with students: don't reply too quickly or not at all if you deem the enquiry to be irrelevant or unnecessary. After that, there's a sliding scale, depending on how closely the email fits with your personal interests. Research assistants on your own projects, plenty of attention (your career depends on them), research assistants on projects you are merely involved in are someone else's problem. One-liners at best. This is where your smartphone comes in handy. 'Sent from my ibrand' works as code for 'I'm busy, on the go some-where, don't expect me to engage profoundly with this now'. In your mind there is a dream as fondly nurtured as those dreams of 'intellectual connection' you had when you were a student, and still naïve. You dream of the big one – the research project so huge and significant, it allows you to buy yourself out of teaching entirely and dedicate yourself to your opus.

If I haven't yet met exactly that person, I've come across the cli-mate. It might be fine for some disciplines that are perhaps well-matched with a business-like approach to work and people. But there are other areas where sometimes I worry that things might get lost. Social theory – social ideas – is one of them, because of the way in which social ideas are also political and the way politics are helped if there is some experience, even if only vicarious, to help people to connect to them. Often, an insight into what is at stake in the politics of a particular set of ideas comes from the sort of personal connection that can only happen outside, or at best, in the margins of a hyper-professionalised, productivist model of intellectual work such as the one I have described. And without a sense of what is at stake it becomes more difficult to get to grips with the complex thought that is often found in writing about social theory – indeed, it becomes more difficult to work out why you should bother.

That's the struggle I have had. Back when I was a student of Gail's, I was introduced by her to some really challenging ideas that proposed we look at nature completely differently, that we start to break down that black-box of a category 'nature', and other categories, and take seriously the influence things, and animals, have on the social and political processes play out. But although I could see how the ideas were important, I couldn't see how I could bring them to bear on the political stakes that seemed important at the time: war and climate change. I carried with me an ever vaguer understanding that a naïve valorisation of nature as good was not, perhaps, very helpful, but that paled against the urgency of thinking about how to make something happen on something as important as climate change. After a few years living on air and trying to find a place in environmental campaigning, I got into a PhD about how the environmental movement had influenced climate change debates, thinking it could easily enough be turned into something to say about how to influence climate politics, but the categories of thought and the mode of doing research remained pretty much standard. Something was getting lost, and despite my frustrations with the PhD, I also felt Gail had been leading me down an intellectual cul-de-sac. Coming to Exeter, where I found Gail, and now Steve, still developing that line of thinking, I was shocked to find that here was something happening that felt like it had some real intellectual content to it, something to say rather than just playing a numbers game – but at the same time the message and messengers were somehow disempowered by the complexity of what they were saying and the absence of any background, any marginalia of social interaction around and about work, the sense of a political identity that supported a shared understanding what the stakes were and why they mattered.

So I have to get over a certain amount of animosity to what has for a while seemed like needlessly esoteric work before I can start to engage – but I have to, as Steve is part of the team. Here goes – I'm reading his book.

There was an old lady who swallowed a fly. I don't know why she swallowed a fly, perhaps she'll die.

This won't do. Steve – ten years ago now – clearly made an effort to write clearly, to approach difficult and strange ideas slowly so his stupid student readers could keep up. But it's not helping, the new terms stay somehow underdefined, and although I'm used to letting unfamiliar words hang over a text until they are explained, they are too many, too strange, and too crucial to understanding what's going on. One word really starts to bug me, because it seems straightforward, and Steve uses it in a passing way as if of course I understand what he's on about so he doesn't need to tell me, which is making me feel really stupid, and cross. This term is so straightforward is doesn't even deserve an entry in the index. Folding – simple, isn't it? It's what you do to clothes or paper. Well, try this:

"- according to the prion hypothesis, rogue prions (the malign versions of the proteins) are characterized through their relations rather than by an essence, substance or sequential structure. That is they work, or contribute to the production of disease, through their complex of relations which cause them to fold differently to normal prions" (Hinchliffe 2007, p. 82).

Prions are the proteins implicated in things like BSE and Kreutsfeld-Jakob Disease. This little extract of sentences is fine – things are defined more by the relations with other things that situate them in the world than any innate quality (like the way Derrida thought about meaning and words) – but then at the end comes "through their complex of relations which cause them to *WTF?* differently -" *Fold?*

It's so odd it must mean something; there must be some reason for using 'fold' instead of 'act' or 'behave' or 'respond' or 'have different consequences'. To be fair, Steve has given some clarification a few pages earlier (although it hasn't stopped him scattering the term around throughout the preceding pages). Typically, though, we get the clarification *a propos* of something else. Here goes.

"Another term that is useful here, the progressive meaning of which is derived from Deleuze and Guattari (1988: 238), is 'involution'. The terms evokes the contagion of the world, and it is rather different to the standard notion of evolution or change by

filiation, by hereditary ... involution signals a becoming whereby species are folded together to form blocks of becoming. 'There is a block of becoming that snaps up the wasp and the orchid, but from which no wasp-orchid can ever descend (Deleuze and Guattari, 1988:238). It is evolution by symbiosis rather than filiation" (Hinchliffe 2007, p. 73).

There was an old lady who swallowed a spider. It wriggled and jiggled and wiggled inside her.

This matters intellectually, of course – if I can't understand this, I don't understand it, and can't do anything with it (although that hasn't stopped people in the past – academics are the worst). But it also matters socially and politically. The BBC ran a radio play, oh years ago, featuring a clever middle-class academic who was tutor to an undergraduate – a young woman with a working class background and one or two things on her plate. She was bright but she didn't have the background that gave her a terminology, or even just the confident, commentating attitude towards literature of her public/grammar school peers. The tutor would throw his head back and disport upon some fine point of Shakespeare – or was it Lawrence? And she would say 'what? What do you *mean*?', and he would condescend to explain (he likes her), at which point she would explode with (winsome) rage – 'so why didn't you *say* that?!'

I don't have to reduce academic work to a contest between social classes in order to say that privilege matters. These days there are more academics who started with a working class background – but there is something more to this than class privilege. Academics get paid to explore questions that interest them in depth – there are all sorts of constraints, but they can still pursue their intellectual interests. Most people never get the chance – most never get the chance even to consider that that might be something they could do. And that process of exploration, especially in the social sciences and humanities, makes a difference to the explorer. Changes them; allows them to consider what is important, what is real, how to act. Most people never get the chance to live that sort of a considered life, they might be able to reflect on parts of it, loosely, up to a point – but all deep thinkers dive from a platform of their forerunners and peers, and most people, most of the time, are isolated from that kind of support, have just to keep buggering on, paying their blackmailers for food and shelter, securing, maybe, a few hundred quid a month pension, a modest freedom, too late for the main chance, all the while coughing up so that some luckier f*** can spend a lifetime at university, broadening horizons of knowledge that you will never see.

So it matters whether or not academics make the effort to allow themselves to be understood without a lifetime's professional effort. Maybe not every one of them, individually, but enough, have to come down and say, for the cost of a book from the municipal library, this is what we mean.

Well, at least I know where to go to work out where all these terms fit together, what they mean, and why they matter. Deleuze and Guattari. Turns out it's mainly Deleuze. Sounds like Delhaize, a cheap Belgian supermarket... I pull a few introductions to his work out of the library.

There was an old lady who swallowed a horse.

She died, of course, because she hadn't put in the necessary preparation. To get to grips with these new ideas, it's necessary to follow them back to their first principles. Here are the start points we need to think about first (ahem): 1) the nature of reality; 2) the place for values in living.

No simple divide is ever clear-cut, but here's one for a start anyway. There's a divide in western philosophy between those who study what there is and those who study being. *Analytic* philosophers worry about how to make valid statements about what there is. They get involved in questions related to linguistic, mathematical, or scientific reasoning. This kind of philosopher is more familiar in the UK and US. *Continental* philosophers believe that analytic philosophers approach things in too narrow a fashion – their arguments imply we should all slavishly follow what science tells us, because it's the best, most true set of statements we've got. But continental philosophers have argued that this attempt to approximate truth is doomed because it's impossible to fix the meaning of words and because many of the things we take for granted, that are simply facts, are in fact the result of historical processes, and as such are only the way they are because of long sequences of actions and events combining together – they are highly 'contingent' – so they could just as well be completely different. This debate is important because it has conventionally been understood that values about how to live your life follow on from the foundations of the nature of reality. And if you can't lay any reliable foundations you can't build a moral edifice that governs how you should live.

(For that paragraph, I've relied on the help of Todd May's *Gilles Deleuze: an introduction* (2005), the following paragraphs are mainly supported by Nathan Widder's *Political Theory After Deleuze* (2012)).

This was what that well-known but little-understood philosopher, Nietzsche, was talking about when he said 'God is Dead'. He was saying that something had happened in society to bring down that transcendental being that we used as a basis for our moral philosophy. He was quite specific: the cause was science. Nietzsche described how he thought Christian moral philosophy emerged. It came, he said, out of the dynamic interaction of the dominant and the dominated. Forced into passivity by the overweening power of the strong, the weak nevertheless possess a 'will to power'. Out of the combination of this will and their passive position, the weak create a distinctive moral system, inventing good and evil, and constructing an identity for themselves around the idea that they do no harm, and that those who do (the powerful) are evil. The idea of a transcendent God emerges to give purpose to their forbearance and endurance. The weak, though, can become dominant by – in effect – laying a guilt-trip on the strong. You can choose, they say, between taking action that would harm us and refraining. If you do act, it's really going to hurt me, but that's ok. The weak use guilt to shame the strong over to their own side. In presenting the actions of the strong as a choice, a new identity is developed for and about the strong. Thus Judeo-Christian religion became powerful. The invention of 'God' by this weak system of power gives it purpose because it represents a higher 'truth' toward which it can aim through a 'will to truth'. Because the weak can't be anything other than negative, passive-aggressive, they can't view the world as it is in a very rosy light, so they invent another world in which everything is nice. But the will to truth can be distorted by the perspective of those in power, even when they are of a weak or passive identity. Religious truth is of a moral nature and will seek to assert itself over different kinds of truth, such as the scientific, historical, or personal (think of the Church's conflicts with Galileo, Huxley, and women, respectively). However, the values that are developed from the will to truth are always behind the times – the conditions of life are constantly changing, and values can't keep up. As a result, these values come into conflict with life itself, denigrating it, failing to value it as it really is, at all. That is what Nietzsche calls 'nihilism'.

Far from being a release from an oppressive religious moral system, science has failed to get away from the idea of truth as a moral virtue, and still can't keep up with the conditions of life. Why aim for singular truth, Nietzsche asked, when life seems to be cosmopolitan, flexible, wily and varied? But as science asserts that there is no 'other world', only things and true statements about them, all attempts to construct a system of values on the basis of science fail, and we become resigned to nothingness – another version of nihilism. It is from this point that Nietzsche argues that a "revaluation of values" (Widder 2012, p. 85) has to take place to overcome the state of nihilism. And this is the point at which Gilles Deleuze steps in. The problem, he says, is not the values in themselves, but the basis on which the values are built: the suffering subject that develops a value system based on their powerlessness. How can those who suffer get over their resentment of those who have caused it? The answer is to embrace the process of suffering as inevitable, to make the suffering an act of will (bring it on!), but rather than allow oneself to be defined by it, overcome it, letting go of the identity formed through it, and recognising, not just that one is different as a result, but that one's self is made up of differences. Nietzsche shifts the fundamental question of western philosophy from 'how should we live?' to 'how might we live?' (May 2005) and Gilles Deleuze sets out to answer it. His answer is to say that a view of reality made up of things with distinct identities is the problem, and the solution is to get rid of identities and view reality as made up of difference. Two – well, a lot more than two, but two for now – very important things follow from that thought. The first is that humans – and indeed any*thing* – can no longer be used as discrete or stable units for the purposes of thought and analysis: values and thinking go at last in the direction Nietzsche was pointing, 'beyond the human'. The second is folding.

Enjoying your horse?

According to a taxonomist, the wasp and the orchid are completely different forms of life. One insect, one plant – the point at which their branches separated from the evolutionary tree is way back. If you wrote 'wasp' on a piece of A4 paper, and then wrote 'orchid' somewhere on the paper that reflected how different they were, they'd be quite far apart. But it also happens that this wasp feeds on this orchid and fertilises it in the symbiotic relationship Deleuze and Guattari wrote about above. So how are you going to represent that with your piece of paper? Deleuze and Guattari suggest you fold the paper so the two words come together. 'Involution' means the act of becoming enfolded or entangled, and it also means 'complexity': involuted means that something is tangled and turned back on itself in a complicated way. So think of that piece of paper again, with a lot more different things written on it, screwed up so there are hundreds of folds, representing the complexity of interactions that we observe in the world. That's how Deleuze and Guatarri, and after them, Steve, are thinking of the world – except the folds are constantly changing, and the words written on it are constantly changing, and their meanings, recycled, re-written and re-folded all the time.

And if that's the case, why should we expect one clear, right answer – cattle or badgers, or even cattle and badgers? And how the hell do we work out what to do?

Chapter 7

Police

The farmers I've spoken to so far are not happy about the police. They say the police haven't done enough to enable them to get on with their lawful activities (killing badgers) without inference. The Wounded Badger Patrollers, and the other folk I've spoken to up at Camp Badger, are also unhappy about the police – they feel the police are too close to the cull contractors. Helping them, passing on information. What else could all those dangly, fishing questions be for?

The attitude of the police in relation to political protest has 'come up' in the last few years. For those involved in political protest, it's always a topic, so there's no real beginning to this story, but I need to start this somewhere, so let's take 2008. In a field in Kent, environmental activists have taken over a field not far from a coal-fired power station and set up camp. It's the third year this protest event has happened, and it's got quite big – a few thousand people turn up. A few weeks earlier a small group of activists had stopped a coal train on its way to a power station in Yorkshire, and symbolically unloaded some coal before being arrested, calling on the government to 'Leave it in the Ground'. With activists converging in Kent with the expressed intention of somehow shutting down the power station, the police are keeping it tight, stopping and searching everyone in and out of the site. Most of the people who go there are probably not going to do anything spectacular, maybe get dressed up and walk in the direction of the power station: quite a few families have turned up, and first-time protestors. And then the police make a find: a 'stash' of knives in the woods near the camp, and they display their discovery to the media, claiming this proves that the activists have violent intentions. Journalists dutifully take pictures. The pictures show a selection of what look like cooking utensils. Because that's what they are.

But the police have their justification for a very heavy operation. Dummy night raids on the camp, constant overflights by helicopter, heavy searches, and jumping on anybody who steps out of line from confusion or frustration, wrestling them to the ground using pressure points and half-nelsons. And then the activists make a discovery of their own. Someone has dropped their policing manual. Not just any policing manual: a NETCU[30] manual – the domestic extremism lot. Someone has decided that these environmental campaigners fall into the domestic extremist bracket. Fears are confirmed in an article in *The Observer* a few months later, when a reporter is duped into regurgitating what he is told by the police (*Police warn of growing threat from eco-terrorists*, November 9th). The *Observer* receives a deputation of activists who explain the real character of the British environmental movement, its long traditional of non-violent direct action. A group of academics also write in (*Don't slur activists with the eco-terrorist label*, November 16th), including Clare, pointing out that neither in the US nor the UK have environmental activists been associated with violence against people. A network advocating property damage did get going in the US, but not in the UK. Principally, though, the term eco-terrorism was used in the US as a means to justify an attack on civil liberties.

The tensions between environmental activists and the police rose when in 2009, the police arrested over 100 activists while they were deliberating over plans to disrupt Radcliffe-on-Soar coal-fired power station in Nottinghamshire. It emerged that the police had an undercover officer working among the activists. He blew the whistle on himself when he felt he could no longer support the way in which these non-violent activists were being policed, and in doing so, he undermined a series of cases that had been brought against the activists. But that wasn't all. He, and a number of other undercover officers, had been having relationships – in some cases long-term relationships, with children – with the activists they were spying on. Amidst the media controversy (*The Guardian* and *The Observer* now understood which side they were on), there was a feeling among many activists, men and women, that what had happened was state-sanctioned rape.

But this isn't about climate change – it is, if anything, about animal rights. And unlike the environmentalists, there do seem to be some animal rights activists who don't mind going further. Here's

---

[30]   National Extremist Tactical Coordination Unit

an example, although it's only one of a number I could pick. Darley Oaks Farm bred guinea pigs for animal testing. In 2004, as part of a long-running campaign to get them to stop, a group of activists dug up the grave of the breeder's mother-in-law and hid it on Cannock Chase (BBC 2006). Then, following what has become the standard pattern of animal rights activism, they turned their attention to anyone with a connection to the farm. Like the cleaner. She received bricks through her windows, incendiary devices, and threats attached to voodoo dolls. And then her children suffered attacks on their property – at which point she was forced to resign (*Guardian* 2005). The better-known case is Huntingdon Life Sciences, the animal testing laboratory. There it is companies connected – even indirectly – with the lab that come under pressure with protests, threats, property damage and dangerous devices, as well as that classic instrument of terror, the phone call.

It could be just an innocent phone call. Well, innocent-ish. 'Hello, I'd just like you to tell me why you supply such and such. Are you aware that....?'

Imagine it repeated 10 or fifty times in one day, coming into the same office. The thing is, we get so used to being told that terrorism is some spectacular act that if not intended to kill, is supposed to create fear. But it isn't just that. In a context in which it is known that people who share your concerns are willing to dig up relatives, throw bombs or bricks, trash cars and gardens, protest, and harass, one phone call, sounding innocent enough, can create fear. Now, with violence so well embedded in the public memory, it's hardly necessary to do anything violent or even particularly threatening to create terror. All you need to do is pick up the phone and withhold your number. That fear stains ordinary innocent concern and protest. Because, in fact, what would be so wrong, if you were concerned about an issue, with giving the company or individual a ring to register your concerns?

I manage to speak to two high-up-ish people who had something to do with the policing of the culls. They have slightly more elaborate concerns about anonymity than the other people I've spoken to so far, which means they've vetted the transcripts of the interviews. Any of the interviewees could have done so if they wanted, but only these respondents did. Just the other odd thing – both of them found it necessary to have someone else sit in on the interview for some reason. Might have just been one of those things.

It doesn't take long, during my first interview with 'Nathan', to discover that, if shooters and Wounded Badger Patrollers are not happy with the police, the police are not happy with the cull.

- my view of the way government prepared or shall we say disregarded the policing element is exactly that, they just did not take the policing element of it into account -

This is interesting. Do go on.

They didn't take into account what was bleedin' obvious, there are going to be dozens of protestors ... the fact that it's the middle of the night and the fact that you've got two opposing views, both of which are legal and that's the key thing, they're both legal.

Just to clarify, you view that mistake, that error to be located in DEFRA rather than NFU or Natural England?

Good question. Whether it was a mistake or not or whether it was just arrogance, it's a very interesting line of command. ...

You've got a government policy which is basically to be delivered by DEFRA, they then delegate that down to Natural England, who then say it's a private industry led event which is the NFU and lobby group, who then have a ... company ... who then recruit individuals or subcontractors to carry out a cull.

Well actually, that doesn't look like a government policy anymore, it looks like something's been made legal and is delivered by some contractors on the ground. That's how the accountability looks to me from one argument ... so I think the accountability was missing. So yes, I do blame DEFRA for that.

How big a problem is it?

What do you think the consequence of that was? What problems did that cause?

The consequences are despite what they say, it doesn't look a great success to me. ...

I think the consequences were several, I think first of all, people's expectations of what would be achieved with regards to law and order were completely unrealistic. One gets the impression that the farming community were told that that police would do this, the police would do that, the injunction would deliver this, the courts would deliver that, without any real understanding of what they really would actually achieve. So I think a lot of the community were led to believe that the police's role was very different to what it is -

But, Nathan says, it's not just about practical consequences. It's about the fundamentals of democracy.

- getting on my high horse, it's the independence of the police that has got to be maintained and I think there is a big wake up call, since the miners' strike, we introduced the Human Rights Act and accountability because I think there are some in government believe that we are their puppets and we're not. They don't want us to be enforcing government policy, they want us to uphold the law.

This, I must say, is reassuring, coming from someone like Nathan.

But then, after the recorder is off and I'm packing away, and we're chatting, he says something that opens a pit in my stomach. He links the anti-cull activists to 'ecoterrorism'.

I rant at him in the car all the way home. Whatever animal rights people get up to, it's not ecoterrorism because, as Chris Rootes has pointed out (Rootes and Miller 2000), there are no meaningful links between the animal rights and the environmental movements, and there has never been 'ecoterrorism', either here or in the US, where the term is used. Environmentalist and animal rights activists are not part of the same network. So, even if people with chiefly environmental concerns are getting involved in protesting about the badger culls (and that's what might be interesting about it, that finally, links are being created), and they get involved in actions related to the cull like the ones animal rights activists have taken in the past, *it's still not 'ecoterrorism'*, it's 'animal rights terrorism', if that's what you want to call it. The distinction is important, because if you think of it as animal rights terrorism then you stay focused on the animal rights networks that have historically been responsible for the actions that you're labelling 'terrorist'. But if you say 'ecoterrorism', you capture a lot more people in a much wider net of surveillance under the auspices of monitoring 'domestic extremism', putting entirely innocent and ordinary people at risk of anything from the slight discomfort of suspecting their computer is being hacked to the utter destruction of their entire lives. All because someone in a police unit read a book once about Americans by an American that was politically motivated and, in any case, wrong.

It also matters because the broader term absolves political leaders from responsibility should the tactics become more widespread by allowing the falsehood that they were widespread (though uncommon) in the first place. No-one is asked 'why on earth did you go for a policy that would create the conditions for the enlargement of ultra-radical animals rights networks and the dissemination of their tactics?' or 'why did you create two massive training grounds for violent direct action in the animal rights mould?' Because they're all hippies and nutters, anyway.

You've been framed. A neat little play on words that, great for a laugh-out-loud telly programme. You've been set up and you've also been caught on camera. Social scientists also talk about framing, and the play on words is very similar. A frame is a way of looking at the world around so that some things are excluded and others kept in the picture in order to give a particular meaning to a subject. It's not the truth about it but it's not a lie either, like the dad who is filmed stepping on baby's toy truck and landing on his arse to the hilarity of 1.3 million viewers. He's not normally a complete klutz, but he did go over, and we'd never have got it on video if young Billy hadn't put the truck in just the right place and waited patiently for the perfect shot.

With frames the 'truth' about 'reality' isn't really important. It just matters that people's frames about something match up enough. The video about the day dad broke his coccyx gets screened on TV because the family think it's funny and sends it in, and then the programmer producers and the audience agree. It works because it doesn't end in a screen explaining that Dad spent the next six weeks in agony, trying to keep going at work while chewing painkillers, throwing money he couldn't spare at a private crack-bones, and cursing Billy's cherubic little hide for what he innocently considered to be a great practical joke.

Erving Goffman, the American sociologist who proposed the idea of frame analysis (Goffman 1974), was basically saying that frames in the human mind work in the same way as the frame around a picture or a shot of video. A frame excludes unnecessary or unwanted content, and helps us compose the picture in a meaningful way. Just as Billy's shot edits out the fact that Dad's fall was in fact a carefully set up practical joke, not a hilarious accident, and ignores Dad's long struggle with the consequences of the fall, the idea that the video is funny does exactly the same – it's only funny if we ignore or are unaware of those facts too. So cognitive frames organise the way we think about our experiences, and the framing of pictures, movie scenes, or newspaper stories project a way of thinking about a particular set of experiences. And unless you're always on the lookout, watchful to the point of paranoia to protect your independence of mind, it's easy to go along with what you're being told – or more to the point, the way you're being told it.

The car sweeping along an empty road at 80 gets you to focus on the car and its abilities and edits out the realities of potholes and congestion that reduces most cars to sophisticated carts; the immigrants nicking all our jobs and hospital beds gets you to focus on migration and the rules of the EU and edits out the fiscal attitudes of the Treasury and corporations that contribute to the shortages in the first place. The gory picture of a beagle suffering vivisection gets you to focus on the suffering of the animal and edits out the suffering of the cancer patient.

When frames agree you get frame resonance, a kind of choral 'Aha!' when people realise that, when you put it like that, it seems just so true. Not because it is, necessarily, but because, in unexpressed form, that's what they were thinking anyway. Copy-writers in advertising and PR, journalists, politicians, campaigners – a lot of these people know about 'frames' and most of the time it remains their shared secret while they try to create a frame that will resonate enough with you that you're persuaded to buy what they want, think what they want, donate what they want – or even, just now and then, protest.

Cries like 'We [women, black people, gay people...] have a right to equality with them!' get you to focus on what you have in common with a group and encourages you to take action in its name. It's a collective action frame. Robert Benford and David Snow are another two American sociologists, who, bored with what social movement scholars had hitherto been saying about social movements, suggested applying Goffman's ideas (Snow and Benford 1988). Collective action frames and frame resonance are their proposals. Until then, social scientists thought that social movements were responses to political opportunities, or that they arose because someone organised the resources for them to exist – not just the money, but the social networks where the money and support could come from. But using the idea of frames raises a few doubts: who's to say what is an opportunity? How do social networks get recruited to the political aims of a movement? Instead, it's frames that define (and limit) opportunities, and frame resonance that builds identity among social networks: collective identity

Introducing the idea of frames, then, led people to realise that collective identity was very important to what a social movement is. Some people began to think that collective identity was what defined a movement, because without it all you had was an aggregate of individuals, not a social movement. In fact, one Italian scholar, called Alberto Melucci, argued that collective identity didn't just define a movement, it was one of its signal achievements (Melucci 1996). If the animal rights activists on the one hand and the conservative nature-lovers of Gloucestershire and Somerset on the other manage to come up with a shared collective identity, manage to develop from being pretty much unconnected into a something like a coherent movement, that will be an achievement. The question is, whose? Their own, or the government that created the conditions where they felt they had no other alternative?

Still, if they do come together, no matter how much of what they do could be described as 'terrorism', it's not 'eco-terrorism'. 'Eco-terrorism' is not a collective action frame – it's the inverse, a collective punishment frame imposed from the outside that says 'those people are all the same, and they're up to something bad'.

By the end of the drive I've calmed down. So far, I haven't seen anything that suggests to me that violent or intimidatory tactics are being spread as a result of the cull. There are a few worrying stories going round that suggests they've been used, but nothing to say it's something new. I'm still worried about the eco-terrorist frame, though – the fact that someone like Elizabeth could have had a series of experiences that bear no relation to her approach to opposing the culls or to other people in general. But then, that is exactly how terrorism works, isn't it? The left hand has been letting off a few reminders of the worst they can do – a possible arson in Somerset (Barkham 2014, p. 339), a bit of pointed defamation, a bit of telephone harassment, and suddenly, even the well-meaning and non-violent right hand begins to seem scary, even when it doesn't know what the left hand was doing. And then, back home, stirring around in YouTube, I find something that complicates my simplistic thoughts about the good and the evil. A *Guardian* journalist, Patrick Barkham, has managed to persuade the headline anti-cull activist Jay Tiernan to let him come along for a night of trying to disrupt the shooters. He's even managed to bring a camera operator. After a few shots of driving around at night, running in the dark, and blowing whistles, they stop and Jay gives an interview. Patrick puts it to Jay that farmers and local people are frightened by all this night time activity. Here's Jay's chance to draw a line between Huntingdon Life Sciences and the opposition to the badger cull. I understand why people are afraid, he could say, but everything we're trying to do is non-violent. There are a few idiots and given the history it's going to take some time to clear them out, but 99.9% of people against the badger cull are non-violent. He could, but he doesn't. Instead he says, 'I don't think it's a bad thing to be honest' (*Guardian* 2013).

It would be easy to say of him, 'well, he's just another of those crack-pots'. But when I was at Camp Badger I observed Jay in the marquee, joining conversation about how to manage the social cases that come to the camp over breakfast. He seemed, of all the people I saw there, the most level, sensible. Leader-like. What can I say about this without merely pointing a tabloid finger? How about that, as well as displaying admirable qualities, courage, a sense of justice, moral authority, he also seems somehow diminished, degraded by the conflict he is in, forced somehow, to deny the suffering of others in order to sustain his motive for action?

But this isn't what we want the police to get caught up in, is it? What we want is for them just to police the facts. My second informant, who volunteered himself almost enthusiastically a while after receiving an invitation, reiterated the difficulties that I had heard before:

[We were] trying to get some understanding into the communities, about what had actually – because there was some people within, even the police, that thought that our AFOs – our firearms officers – were the people that were going to be out shooting the badgers.

So it started off from that real lack of understanding about what this meant, how it was going to be delivered. There are people that thought that's what was happening and then people thought that the police's job was to protect the contractors that were doing the cull and that clearly wasn't the case.

Our job was very simply to keep the peace, what we do normally, to protect life and property and to investigate crime.

And they did the job. Everything is under control, his voice tells me, in uncontroversial words and a strong, on-top-of-it tone of voice. No problem. Safe.

There is just a hint, though, of that framing thing going on. A short while later we move off the question of the police's role in safety and licensing, and get onto crime.

- we worked really hard to speak to lots of these different groups, understand exactly what their intentions were, whether it was to do a ramble on a set route [through the countryside] on a particular night, or whether it was to have a telephone campaign to harass people that live in the area, to potentially cause damage, to potentially sitting on badger setts and we were keen to point out to people, what would be criminal activity and what wasn't criminal activity because we found that lots of people engaged in the protest, didn't want to criminalise themselves, so part of keeping people safe was also keeping them safe from prosecution, so that they were armed with the best information, if they wanted to get themselves arrested, "this is how you get yourselves arrested but if you don't want to get yourselves arrested, this is the line you can come up to", I think that was pretty successful -

It looks like the protestors are framed as the potential criminals, while the shooters are not. The Wounded Badger Patrollers that I have spoken to, at least, seem to have been learning otherwise. It's not just the car chases and the crow scarers, it's about the way in which the culling is done. Where it's done. Because the Patrollers I'm speaking to are beginning to ask questions about some of the things they've seen. Like the night we saw a shooters' van speed off as soon as it saw us coming, walking up a path in a wood managed by the Wildlife Trust – who haven't given permission for culling to take place on their land. If culling has taken place where it shouldn't, isn't that a breach of the licence? And if a shooter has breached their licence, why wasn't what they were doing also against the Badger Act?

A little later on, two incidents come to light that simply could not have been made up, not even by Terry Pratchett.

1) So, there's this guy who's known on TV and who sometimes goes out with a famous model who is often featured on a particular page of some newspapers and not others. For a reason that is beyond both you and me, he's got a job driving dead badgers from Gloucestershire to the incinerator. He's driving a van full of about

200 dead badgers when he hits a bus shelter, causing a nasty mess. There are all kinds of distracting details about this story, such as his lack of a valid driving licence, but this one in particular stands out. He claims that a radio got stuck underneath his brake pedal, causing him to lose control. It's the radio he's been using to listen to police updates about where the protestors are, and thus, how to keep out of their way (*Independent* 2014).

2) Down in Somerset, there's a man – a Wounded Badger Patroller – standing near the spot where a dead and wounded badger had been found and whisked off to the animal hospital. Some shooters arrive, belatedly, looking for their badger. The exchange goes something like this:

"Looking for a badger?"

"Give it back!"

Thump.

I'm not making any comment about who hit whom first. Ask the nearest primary school teacher. Anyway, the Patroller phones the police to report he's been assaulted. The shooters phone their control to report an assault. Some police arrive, and start to investigate the Wounded Badger Patroller, treating him as if he was the suspect, which, given that he thinks he's the victim, gets right up his nose and an awkward half-hour ensues. Luckily for us though, the Patroller recorded everything on his handy voice recorder. How was it that the officers responding to the shooters' call should arrive some thirty minutes before those who were responding to the Patroller's call? Surely, someone would still have had to pass the message on from the shooters' control room to the police.

No. Because the shooters' control room was the same room as the police control room. The police officers responding to the Patroller's call were dispatched late, then got lost, and then were distracted by a couple of suspicious figures dressed in black running across a field. They thought they might have nicked a badger (Avon and Somerset Constabulary 2014).

One of these stories is ripe for a conspiracy theory, the other has got a punch-line. But that's for later. For now, they're just here to show how strongly that frame about protestors was set up, how far it went in seeming to influence how people really behaved, on the ground, during the culls. The reason, when I put it to him, that my second informant gave for sharing a control room with the NFU was straightforward: public safety. They were keeping shooters out of the way of protestors for the sake of public safety. And perhaps they were justified. It doesn't take long, reading around the subject (by which I mean searching online), to find out the level of danger the police might have been worrying about. As recently as 2012 a group was letting off firebombs in the area around Bristol. They hit a bank, a car sales yard, and a police site. The attacks were connected with anarchist rhetoric not alien to animal rights networks. With people around who were willing to say that 'people should be afraid', why shouldn't the police be taking the threat seriously?

But then again, there are big differences between having a strong view about something, thinking something ought to be done, doing something about it, and doing something violent, and the police ought to be able to work out the difference. There's also a difference between protest and direct action: not all protest is direct action and not all direct action is protest. So if a bunch of people want to go and walk around footpaths at night and look out for wounded badgers because they've got reason to think there might be some, and you steer them away from the places the wounded badgers might be, or you're unable to give them the same level of service as the people trying to shoot the badgers, then regardless of your intentions, the effect of, say, having a co-ordinator of the shooting in your control room is political bias.

But then again again, I wouldn't want to be the police officer having to stand up in a coroner's court trying to explain why, in the strict service of neutral policing I found it necessary to tolerate a slightly higher risk to public safety and allow Wounded Badger Patrollers to enter areas where I knew shooters were trying to kill badgers. Being in that position, and trying to palm the blame off on the shooters and their safety procedures which, when applied correctly, would have prevented the death of the individual in question would be, in my mind, a touch too late. Damned if you do and at best, out of a job if you don't. But above all, I would resent being put in that position in the first place.

Chapter 8

Results

It's April 3rd. I'm off on one of my long journeys, keeping the family together, when I get a call from my wife. 'The report's out.' What does it say? 'The cull wasn't effective or humane.' Are they going to roll it out? 'No, but they're going to continue in Gloucestershire and Somerset.' What? 'Paterson's just been interviewed on PM. You should listen to it, it's amazing.' I have a couple of days back at work before I'm off for Easter again, and I spend the time catching up. My parents are around; they do the child-care. There's not just the Independent Expert Panel (IEP) report (IEP 2014), there are also three AHVLA reports (AHVLA 2014a, 2014b, 2014c), DEFRA's response (DEFRA 2014b), and their new strategy for tacking bovine TB (DEFRA 2014a), published on the same day. Dad says I've missed an interview on the Today programme but that's 3 hours long, the item isn't flagged on the website and I haven't got time. First of all, then, I hunt down Eddie Mair's interview on the BBC's PM programme (BBC 2014). He starts off speaking to John Krebs, who advised on the RBCT, and then turns to Owen Paterson.

Mair: - The government's been trialling the cull of badgers in two areas of Gloucestershire and Somerset with a view to spreading the cull to other areas but today the Environment Secretary Owen Paterson announced the cull would not spread elsewhere but it would carry on in those two parts of the country. So how did these trials fail? Lord Krebs is an expert on and critic of culling badgers.

Krebs: The pilot culls failed on two of three counts. They failed on efficacy. They managed to kill in the six-week period fewer than half the number of badgers they were supposed to kill. On the humaneness count the pilots also failed in that somewhere between 7% and 22% of badgers lived longer than five minutes after being shot. Really this is the moment when the Government ought to step back and say, 'Is it right really to focus on trying to kill badgers or should we focus on biosecurity – keeping badgers away from cattle and cattle away from badgers, and preventing cattle-to-cattle transmission.

Mair: Well, the Environment Secretary has been speaking to PM. Owen Paterson, these pilots were designed to test whether controlled shooting of free-ranging badgers was safe, humane, and effective. Was it humane?

Paterson: These were pilots to establish the technique of free shooting and the cull companies themselves learnt obvious practical lessons and the Independent Panel report has given us some clear recommendations on how we could improve on humaneness and on effectiveness. So on humaneness, 68 out of 69 badgers died pretty much instantly, but a number didn't, and the Panel have come up with a number of helpful recommendations which are really practical, on how we can improve that technique.

Mair: On the basis of the culls that have taken place, were they humane?

Paterson: Er – I have said 68 out of 69 died almost instantly -

Mair: And in your view, is that humane?

Paterson: - a number didn't. You are talking about shooting a wild animal in difficult rugged countryside, in the night, in difficult weather, and perfection, sadly, is impossible.

Mair: I'm thinking about this from the badger's point of view, not the point of view of the shooter. Was it humane?

Paterson: As I've said, if you're one of the 68 that died almost instantly, yes, that was humane. If you were one of the smaller number that took longer, it is quite clear from the Panel report, who set a five minute threshold, that they want us to improve on that.

Mair: Well, they said as many as 20% of the badgers that were shot at were still alive after five minutes and therefore risked experiencing marked pain.

Paterson: Yes, they did take seven where no-body knows what happened to them. We don't know whether they were hit, we don't know whether they were all missed, so that has made that ratio, out of the 88, that's a significant proportion. The real lesson is that there are some improvements to be made. Er – shooting is never going to be perfect, but we will always want to improve our techniques.

Mair: Let's talk about effectiveness, which you've touched on. The Panel said it's extremely likely that combined shooting and cage trapping removed fewer than half the badgers in the trial areas. That's not very effective, is it?

Paterson: No, but these are pilots, and they got off to a slow start. These pilots are intended to go on for four years, and we mustn't lose sight that this whole exercise is to bear down on disease.

Mair: Understood. I do want to ask you about these culls, though. Not as humane as they could have been, certainly not as effective, and yet they're going to carry on in these pilot areas. Why?

Paterson: Because they're pilots, and we cannot sit on our hands and do nothing -

Mair: No-one's suggesting you do, are they?

Paterson: We have to recognise that we have a problem of disease in wildlife and we have to address it, so -

Mair: Not [inaudible, 'humane', presumably], not effective, but they carry on, and this time, it should be said, with no independent oversight to assess their future performance. You have something that doesn't work, leaves animals in great pain, you're going to carry on doing it, without ever knowing impartially what's happening.

Paterson: Eddie, you're ignoring the tens of thousands of badgers dying hideous deaths from tuberculosis -

Mair: That doesn't justify carrying on with the culls in these areas.

Paterson: No, you've made a very broad statement, which I've said is inaccurate. I'm quite clear that it is prudent and sensible and responsible to continue these two pilots -

Mair: With no independent oversight.

Paterson: - which I've always intended, having learnt the lessons from the cull companies themselves, and from the Independent Panel, and there will be oversight

Mair: No independent oversight.

Paterson: - part of the licence. Yes, there will, because Natural England has a role to enforce and oversee the management of these cull pilots.

Mair: And is today's announcement something you personally are entirely happy with?

Paterson: [takes a deep breath and speaks with a sigh] Well, obviously, I would prefer to move much faster on the goals of disease in the high risk areas, I would much prefer to have gone on – but that is only a delay, I'm absolutely clear that if you look at other countries, Australia, New Zealand, and above all the Republic of Ireland, the Republic of Ireland has seen a spectacular drop. How? They've followed exactly what we're doing here, very tough testing regime, cattle movement controls, slaughter of reactor cattle, but they have removed diseased badgers. And I'm happy to say, as someone who had two pet badgers as a child, the average Irish badger is one kilogramme heavier than before the cull, so they've ended up – or headed to a destination we want to get to. I want England to be TB free.

Mair: In all of your years in politics, have you ever seen a more disastrous pilot scheme than this one?

Paterson: That's a rather inflammatory question

Mair: What's the answer?

Paterson: - a rather tendentious question. The answer is, it's a nonsense question. The answer is: these were pilots. They were set up to trial a technique which has never been undertaken anywhere before, and I really take my hat off and I do praise those who carried out the pilots under very severe provocation in some cases from protestors. They are determined to try to establish a technique which can remove diseased badgers in a humane, effective and safe manner -

Mair: Mr. Paterson ... – Isn't it appropriate for politicians to test anything? And these tests go on in all walks of politics, all parts of public life, to test whether new things work. We've had this pilot scheme, it's not only the Shadow Environment Secretary who calls this pilot disastrous. The Institute of Zoology wonders whether the pilot culls are making a bad situation worse, the Humane Society says its indefensible you're carrying regardless with your, what they *call, discredited cull. Don't you look at these results and say 'this isn't working, we need to stop this'?*

Paterson: Er – I look at the numbers of cattle – 314,000 cattle hauled off to slaughter quite unnecessarily -

Mair: That's the problem, this is your proposed solution, which I'm suggesting is not working.

Paterson: Last year 13,620 across GB, that's over 90 a day.

We have set up these pilots with a view to see if we can establish a method of removing diseased wildlife.

Mair: They've failed.

Paterson: We have learnt lessons ourselves. There is some very helpful advice from the Independent Panel, we will make improvements, because I am quite determined that we will follow the example of other same countries that have borne down on this disease, not just in cattle but also in wildlife.

Mair: You brought up your badgers, tell me about your two badgers as a boy.

Paterson: Well, it was a very long time ago, and I had two pet badgers for a not terribly long time, so this picture that I'm not keen on having healthy badgers is false. I very much see the badgers as a key, an iconic creature in the British countryside, but I want to see healthy badgers.

The problem with the political interview these days is that it has been debased by media training. Politicians, executives and PR professionals have been taught their ABC of media interviews. It stands for 'Acknowledge, Bridge, Comment'. It basically means not answering the question, instead segueing into whatever you have prepared to say ahead of time – your frame. The interviewer has to ask the same question again, creating the risk that they make the politician look bad by refusing to answer. That's OK for a short interview because the politician can just bluff out the seconds, and bet that the journalist will have to change tack at some point in order to get something out of it. But this interview is between 7 and 8 minutes long, a broadcasting eternity. One reason why Mair is good is because he doesn't just repeat the question, he unpicks the comment, so he's highlighted that Paterson is trying to avoid something, and he's showed that Paterson's comments are less than tasteful (humane for badgers, not shooters), and that they are, shall we say, incomplete with the facts (68 out of 69 versus 20%). The game Mair starts out with is a labelling game. The IEP said too many badgers took too long to die – so, the culls were inhumane. If the culls were inhumane they shouldn't continue. Paterson, though, concentrates on the strict implications of 'humaneness' – it's a matter of degree, or learning to get better. He has no choice but to avoid answering the question head on, because the cost of admitting the 'inhumane' label is too high: the end of the culls. He has to take the hit and move on to the next question: effectiveness. He acknowledges, "No", bridges, "but these are pilots, and they got off to a slow start -" and comments, "These pilots are intended to go on for four years -" but it's all been done too quickly, and Mair cuts in. He's got his acknowledgement, so he's moving on, but he does so in a way that prevents Paterson from going back over the previous ground, thus avoiding the big question, the one just about to come up. Instead of asserting that the culls were 'inhumane', Mair appears to cede ground to Paterson's frame. He says 'not as humane as they could have been' – but as he does so, he phrases it to contrast the stark humanitarian ethic and the leisurely implications of 'as it could have been' – as if he were reviewing a football match. The next question seems like the big one, the one he's been building up to by preparing this ground: why are they continuing? But it isn't. Another reason why Mair is good is because he's done his research – or at least someone has done it for him (they've had all day at PM after all, unlike John Humphreys and others on the Today programme). He interrupts, preventing Paterson from sliding into a pre-prepared comment, and insists that he is going to get an answer on independent oversight. He pushes Owen Paterson to answer with 'Natural England'. Conscious listeners will have been wondering 'and how, exactly, is Natural England *independent*'?

From then, Mair could have gone on about independence, but Radio 4 listeners are presumed to be relatively intelligent, and pushing Paterson into full defensive was not going to help. Mair lets Paterson deliver a bit of script, lets him relax a bit. And then Mair asks what looks like a stupid, awful question. This is Paterson's opportunity to take control. He could have said 'Well, in fact, pilot schemes don't go as well as hoped all the time for lots of reasons, but that's no reason to junk the whole policy. A sensible politician will look at the details, take advice, and try to improve it. For example...'. But no. Instead, Paterson feels he has to tell the audience what to think, and starts being rude about Mair's professional abilities ('a nonsense question'). He is, in short, exposed as arrogant. And of course, because Mair doesn't ask nonsense questions, he's fallen into a trap – research again. It's not just me, says Mair, but these respectable institutions. Paterson forgets to acknowledge and bridge, unless 'er' counts, but eventually Mair lets him 'comment', because the job has been done – and at last comes the easy question. Tell me about... Coming at the start it's used to put interviewees at ease. Coming at the end, it's the payoff. Perhaps he's just exhausted after several tough interviews. Paterson does something for which he has only himself to blame, he says 'not for a terribly long time'. He undermines everything he has just said by demonstrating that he is quite happy to pretend that a minor part of his childhood is a source of credibility on government policy.

*

Back at work after Easter, and it's time to read the reports. I start with the AHVLA (APHA) reports – they're the ones who have actually done the monitoring – and with effectiveness. There are two reports, as the AHVLA also has results for the extension period even though these weren't available to the IEP when they were evaluating the culls. I look at the report on the first six weeks (AHVLA 2014a). The prose is desiccated, but the basic points are that it's very difficult to estimate the total population of badgers and that the culls got nowhere near their target. They weren't even close to 60%, which is what Peter Kendall, the boss of the NFU, was claiming at the time of the extension. The AHVLA, at the request of the IEP, have used two methods to estimate the badger population. First, they set up traps along badger-runs and near setts in 50 1km x 1km squares in both cull zones. They traps were not for badgers, but badger hair. They were highly sophisticated. They were made of two sticks and a piece of barbed wire. The hair traps scraped hair off passing badgers' backs and the researchers collected the samples and extracted DNA, using a Genetic Analyser to identify individuals, just like they used to do on Blue Peter. They used this data for two kinds of analysis. In one method, they used the number of times the hair of individual badgers was recaptured during data collection to generate an estimate of the population. In the other, they matched DNA profiles of the badgers culled with the profiles they had collected and developed an estimate from there (based on probability: the higher the badger population, the less chance any single badger would turn up in the cull, so, for any given number of culled badgers, the fewer the matches, the higher the population). This second method, was, according to the AHVLA, the primary method. They thought it was better. They didn't use hair to get the DNA profiles of the badgers that were culled though. They used ear tips. Something about that, as I scanned through the report on the extension and the cull as a whole (AHVLA 2014b) – same story, effectiveness around 45% in Gloucestershire and 35% in Somerset – was niggling me. Must have had an effect on me as I started on the report about humaneness (AHVLA 2014c).

It's a long report, and the authors have broken the job of assessing humaness down into seven parts:

- Objective 1: To determine the time period between the first shot taken at the badger and death of the badger.

- Objective 2: To determine the proportion of badgers that are not recovered after being shot at with a firearm, and have firearm injuries.

- Objective 3: To describe the behaviour of badgers after being shot at with a firearm.

- Objective 4: To determine the location of rifle/shotgun entry wounds in the badger carcases recovered from observed and unobserved shootings.

- Objective 5: To determine the extent of internal firearm injuries in the badger carcases recovered from observed and unobserved shootings.

- Objective 6: To investigate whether there is any evidence of correlation between the times to death determined by Objective 1 and the firearm injuries recorded in badger carcases recovered from observed shootings.

- Objective 7: To compare the firearm injuries in badger carcases recovered from observed shootings with those in badger carcases recovered from unobserved shootings" (AHVLA 2014c, p. 11).

I can see that the first five objectives would bear on humaneness well enough, but I've got to think about six and seven. Six is about working out if it makes much difference where the badger is hit. Seven is about checking whether the shooters were any better or worse at their job when an observer was around.

OK, well, I'm not expecting this to be fun, so let's get on with it. I get through objective 1 and 2 all right – they're a matter of statistics. A few badgers were picked up a long time after being shot, a few weren't recovered at all, but there's not much evidence to say they had been hit or spent much time suffering. I move on to the badgers' behaviour after being shot. This is where I start to struggle.

"The behaviours displayed by badgers after being shot at included running (galloping and trotting), standing or sitting with fast erratic movement of the head, body and legs but no lateral movement, recumbency with smooth movement of the head, and recumbency with apparent involuntary movement of only the legs. Nineteen of the 74 badgers whose carcases were recovered and for which detailed behaviour was recorded ran after being shot at; the mean duration that badgers ran before collapsing was 7.5 seconds (range 1 to 15 seconds). Nine of the 10 badgers that were not recovered also ran after the shot was fired; the mean duration in view was 23 seconds (range 4 to 90 seconds). One of the non-recovered badgers initially collapsed, but had moved away from the shot site after a second shot was fired. Movement indicative of consciousness, including running, was seen in 58 of the 73 badgers whose carcases were recovered and detailed behaviour recorded. Behaviours indicative of consciousness continued for a mean of 30 seconds after the shot was taken (range 2 to 823 seconds). Badgers collapsed and showed only involuntary movement, if any, in 15 (18 %) of the recorded events. The mean distance that badger carcases were found away from where they were when the shot was taken was 3 metres (range 0 to 25 metres). Fifty (64%) of the recovered badger carcases were found at the site where they were shot. Vocalisations were heard in only a single event (1% of events). The vocalisation was described as a chatter" (AHVLA 2014c, p. 31).

I plough on. Lots of tables about where the badgers were hit. Something soothing about tables of figures. Everything's under control. And then this.

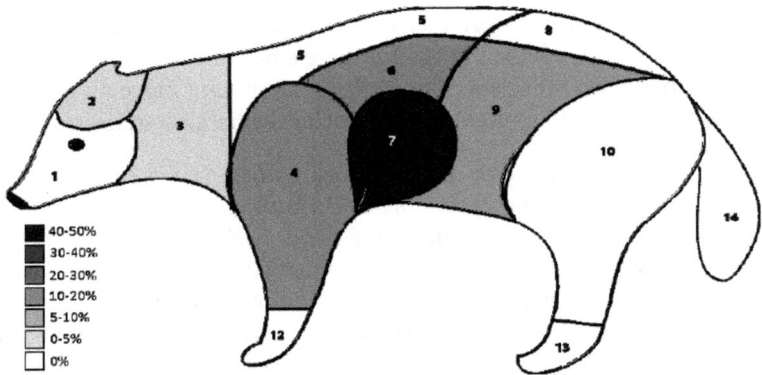

Figure 8.1. Diagram showing proportions of first entry wound locations by anatomical unit, for observed badgers.

Source: Figure 9, AHVLA 2014c, p.41.

The report continues:

"For carcases where the target area set status could be determined with certainty, the proportion of first entry wounds that was 'inside target area' was 36.1% (28.6-44.2%). Assuming the 'best case scenario' (that the carcases of uncertain status actually had the first entry wound location in the 'best' of the possible set options (the 'inside target area' set)), the proportion of first entry wounds that was 'inside target area' was 37.3% (29.8-45.4%). Assuming the 'worst case scenario' (that the carcases of uncertain status actually had the first entry wound location in the 'worst' of the possible set options (the 'outside target area' set)), the proportion of first entry wounds that was 'inside target area' was 35.4% (28.0-43.4%)" (AHVLA 2014c, p. 42).

But that's as far as I get. Figure 9 has made my eyes fill up. I sit, staring at it on the screen, and in those moments, everything changes. The arguments fall away. This is all wrong.

In those moments I realise that the report, the IEP, DEFRA, everyone, have got humaneness the wrong way round. Free shooting might have caused suffering for slightly too many badgers, but it's inhumane for the people involved. For all that the AHVLA scientists have applied their clear, objective, professional analysis to the problem, they've still committed the cardinal sin of biology: imposing human categories on animals. I try to think what it must have felt like to write the report. To write the word 'chatter'. Did they feel anything at all – brutalised, at all? Worse if they didn't. We can cause suffering in animals, we can be cruel to them, but we can only be humane to ourselves.

I change, just as when you drop acid into a pH indicator. Except it's not acid. It's pain.

Now that the IEP report is out I need to speak to everyone again and find out what they think about it. Not too quickly – I leave it a few weeks to give people a chance to read it and work out what it means. Then, through May and June I phone around, crossing a name off the list now and then, and listen, down the line, to what my respondents have to say. After a few goes I realise I have to watch out. The thing is that I'm bored. Not just slightly bored, but intensely, deeply, psychologically unable to concentrate on what the person on the other end of the phone has to say. I notice that I must sound bored, too, and that I'm missing cues for keeping up my end of a lively, if intentionally one-sided, conversation. I have to force myself to stop doodling and at least act interested.

The problem is that a lot of what I'm hearing is all so predictable. Some of my respondents have simply been unable to keep up with the policy events, and don't know what's in the IEP report. The opponents of the cull I speak to are enraged that the government are ignoring the conclusions of the report and carrying on with the culling. The cull's supporters criticise the report for imposing unrealistic and unfair criteria for judging the humaneness of the culls, in particular, and insist that this was just a pilot, that it'll be done much better next time. Everyone feels their views have been vindicated, somehow. Independent scrutiny of the culls – 'science' – has, in other words, done nothing whatsoever to move the policy debate forward. Instead, as a contribution to the policy process, it has simply acted as yet more terrain around which the warring sides can entrench their positions.

The view of the cull supporters is put by Henry – Farmer Spoligotype. The pattern of his response is exactly the same as before. The protestors are the ones causing the problem with the cull, and the 'science' is rubbish.

So what is your view of the outcome of the cull then?

*I think certainly ... we had quite a challenging time with protes-
tors, and there's no doubt that their influence was quite significant
in terms of the efficacy and possibly to some extent the humaneness
of the effort that we put in. That really doesn't seem to have been in
any way taken note of by the independent expert group other than
their comments on safety that all things considered it appears to
have been done pretty safely. But certainly in terms of effectiveness,
this is numbers of badgers taken overall, and on occasions possibly
certainly the monitoring of the humaneness, there was quite an
influence from the protestors probably more so in Gloucestershire
than Somerset.*

*One of the other things that they said about humaneness was that
they commented on problems with shooting accuracy. I suppose
the thing about humaneness that might have been an issue with
protestors was the difficulty in retrieving some of the shot badgers.
So there's a big question mark about how long they took to die
which kind of enters into things, but there was also a question
about shooting accuracy with relation to humaneness.*

*I think the majority of evidence of the ones that were directly ob-
served and post-mortemed, I think there was only one that their
estimate took longer than five minutes to die. To my mind that's a
pretty good assessment of the capability of controlled shooting. As
you say, the question mark comes over these ones where they were
uncertain because they weren't collected in time or observed in
time. IEP seem to have taken a hugely cautious view on this one,
and of course the worst of their outcomes are the ones that always
get quoted in the press. Whereas no other wild animal assessment
of humaneness has ever gone into this sort of detail.*

*I think if standards had been applied to deer and foxes and other
animals in the past where there's a licence and you're allowed to
shoot, I don't honestly think the outcome for badgers would have
been assessed as being any different, it would have probably been
regarded as perfectly humane. But of course this was because of the
politics involved with the badger cull was under such a microscope,
and then their assessment was hugely cautious, in our view made
some ridiculous assumptions on the cautious side, then it obviously
skewed the figures in our view.*

Which assumptions did you think were problematic?

I think the fact that they couldn't find – I can't remember exact numbers – but I think there were nine or so badgers that were indicated they might have been shot, or shots were taken at, and then they couldn't find them. I think there's only three that they actually ... were pretty certain were actually hit. The others might well have been missed, but the independent expert group seemed to assume that they were probably hit and then took a long time to die, and of course that hugely skews what's a relatively a small sample the overall thing. The other evidence which is just the wider post-mortem of badgers seemed to indicate that humaneness was pretty much guaranteed with the shooting. So we think it's these observed but not seen afterwards' ones that really have to some extent skewed it quite badly the wrong way.

Just about the only thing keeping me sane during these interviews is the opportunity to come back on one of the points the respondent made in the last interview. Challenge them a bit. For Henry, then, it had to be spoligotypes.

When we spoke last time you talked about the spoligotype maps that showed clusters of different strains of bTB, which to your mind fit very well with the idea of there being a local host, the local host being badgers, and that producing a cycle of these strains staying in those areas. I went back and looked at the paper and they've suggested two things. Because the other thing that was interesting about that was that 85% of bTB was actually one spoligotype, Type 9, and they were trying to get a hold of why that might be. Basically they talked about there having at some point been a bottleneck in the population for bTB, so for example when policies got the incidence of bTB in cattle down to a very few, and that this particular type, Type 9, had the genetic adaptation for some reason to carry on through that.

The two possibilities they talked about were that it could be that they are somehow specially adapted to badgers so that it was being hosted very well. The other possibility was that this Type 9 is actually distinct genetically from the type of bTB that was used to produce the tuberculin that's used for the test, so it's just possible that the test isn't picking up Type 9 as well as it does other types of strains of bTB. I just wondered what you thought of that kind of alternative possibility?

Yes, I suppose those are theories which they ought to be doing some experimental work on to try and find out. I have not read that 80% of all TB is Type 9[31], I must admit that's news to me. Certainly in our area Type ... is the predominant one and a large number of farmers in my area have that, and there's a hell of cattle taken out of ..., maybe not as much as Devon. It's possible. There's sub-typing beyond spoligotypes, VTNR work and that sort of thing, which the experts can trace an awful lot more of.

But I think the key thing about all of this is that while you can pick up TB that's been moved by cattle into the clean areas in the past, the clean areas getting smaller over time, but if you go back to when I started farming, the dirty area was about a few square miles in about three counties, and it's just got completely out of hand. Once they've started doing spoligotyping work you could pick up exactly where animals have come from, if they've move to the clean areas. But the evidence, and particularly when they were mapping badgers and cattle side-by-side ... and that's the thing that's missing under current spoligotyping is that they're not really getting the evidence from the badger population.

That's when you got this very discrete picture that if it had been just cattle causing the problem, the way we trade cattle and move them about, although there's evidence that cattle don't necessarily move that far, we know they do move some pretty big distances. If it was cattle driving the disease you'd very soon get a pretty homogenous mix of spoligotypes all over the place. But you don't get that, it has stayed remarkably persistent, even when you just look at cattle alone within areas.

One of the counter-arguments I came across for that was that actually most cattle movements are local, so actually cattle

---

[31]   No indeed, because, if you compare what I said here with the actual article, or indeed my summary of it above, you can see that I've miss-poken. I've got the overall point of it, but not the detail, that it's the clonal complex of Type 9 that is responsible for 85% of bTB cases.

movements themselves could also just as well produce ... What do you think about that?

I don't think that's actually true. A lot of that's extrapolated data from BCMS[32]. The problem there is that because every time you move an animal to market and back again, yes it does appear, and sometimes when you move it from farm to farm it appears as local movements. But actually cattle trading as witnessed by the sort of outbreaks that have taken place over many years in the eastern counties from cattle traded out of the west country, none of that has ever led to persistent recurrent TB. It happens all the time. It's happened every year for about the last 30 years, but it's never ever led to persistent TB taking place there.

But even within the cattle areas that we know about, there's still a very significant amount of TB that moves quite large distances with cattle. Yes, probably the majority of movements are relatively local, but relatively local is still 40 or 50 miles, and some of the spoligotypes are even tighter than that. Cornwall for instance has got three very definite spoligotypes in it. You can't say that there isn't a fairly profound movement of cattle around Cornwall and from Cornwall into other parts of the south-west, so to me that argument just doesn't really stack up.

You could almost say that Henry would have made a decent scientist in another life. The science is rubbish, we need more science. Scientists are allowed their pet theories, convictions, even obsessions about what the as-yet-'unrevealed' fact of the matter is. The difference is that Henry is not prepared to wait for the scientific uncertainties to be diminished before committing to a controversial political action, because he believes that he has privileged access to a better knowledge. Concrete, on-the-ground, reality, the facts.

But Henry has been committed to his view for such a long time that we can hardly expect him to be shaken by the findings of what is merely the latest in a long history of independent reports on culling badgers. But what about someone who had seemed a little more balanced about their support, someone, perhaps, who might

---

[32] The British Cattle Movement Service.

be more susceptible to what a group of fellow scientific minds had to say?

Larry, I thought, was like that. When I spoke to him first time round he was not opposed to the cull, but then he didn't like the idea of killing badgers either. He held some hope that the culls would make a difference to the drudgery of testing, so how would he respond to the independent panel's findings that free-shooting, at least, was ineffective? As he's a vet, though, I decide to start by finding out what his farm clients have been saying to him about the cull.

What have they been telling you about how they thought it went?

Most of them felt very positive about it actually, they went very well, many said there were far more badgers on the farm than they ever imagined, some farmers had contractors in and others did it themselves and in some areas there was lots of disruption from protestors, to the extent that they didn't do it as successfully as other areas that were far more remote, they had night vision stuff and they reckon they got all the badgers and said, "we've been feeling better since", so very mixed really.

The big message I got was they felt positive and it was a success but on the other hand, others would say interference from protestors was a significant hindrance and some were quite aggressive and confrontational.

What's your view of the outcome then, having heard all of that?

The only view I can draw is what I've been told from the farmers, from their point of view it's been successful when it's been allowed to happen. The protestors are a bit of a frustrating sector. In terms of the long-term effect of the cull, we haven't really seen that yet I guess because we've not had a chance to test the cattle in a long period of time after the cull to see whether there's any benefit. That's my main thought I guess.

Could I ask you about the independent expert panel report into the effectiveness, humaneness and safety of the cull, what's your reaction to its findings?

I think there's been a hidden agenda somewhere, I think it misrepresents the true situation, [Inaudible, talking about criteria for humaneness]. I'm not sure where they got the data from, there were a few observers out there as far as I'm aware but I think in most cases, it was probably quite successful and I think maybe there was a hidden agenda by the people who wrote the report, I'm not a conspiracy theorist, I don't know whether that's really the case but the farmers seem to think it was doomed to fail, we did this to tick a box and now they say "You can't do it this way".

I think it may be an inaccurate version of events or been skewed in favour of not continuing the cull, so all in all quite disappointed really.

In terms of effectiveness, you say they didn't deliver the level of culling that had been set by the government?

No, in some areas people have said "there are no more badgers to kill", maybe because the estimates were incorrect, I think if they did get al.l the badgers and they may have been accurate or inaccurate numbers, in other areas where protestors, if you averaged out the total number of badgers in a given area, maybe they didn't reach the target, mainly because of protestors. There was no mention of any of this in the report, the perturbation effect by the protestors really, it's just been the people, they obviously put the guns away as soon as protestors appeared and also the cost of the whole exercise, it's cost X millions of pounds and so much per badger and you haven't got the numbers required, well not once was it mentioned that the protestors were a significant spanner in the works in many locations, ... that was never mentioned in the report.

I'm quite struck by the way Larry acknowledges the limitations of his perspective, or at least seems to, when he says 'the only view I can draw', but then goes on to demonstrate the level of his commitment to it, going as far as to entertain the fringe of a conspiracy theory about the independent panel. But maybe I'm misreading him: maybe he believes the view of the farmers he's spoken to is the best perspective on which to base his thoughts: like Henry, then, he believes that the raw on-the-ground, from-the-coal-face data of farmers' experiences are the best data available. And who is to say they are wrong? But then, a little later on, as we're talking about the details of the government's response to the IEP's report, Larry says something that makes me wonder.

The last one is talking about working around the challenges of measuring badger population in a cost effective manner, so no

longer using the DNA hair trap test but doing something else? What do you think of that?

They can improve on the accuracy if they have a better idea of the numbers of badgers present, it would be good ... The DNA thing, I suppose they're obviously taking DNA from each badger that [is killed]. Is it really relevant though? Do you need to know how many numbers are there if you just keep shooting until they're gone? I think setting the target perhaps was a mistake at the beginning really, they had no idea how many badgers were in certain locations. [They had a target, but] when that failed to be reached, they classed that as a failure ... the numbers may still be totally wrong, they were revised down as it was so ... it would be nice to know the exact numbers but is it relevant to the cull and is the percentage relevant even? I think if you just allowed a longer culling period, I think it doesn't really matter how many are there, if they keep at it, they'll get them all eventually.

Maybe he's just talking, and not really saying things he's thought through. But maybe that's what makes it more telling, not less. Last time I spoke to him he said he didn't like the idea of killing badgers. This time he appears to be saying that he doesn't mind if they're all gone. Perhaps there's been a process of identification going on – Larry identifies with the farmers he works with (why shouldn't he?), so in the process of empathizing with the struggle his clients are going through, he begins to adopt some of their way of thinking – his thoughts begin to resonate with theirs.

If that is what has happened then Larry is not alone. It happens to about seven billion of us, except for the odd hermit. It's been happening to Fran.

Could you tell me a bit about what you've been doing in relation to the badger cull since we spoke last October?

I finished up at Camp Badger. Then I was invited over to the Gloucester cull zones. A chap there had got a disused pub that he offered various sabs the use of, and I was invited over there ... So I did that until they finished in Gloucester, which was the beginning of December. My physical actual involvement with the cull was pretty much all of while it was going on in Somerset, and then the overlap with the extension in Gloucester. So I didn't finish until beginning of December, it was about the 3rd or something. Yeah, I was pretty knackered.

Yeah, it's a long time.

Pretty knackered by the time that all finished. Subsequently, I've been raising awareness locally within my own area and recruiting for the Badger Army amongst my friends and family, and quite honestly perfect strangers that I've met and engaged and told them what's going on and how appalling it is. I've continued with the online petition monkey stuff, and again just sharing and disseminating information, writing to my MP, writing to various people. Just background stuff but it's all part of it. I shall continue to do that. And if it happens again I'm going to have to go and do what I can.

So what's your view of the outcome of the cull then?

It's a disgrace. This report that the government kept sending back because they didn't like it, it shows unequivocally that it is cruel, which we knew that it is inhumane, which we knew that the cull operators were basically acting without thought or consequence for the wellbeing of anyone who may be in that area. They were breaking the rules. The police were unaware of these rules and the fact that they should be policing them. The police have been collaborating and assisting with the cullers, this has now been shown beyond a doubt.

The dead badger crash man said in his statement in court that he had a police radio in his vehicle and that there was an NFU operative in the police control room. The police said that's absolute nonsense blah-blah-blah, but this chap wasn't done for perjury, was he, it was all dropped very quietly. So it shows that they have been quite frankly in the pocket, they've been acting as private security without thought or regard for law. Protestors have been harassed, they've been arrested, removed from the area, and then conveniently de-arrested, just to get them out of the way. There's untold cases now going forward to the Police Complaints Commission about wrongful arrest and all the rest of it.

Fran's talk was pretty angry in the first place, but she's shifted from complaining about what's wrong to simply stating it. These things are no longer a discovery for her. They are the reality. Fact: this is shit. But then, while I am going through the motions of prompting Fran through the next set of expected critical phrases, she comes out with a story that seems to move us onto some other plane of existence, a world in which weirdness such as this could possibly happen.

There was a tracker on this badger shooter at Stonehenge. You need to Google it. You need to go onto I think it's badgerkillers.org or something. I can't remember which site it is. Last summer during the cull one of the shooters from Gloucester was making trips three or four times a week to one of the burrows just outside Stonehenge. I can't remember the name of the burrow. It was illegal badger trapping basically, illegal badger shooting. Natural England are claiming not to know anything about it, it's all gone quiet now.

Were these trapped badgers then shot and included in the numbers for Gloucester?

I'm not quite sure what to say. I have to wait until I speak to Elizabeth to find out more. She too has cemented her commitment and become more involved in her group. They're using all their accumulated experience and skills to be good and thoroughly annoying citizens. That doesn't mean that Elizabeth doesn't entertain the idea of conspiracy – in fact, far from it. It's because she's prepared to imagine there might be something conspiratorial going on that she must be such a nightmare for the authorities. There's something in her voice which even suggests she enjoys it. And it's that commitment to rigour – the ability to say 'no, part of this was above board, but...' that makes me sit up and listen when she does tell a story. Of course I have to be careful about being too credulous, but my credulity is not the point. The point is that the people involved in this conflict are operating with these understandings of each other.

With the badger van crash in Gloucestershire, the police dealt with it as a classic offence, they didn't actually do anything about the badgers that were in the van and I'm trying to get them to reopen this now because I think what it was, was badgers being transported in.

So this is the controversy about it is it?

It wasn't investigated at the time and yet al.l the evidence is held by the police and the city council, so I think the evidence is there, we just need it to be examined, analysed and on the back of these IEP reports, the police aren't prepared to do that, I think they hadn't, I don't think last year, they had expected the NFU and the cullers to commit crimes. I just don't think they thought that, I think they thought they were cooperating with the government, as I did, I was just there because I was anti the cull and it's just opened up this huge gulf of what the law is and how the country people seem to operate and they seem to operate outside the law. It's just their normal way of operating and the police aren't really present in the countryside very much and I think it just all goes on and no-one knows it's happening. It was just a fluke that this crash in the centre of Gloucester that we seem to have some examples of it. ... This year, we will be watching for it very carefully but it's really difficult because we are only responders, we are not running it, so all I can do is give the police as much information as they can have on the crimes cullers are committing, so that they can act in a completely neutral way.

Have you heard about this story on badger cullers, about a culler's vehicle being tagged with a tracking device?

Yes.

Being detected going down to Stonehenge of all places ...?

Yes, I have heard that and someone in our group did a Freedom Of Information Act request to English Heritage, to find out a little bit more about it and we understand that there was, English Heritage did have a licence for catching badgers at the time so it does all seem to tally because it does seem that someone was there catching badgers, so it's just a fluke that that came out, so I think that's right, that it did happen.

So, the tracking device revealed that a trapper was legitimately catching badgers at Stonehenge and then making his or her way to Gloucestershire. It seems fair enough to ask why and even to come up with a hypothesis about it. Of course, the innocent explanation is also possible, that, as someone whose profession it is to trap and kill badgers, they had something to do with the culls. I'm pretty sure that if the last, perfect, golden thread of conspiracy thins to a whisp,

Elizabeth's interest will thin with it. But then there's the other story. Sit up.

There was an article in The Guardian[33] a couple of weeks ago which you may have seen, which was a specific incident ... where the cullers had shot a badger and then they'd left the scene and returned four hours later and it ended up being investigated as a police complaint and the investigation of the complaint – into the complaint, was given to The Guardian by Mr Tasker who was the person that made the complaint and there were a number of quite staggering things about it. The first being that he was beaten up and he wasn't actually there when the badger was shot, he was there three or four hours later because he was watching a sett, he was sett monitor and the cullers came back and beat him up and he rang 999 and they rang the NFU who were in the police control room and when the police eventually turned up, they arrested Mr Tasker rather than the cullers, which is all very, very peculiar ... and there's a lot more background information on that case that's been submitted to the papers now.

But it seems that why they went away for four hours and then returned was that the culling company had shooters in that area that week, and because of the way they were acting, their licences were revoked. So a new team came on that night and they were shooting between these fishing huts and there were actually fishermen fishing there with little head torches on while they were doing it and when they fired one of the shots, someone screamed and they thought they'd shot someone, so that's why they left for four hours, was because they thought they'd shot someone! And I think they then took those four hours to contact the culling company to find out if there'd been a report of someone being shot, when they realised no-one had been shot, they came back to the scene and picked up the badger. So that in itself is a classic example of how dangerous it was. Because these fishing huts they were firing between were just wooden structures.

---

[33] See *Guardian* (2014)

Despite the involvement of scientific analysis about culling before and after the culls in 2012, and a constant flow of science on bovine TB, it has done nothing to help alleviate the differences between people who are mostly worried about farming and people who are mostly worried about badgers. It seems that if there is some scientific research that seems to agree with what you're saying, you can use it to batter your opponents with. If you don't like the implication of what science is saying, or you think your source of data is better, pick it apart, or ignore it. It would be easy to blame government: *they're just ignoring the science for political reasons!* But that would be to join in the battle, to make just the sort of ideological intervention that you're criticising.

Pardon? How can it be? Science is objective. We turn to science for the value-neutral, free-from-political-interference, most-up-to-date, hard *facts*.

Here's a challenge. Think of someone you reckon is just in it to play a cynical political game, to look after the vested interests they represent. Having conjured up your least favourite politician, now assume that they at least mean to have good intentions. Now answer the following question: why do you think this well-meaning person would ignore the hard science?

One answer is that they're defending something they feel is more important than a small piece of attempted knowledge represented in a scientific article. A core belief. A deeply held value. That's what political scientists Martin Lodge and Kira Matus suggest in their paper about bovine TB (Lodge and Matus 2014). They think it's helpful to think of the sides caught up in the debate about culling badgers as advocacy coalitions. Advocacy coalitions are made up of people from different areas of life, such as politics, the media, science, or affected members of the public who share beliefs at some level which results in them all supporting the same or similar policies, despite not necessarily having much to do with each other otherwise (Sabatier and Jenkins-Smith 1993). These beliefs might be fairly superficial and easily altered in the light of new information, or they can be very important to the people who hold them, and be resistant to change, even when new and challenging information comes up. Lodge and Matus found that out of eight relevant groups of speakers reported in news stories over a 27-year period up to 2012, only two shifted their view from supporting to opposing culling after hearing the results of the RBCT: independent scientists and the Labour Party. Farmers, DEFRA, government scientists, and the Conservatives all maintained support for culling despite the negative findings of the RBCT. On the other hand, the Coalition Government, on coming to power, did take account of advice from scientists that built on a review of the RBCT by the former Chief Scientific Advisor, David King (DEFRA 2011, King 2007) for how culling could be done more effectively, bringing in hard boundaries and the target of 70% of the badger population to be killed in a large area.

If your rule for judging good government is that they make policy that reflects the available evidence you might say that the Labour Party had done better in following the recommendations of the RBCT panel (but then again, there's the King review, and the review of the review – the ones the Coalition claimed as support for their position on culling). Oddly enough, that might be because the Labour Party is not, politically, terribly interested in rural issues as most of its voters and activists are urban-based. Having no particularly strong views about the topic embedded in it, surely the best thing was to follow the advice of some experts. The Conservatives, on the other hand, have close historical and electoral connections with the countryside and come to the question with a view – with core values – informed by rural constituencies and activists.

If. The Advocacy Coalition Framework that Lodge and Matus are working with treats scientific knowledge in a fairly neutral way. Yes, scientists can take part in the political game, but scientific information is neutral, and is then interpreted in different ways by groups with different sets of core beliefs. Remember Nietzsche and the horse? Nietzsche believed that science was no such thing. The Truth that science lays claim to is a moral claim, a fragment of the morality that was the battle strategy of the weak against the strong. But according to Nietzsche, what became a moral injunction on people to report things as it was, or to do what they said they would, and later became a scientific claim that things really would do what they had done before under the same conditions, started out as a simple description of a state of affairs – a metaphor. Truth wasn't good, it was just true, in the sense of being consistent or straight. There is, in fact, no need to say 'badgers give bovine TB to cows *and that's the truth*', or 'culling can't make any meaningful contribution to the control of bovine TB, *scientifically speaking*' because you haven't added anything to the truth of either claim by adding a reference to truth or science. All you've done is made a battle cry, asserting that action should be taken in accordance with that truth. This is what

Nietzsche meant when he said science was nihilistic. Because, if your value is life itself, then truth or science just limits your choices, or limits your ability to see that things might be more complex and changeable than you imagine.

Another way of looking at science in policy-making is as a collection of knowledges and interests that are woven in with other knowledges and interests in different ways. That's what another academic commentator, Gareth Enticott (Enticott 2001), has tried to do in his accounts of the different perspectives caught up in the debate. Gareth draws on ideas from another French philosopher-ish academic called Michel Foucault (Foucault 1979), who owed a lot to Nietzsche. Foucault was interested in the link between knowledge and power, and came up with a term to describe one particular intersection of the two. For if, according to Nietzsche, the type of knowledge that gave the weak power was morality, the type of knowledge that helps those in power maintain it is governmentality. With the help of a lot of other academic references (for, these days, writing an academic article is as much as act of collage as it is of sustained argument), Gareth tells us that statistics helps governments do government. The collection of statistics helps legitimise government (think Domesday) and helps a central power act from a distance. Government has enrolled science to create a statistical portrait of bovine TB, the scale of the problem, its causes and possible solutions. It is on such numbers that government policy on bovine TB is based. There are, though, two small problems. First, Enticott points out, the statistics are generalisations. Working with one single statistic to represent the probability that badgers in general might infect cows in general with bovine TB, or to represent the impact culling badgers (randomly) may have on the incidence of the disease, denies the complexity of badger biology and farm ecology. Not all badgers and not all farms are the same. Second, the government view is not the only perspective that thinks it has got the facts, or at least, the ones that matter.

Farmers have their own set of observations. The problem is that these observations don't translate very well into numbers. They have to do with weather conditions, the seasons, herd and land management, and individual, on-the-ground sightings of badgers near cows or around farm buildings. They are 'merely' anecdotal, but they are direct and between them farmers stack up their evidence against badgers. Conservationists and ecologists have yet another way of seeing the issue, one that emphasises the links between a multiplicity of different actors and factors. It's impossible, in this view, to reduce the cause down to the individual species when there's so much complexity in agricultural and landscape-scale ecologies.

Coming back to work on a case-study about biosecurity some years later, Enticott (Enticott, Franklin and van Winden 2012) explains why the existence of these different forms of knowledge about nature makes agreement about what to do so difficult, and how science is awfully tangled up in it. He describes two strategies for treating a disease, the population approach and the 'high risk' approach. The population approach is the sort of large-scale strategy that would be most straightforward for governments to carry out and is based on scientific research such as that carried out during the RBCT: it's a form of governmentality. The population approach is about trying to reduce the average risk of infection by getting everyone concerned (farmers) to change their behaviour, removing or reducing the most likely reasons for cattle becoming infected. Basically, it's a public health campaign for cows. It involves leaflets.

The problem is that different farms have different levels of risk of bovine TB being passed to their cattle from wildlife by any one route. Let's imagine the health advice leaflet says 'make sure your feed store is locked and secure'. Every farmer does it (they don't, really). The ones who do and are at low risk of the disease because it's not present in their herd or in the surrounding wildlife don't get any incidence of bovine TB. *See, it works!* The ones who don't and are also at low risk also don't. *See, it doesn't work!* The ones who do it, but have a hard case of hidden bovine TB in their herd that isn't detected by the test keep coming down with bovine TB. *See, what a load of rubbish! You can't keep badgers and cattle apart.* The ones who do and also have a load of bovine TB-infected badgers on the farm: well, maybe there was a slight fall in the number of cattle reacting to the test, but all it takes is one to shut you down, so what's the point? So what about the one who doesn't and has infected badgers and infected cattle? *Well, who can blame her, it's all a load of crap anyway.*

That clash of large-scale statistical observations and direct experience leads to a loss of faith in government health initiatives and advice, and to a sense of fatalism among farmers. It can even serve to confirm farmers' own theories about what the problem is (badgers) even when it isn't. The alternative is an approach based on the model of the doctor-patient relationship, in which vets work with farmers to tailor a treatment for bovine TB that is suited to the particular farm and circumstances, building trust and understanding the particular problems and challenges – be they farming-related, social or personal – that might contribute to the problem or stand in the way of improvement. It's risky, because the farmer-vet relationship might not be that good and because it doesn't address the root causes of infection, only responding once infection has occurred. In fact, the high-risk approach isn't just high risk. It's heretical. It suggests that instead of attempting to eradicate bovine TB, we learn how to live with it.

This is madness, surely?

Why? Enticott refers to the example of the management of avian flu in ostriches in South Africa. There, farmers and vets concentrated their efforts on maintaining the immune resistance of the ostrich flock, giving the ostriches extra support during stressful times, and only culling them where the disease spread, so that flocks showing one or two cases of avian flu and no increase were not culled at all, because the other members of the flock were demonstrating resistance to it.

It's inspiring to read someone who is prepared to suggest something that is so against the grain and then go and do the work to back up the point. It's not exactly 'hard science', just 'we tried this and it sort of worked'. I'm always a little cautious when I come up to an article that talks about Foucault. Very few of them seem to acknowledge that his work was controversial, either for being accused of shoddy history, or for being thought too intellectually narrow, or for simply having nothing positive to suggest, no alternative. Here though, Gareth Enticott has taken what seems like a reasonable positive implication out of Foucault's critique of the centralised state: local action. The problem is that things seem a very long way from this point. BTB infected cattle have to be slaughtered, farmers have to go through rigorous testing, and, in a few months' time, the culling of badgers is going to start all over again.

Chapter 9

Shooter

Right from the beginning of the project, I knew I needed to speak to a shooter. But how? There was no way I could approach one in the field, even, as I had hoped, when they were off duty. Either they wouldn't feel safe and avoid me, or I didn't feel safe. The only way seemed to be to ask the people I spoke to if they knew anyone. One person said they might, but backed away later. I asked the farmers, who either said 'no', or 'unlikely'. And then, months down the line, too late to bring into the Q Methods study, my phone rang. No name was given, just a phone number and a time.

The problem is that I know he's been hand-picked. And because he's been hand-picked, I can't know whether his view is reflective of 'a shooters' view'. His is a farming background; others might have had more to do with hunting or pest control, different perspectives. On the other hand, it let me off the hook slightly, as a lot of his views about the issues and the different alternatives are a photocopy of those I'd heard from farmers.[34] His perspective is distinct (though not necessarily all that relevant to the range of views in the wider population) when it comes to his experiences of shooting badgers. But it is about more than just being an alternative, distinct view. The interview expresses the pride and commitment felt by one of those, at least, who went and did a dirty, difficult, dangerous, and ultimately, they believed, necessary job. There can be no sweeping

---

[34] For a more formal look at the problems and approaches to the method of 'snowball' sampling that the recruitment of this shooter and several other respondents represents (and incidentally, an instance of rent-a-quote), see Biernacki and Waldorf (1981). There is clearly a tension between arranging interviews with difficult-to-reach or reluctant groups and the goal of identifying a wide range of different views about culling badgers. It is important to acknowledge it and try to work around it as much as possible.

aside, dismissal with a different interpretation of the facts, or a different set of aspersions caste. I do as much as I can, towards the end of this interview, to challenge him with exactly this point (but put the other way around), that opposition can't be wished away. His response, like the other farmers, is to dilute the opposition, just as the anti-cull protestors have diluted their opponents by saying that the NFU only represent a small percentage of farmers. Both miss the point, that they each exist, with as much pride, commitment, belief, seriousness, logical capacity and error as the other. And, as a corrective to myself and anyone who sees themselves as an objective observer, their wishing away of opponents exists too. If anyone is going to get to grips with a conflict like this, that practice of wishing away cannot, itself, be wished away.

So tell me a bit more about that, about what you were doing.

Well there was a training course, and the details of that obviously are published on the net by Natural England, but it was a robust training course which was a one day course with some fairly in-depth training on badger ecology, firearms safety, practical hints and tips in terms of what would be good and sensible techniques to adopt when carrying out contracting activity, and training on cage trap usage, although the primary method at that point was envisaged to be rifle shooting, but the licence permitted cage trapping as well, it was thought appropriate that all the contractors should have some cage trapping knowledge as well so we dealt with that.

Then that was followed up with a marksmanship assessment on an approved rifle range, where each contractor had to demonstrate their ability in darkness, so either using a night vision scope or with a lamp illuminator, proving their ability to shoot straight.

And then what happened? Presumably you passed those assessments and you then took part in the cull. Is that right?

Yeah those assessments were passed in 2012, so there was obviously a long delay, because culling was postponed in 2012 for various reasons, I'm not sure we'll ever get to know what all of them were, political, geographical, so yeah, there was the Olympics, there was the policing resource, there was weather, there was all sorts of things going on, which all added up to a postponement.

The actual course was a year in advance, so everything was building up to culling and then it was postponed, and then obviously last year it started, and there was a lot of preparatory work went on in advance, making sure everybody was ready and well organised, and off we went.

So without wanting to stray too much, can you tell me a bit about what you were doing then, when you say "off we went" and it got started? Can you tell me bit about that?

I obviously need to be somewhat careful in terms of not wanting to give too much away, but essentially, and our opponents know what a lot of the techniques were, essentially the practice of controlled shooting permitted badgers to be shot at bait points or while free roaming, so the whole purpose was to identify where the badgers resided, and so surveying, working out where their runs were and the primary method was preparing bait points using peanuts to attract badgers to a particular place where it was felt that they could be safely culled.

And so leading up to culling there was a period of pre-baiting being done to try and get badgers into the habit of being in the right place at the right time, and once culling commenced it was a case of getting round your area and seeking to dispatch badgers, either at bait points or while they were free roaming.

There was a very tight set of rules we all had to abide by which was contained in the best practice guidance, although it was made very clear to us it wasn't guidance at all, it was the rules, and contractors were going out for relatively long periods on a regular basis at night, as was myself and my buddy. We all had to operate with a buddy, so myself and a very experienced buddy were going out probably five nights a week to our allocated land with a view to dispatching as many badgers as possible within the rules, and there was a lot of rules to do with how they carcasses were handled.

The rules were quite strict in terms of how you could shoot them, and once you had shot them, you had to make sure that they were handled properly with regard to biosecurity, and obviously they went into a system then whereby some went to post-mortem, but ultimately they all went for incineration.

And how did you find that experience of doing that? You said you were working five nights a week.

It was demanding. It was quite a commitment, but I mentioned earlier on, because I'm from the farming industry myself. I've seen just how much the farming industry is pinning to this project and it's important, so myself and the other contractors took it seriously, and yeah it did impact upon work, it did impact upon our own private lives, but it was six weeks and we felt it was something that we had to give 100% to.

Do you think what you were doing had any effect?

It's far too early to tell is the honest answer to that. TB infection rates in cattle take a long time to actually see the real effects. I mean in the RBCT study, the reactive areas were pulled very early because they interpreted the data to indicate they felt it was having an adverse effect on infection rates, but then when they revisited the data in the long term, it turned out it hadn't at all. So I'm not sitting here drawing any conclusions at all at this early stage.

Interestingly within my patch there's one herd that's gone clear for the first time in years, and another one that's had a breakdown for the first time in a considerable amount of time, and both of them had significant numbers of badgers removed from them.

I don't think it's possible to statistically draw too many conclusions from too short a period of time or too small a set of data. At the end of the day we believe, and certainly I believe that the science already exists to say that culling badgers will have a beneficial effect on bovine TB infections. What we're trying to prove is the fact that badgers can be culled effectively, safely and humanely.

That's the objective of the pilot, and I hope long term those farmers that have been prepared to participate in that pilot will see some benefits, but really there's a much bigger picture here, which is accepting the policy and principle of wildlife control having a role to play in tuberculosis control in cattle.

So in terms of what you were doing specifically, do you feel that what you have done in the cull, were you successful personally for your part?

I genuinely think I was. I'm not going to say how many badgers I removed, but it was a lot. It was certainly at the top end of the *contractor performance results. It's not a league table, but obviously we look at the contractor results and I got very good results, and I also take pride in the fact that I didn't wound any, which I felt was important as well, because that was one of the things we were trying to prove.*

I felt that the equipment that I used, the tactics I deployed and the experience I'd gained previously meant that I had confidence in what I was doing, and there are parts of the area that myself and my buddy were operating in which do not now have any badgers that previously had a lot of badgers in it. There are still parts of the area which still have significant numbers of badgers that need removing.

So yes, I mean it's a four-year pilot. We had interference in places. Personally I feel that we made, bearing in mind that it was the first time anybody had done anything like it, so it was a pilot, it was trialling new techniques on a species that hasn't been culled using that technique before, and so the results were varied, but I think in my area where we didn't have any protestor interference, we were able to get, I would say success or the very start of success. I mean success will be in four years' time when we know that we've done a good job.

The other thing is one of the key indicators was this 70% figure. Now I have absolutely no idea whether I've culled 70% of the badgers in my area or not, because the numbers that AHVLA have provided range so enormously, I mean I don't think anybody can have any confidence in the numbers at all, which means that if one's numbers spell success, I think we need to be just as cynical about that number as if that number spells failure, because I think it's pretty much proven that accurately estimating badger populations is pretty damn difficult.

So to come back to some of these various solutions and things that could be done and things that aren't being done, one of the arguments that people used as a concern against the cull was the idea that these culls are going to cause perturbation of badgers, so clear an area or you'll disrupt a social group and the rest of the badgers will move away, and part of the problem with that is if you don't have sufficiently hard boundaries, then the incidence of TB around the edge of the cull area is going to go up, and when people were looking at the cull zones and trying to work out, well

what were the boundaries, they weren't really seeing them. What's your response to that kind of argument of perturbation and boundaries?

Certainly perturbation I think has been misrepresented largely in the media as being badgers fleeing culling. My experience of perturbation, and I now have first-hand experience of perturbation, is that it's badgers that actually fill in areas that have been culled. It's a myth they all pack their bags and say "I've had enough of people shooting at us, we're going to go and move down the road where it's quieter".

Every night a badger has very few functions on its agenda, one of which is to eat and drink and the other one is to defecate and urinate on its boundaries and to mark its boundaries, and if the clan of badgers next door isn't marking its boundaries; that will immediately prompt an investigative visit to see whether their des res is more desirable than the one they're currently occupying, and I certainly have experience of setts that we have emptied and have been redundant for some time, being populated by animals from other setts in the vicinity.

So that's reality. I've read the research from Woodchester, and there's a relatively recent piece of research that's been published that shows that setts where animals are infected with TB don't always infect their neighbours, because they keep very well defended boundaries, so I'm alert to that, and it's one of the reasons why the people that designed the cull were using this rather arbitrary six week period, which I must admit I don't necessarily subscribe to it having any basis in fact or science, and I think that a diligent and astute badger culling contractor will be able to work out, or should be able to work out relatively easily where there is still badger activity in the area that they're covering, and they don't pack their bags and move five miles down the road. It would tend to be areas where essentially a vacuum's been created, would be where they would move into.

Now I think there's probably a need for more science on perturbation. I don't think enough is known about it and they are obviously animals who change their habits when their neighbours are no longer there to mark their boundaries. I accept that entirely. But at a time of year when cattle are starting to come in from their summer grazing, and I think it's far more important to get badgers removed from an area and it is done effectively and with a recognition of the fact that the type of perturbation that I've described can happen, then you just need to make sure you're putting in sufficient effort and priority to minimising it and making sure that you're checking areas that you think you've already cleared out once.

With regard to boundaries, I do not wish to reveal the boundaries of the ... cull area but I consider them to be, on the whole, suitable and hard. Badgers are not known for their ability to cross major roads or motorways safely or cross large rivers.

Doesn't what you've described though touch on some of the content of the criticism that's been made, which is if you clear out an area of badgers, then another group of badgers might move in, and actually you might, rather than get rid of TB, you might actually import TB into an area?

Well certainly the RBCT, which was in itself to a degree flawed, but that's the most recent piece of science we have on the subject, concluded that reducing the numbers by at least 70% and sustaining that level had tangible benefits.

Now again there will always be winners and losers. I mean just an example I gave earlier on, the fact that we've got a herd that's gone clear and a herd that has had a breakdown; that's far too small a dataset to draw any meaningful conclusions from whatsoever. I think if the bigger picture, which is over four years, significantly reducing the badger population and maintaining at that lower level during that four-year period, we will find out whether that does or does not make things better or worse, but clearly we wouldn't be doing it if we didn't think there was a very good chance of making things quite a lot better.

So have you met people who hold a different view to you about what to do about bovine TB?

Well I met quite a few in the middle of the night when I was trying to shoot badgers, but we weren't really able to engage in a sensible conversation at the time.

What happened when you did meet them? Because you said earlier you didn't have much protestor activity, so what happened when you met people?

Well it's all relative. I had some and other contractors had more. In my experience it ranged from a bit of a game of cat and mouse, we were pretty covert and managed to avoid protestors largely, because we didn't particularly want to, we had no reason to want to interact with them.

But protestors fell into two fairly distinct groups. There was the respectable face of protest which branded itself as the wounded badger patrol, which tended to be quite visible, wearing high vis jackets, and tended to be maybe some of the older and maybe more respectable members of the anti-cull protest.

They tended not to be people that were prepared to maybe get their hands too dirty themselves, or didn't particularly want to necessarily break the law or risk facing any consequences of breaking the law. They branded themselves as the wounded badger patrol. Interestingly they didn't find any wounded badgers because it was pretty obvious what they were doing, which was making as much noise as possible, being as visible as possible, shining torches around, high powered torches around to make it as difficult as possible for contractors to operate.

In other words either the contractor would feel that they weren't able to safely operate in that area, because there were obviously people walking around, or it was fruitless because having lots of people making lots of noise, walking up and down footpaths, pretending to look for wounded badgers that aren't there, tends to mean that unwounded ones don't hang around for very long to be shot at.

But those people were undoubtedly liaising with the more extreme elements that were present as well, which were from the animal rights movement, the hunt saboteur types; that end of the animal rights movement that were prepared to break the law, that were prepared to engage in conflict and confrontation, and there was certainly in my experience and other contractors' experience a lot of incidences where the respectable end of the protest in the form of the wounded badger patrols would find somewhere where a contractor was operating, and hey presto, very quickly the more extreme guys would have been radioed or telephoned for, and would turn up to actually have some form of conflict or confrontation with the contractors that were trying to operate in that area.

My experiences with those were that they were from out of the area, they tended to be younger, they all had their uniform, which was a black hooded top, army combat trousers, boots, balaclava or face covering, and they were abusive. They tried to force contractors into having some sort of a response which they'd try and catch on film, all the usual tactics of trying to wind people up and try and draw a response that they could then film and try and make out that the contractor had done something wrong, and goading them etc, etc.

So are you able to describe a particular or a typical example of an interaction that happened to you with one of these? I mean who did you come across mostly? Was it the wounded badger patrol or was it...?

Sometimes it was the wounded badger patrol and sometimes it was the hunt sabs, and it was obvious that they had a rota and they were literally going round the lanes, they'd found where some of the setts were, and they were literally going from sett to sett, gateway to gateway, looking for contractors, and looking to basically compromise those areas and make them difficult or impossible for the contractors to operate in.

If they came across a contractor they'd be very verbally abusive. They would call you all sorts of names and try and goad you into a response. They'd say they'd put a bomb in your car in one instance. There was...

Sorry, is that something that happened to you?

Yes I was present. I was actually present when another contractor had a, one of the hunt sabs had said they'd put a bomb in his car, and there was a police officer present at the time as well and they did nothing.

And so what about the other things that happened to you in these sorts of incidences?

Yeah there would be other incidences. I mean that was the most commonplace set of circumstances. As I say, I only probably had half a dozen interactions with the hunt sab types, because most of the time I saw them far more frequently than that, it's just they didn't see me. So as I said, there's absolutely no point having an interaction with them. Other contractors actually found themselves in quite difficult circumstances on a couple of occasions where animal rights protestors did actually become quite physical and you want to avoid that.

Again, one of the things we're trying to test here is safety, and there's nothing to be gained whatsoever from having an interaction with one of these protestors, so when you've got pretty good night vision equipment, you use it to your advantage to stay below their radar. They tried to block your access to the field. As I say they were verbally very abusive. They made it impossible on some occasions to actually shoot any badgers. The only thing one could do in those circumstances is to try and safely vacate those premises and go somewhere else to see if you can cull badgers somewhere else, where they're not.

We got followed, and at points there were protestors at strategic points in the area that were looking out for contractor vehicles at junctions, and so often one would get followed, so you'd have to just try and lose your tail, and there were certain places where protestors would turn up probably every hour, every two hours, which made it very difficult to operate, and then also during some cage trapping we were doing as well, we had all of our cage traps stolen or cut up as well.

I can hear it, but I'm going to ask you to say how does that make you feel or think about the situation?

Frustrated. As I say, there's absolutely no point imagining that any amount of rational argument or debate or conversation would ever persuade these people to stop doing what they're doing. The only thing that can do that is the law, and the law wasn't as effective as I feel it could have been in terms of allowing the government's policy to be implemented. It made me very frustrated because we had a job to do and a limited amount of time to do it in, and we were trying to do it to a high standard.

As I said earlier on, I took humaneness very seriously. Our opponents would portray me and the other contractors as being evil, heartless badger abusing scum would probably be their words, when in reality I simply wanted to be part of something that was trying to do something about a terrible disease that affects badgers and cattle, and I took pride in the fact that none of my badgers were wounded, and it was absolutely evident that it was a very, very humane way of killing them.

So what would you do if you were in charge?

In charge of what? If I was in charge of the country, I would probably be having a word with the chief constable and police and crime commissioner ..., and asking him to make sure that his officers facilitated peaceful protest, but did not tolerate any form of law-breaking, and created an environment where contractors were able to operate safely and without fear of harassment, intimidation and hassle in order that they can deliver the democratically elected government's policy.

I don't know whether you saw there was a webcast of a kind of review of what took place between the police and crime commissioner and the chief constable. One of their concerns, they expressly said "we're not very happy about", is they arrested a number, I think it was around 30 people, but they haven't been able to get any charges, one of the problems being that no one who'd been involved with the cull was prepared to come forward and act as a witness, even despite the sorts of measures that the police can take to help to protect them, such as giving evidence from behind a screen. What's your reaction to that concern?

Well the animal rights movement contains some pretty nasty people, and of course I've spoken to fellow contractors on this subject. I have every respect for a contractor that has concerns for his safety and the safety of his family, and contractors were assured by all of the people running this, the company running the cull, the NFU, DEFRA, government and the police that their anonymity would be maintained, and maintaining their anonymity is actually very important, because I think quite rightly they have some concerns with regard to their own safety if certain extreme elements of the animal rights movement decided that they were going to do all of the things they're possibly capable of doing.

Having said that, I think in most instances it's the fear of what they're likely to do rather than what they do actually do, but bearing in mind they have dug up people's grandmothers, they've dug up the 10th Duke of Beaufort and they've conducted seriously vile campaigns that have been described as terrorism at Huntingdon Life Sciences, and bearing in mind that some of the characters that

were involved with Huntingdon Life Sciences are the same charac-
ters that have become involved in the badger cull, I'm not altogeth-
er surprised that some of the contractors are a little bit cautious
about giving statements.

I think, and it by no means applies to all contractors, and I'm sure
some of them, in fact I know some of them are more than willing to
make statements, I think the police having originally told contrac-
tors that their anonymity would be protected, when it came to it,
the criminal justice system doesn't actually provide for protecting
contractors' anonymity, and my own view is I think the police and
crime commissioner is maybe trying to score some cheap points
there, and has absolutely no recognition or understanding of why
that situation would be.

And what about the other concern, which was in terms of the
police's independence? The culls were run as a private event if
you like, run by a private company, and the police aren't really
there to facilitate private events such as the equivalent perhaps
of football matches or something like that. They are there to
police crime that may occur or public order difficulties that may
occur around them, or even indeed emergencies, but they're not
there specifically to facilitate the private event. That's up to the
people who are running the event. What's your response to that,
even in the context of challenge such as in protests and so on?

My view is that the pilot badger culls are the policy of the demo-
cratically elected government of the day, and on the basis that it's a
trial technique being carried out essentially on behalf of the gov-
ernment, I don't think it can be compared the same as an event,
and I think it's also fair to say that we weren't doing it for our plea-
sure. If I go to a football match, I do that for my pleasure. If I go to
a rugby match, I do that for my pleasure.

When I was going out at night shooting badgers, it was because it
was a really important government policy that we're trying to do
something about a disease. I mean the police quite frankly would
not have been required at all had it not been for protestors.

I mean badger culling per se does not require the police, but when
you have significant numbers of people that are prepared to break
the law and will be prepared to go out night after night trying to
basically stop you doing what you're trying to do, then that's when

the need for the police kicks in, and I personally don't believe that the police policed the cull particularly effectively. I totally respect the right to peaceful protest and the right of others to hold views different to my own, but when it comes down to persistent law breaking, and that being law breaking designed to stop something that's a government policy being implemented, I actually do think that's the job of the police and I rather wish they'd done it a bit better.

...

We kind of got started on this subject earlier, but could you tell me a bit more about what your view of the outcome of the cull is?

Yeah, there are politicians and politics involved, so one has to be a bit cynical in some respects, but it's pretty evident to me that the original and primary function was for pilot areas to prove that it's possible to safely, effectively and humanely remove 70% of the population of badgers from an area, and maintain it at that lower level for four years, and if that were proven, over a longer period disease reduction benefits would hopefully be experienced or would in our opinion be experienced, but once you've gone over that evidential threshold whereby the pilot areas have been proven to work, and proven to work isn't reducing TB, being proven to work is the fact that you can do it safely, humanely and effectively; that would allow the policy to be rolled out, which it obviously hasn't, but then we get into the realms of politics.

So what do you mean when you say that, into the realms of politics and politicians?

Oh there's all sorts. I think it's pretty obvious that the Coalition is slowly unravelling itself and they're trying to find lots of things to differentiate themselves from the Conservative party, and this is one of them.

Okay, so you're concerned that the policy becomes a victim of internal division about...

Yeah correct, and the Labour party cannot resist the opportunity to find fault in government policy of the day regardless of whether it's actually constructive or worthwhile to do so. Interestingly the shadow environment secretary did go on record saying that they may well have to continue with the pilot culls if they came into government, but she's also gone on the record saying that she's not automatically, I can't remember the precise word, but not fundamentally opposed to killing badgers that have got TB, but at the same time they were very quick to criticise when the IEP report was published, and again it's politics, it's playing politics. It's not a political issue. It's an animal disease issue. It's an economic issue. It's not a political issue, but unfortunately we're reliant upon politicians to provide us with the solutions.

Okay so specifically then, the IEP found the controlled shooting didn't deliver the level of culling set by government.

Yep, and that's 70% of a very, very, very spurious figure. I can't remember what the exact, but you'll have seen the data in terms of the range in estimated population. I mean certainly from a contractor's perspective, there certainly was not 2,600 and however many badgers it was we meant to shoot last year there when we got there.

It was a very bad breeding year, bearing in mind that some of the ... cull area, and I don't think I'm breaching any sensitive data here, was certainly in flood plain, and anything, whether it's a rabbit, a stoat, a weasel, a badger or anything else, would have either have had to packed its bags and moved an awfully long way or drowned, and certainly it did not appear that there had been a particular successful breeding season the preceding spring, because there weren't that many juvenile first winter animals being culled.

And then ironically last year was a mast year, so there was an awful lot of natural food availability, and I think it's fair to say that trying to accurately estimate badger populations is like trying to nail a jelly to the wall, and I think we'd all be well advised not to get too hung up on the numbers, and I would be just as balanced if we'd had a rounding success, because bear in mind that the population data estimate range ranges to the point that we could have actually shot 105% of what was there, which clearly we haven't.

So we either need to get better at the numbers or accept that for the purposes of this exercise, it's about significant reductions rather than precise numbers being removed.

So on humaneness then, they said that there were problems relating to shooting accuracy and the retrieval of badgers that led to too many badgers taking longer than five minutes to die.

Yeah I think the methodology was flawed. Having read the IEP report, there are certainly some areas in there where I think a small number of individuals contractors would benefit from some additional training and support. On the basis that the maximum distance we were permitted to shoot badgers at was 70 metres, and certainly in my experience it's very easy to get to within 70 metres, or as a matter of fact quite a lot nearer to a badger, and providing that you approach quietly from downwind and you haven't got any members of the animal rights movement in your vicinity, it's actually quite easy to shoot them.

So all contractors were asked to demonstrate their ability to shoot accurately at 70 metres before they were permitted to cull badgers, and they all demonstrated an ability to do so.

I think how this was measured, because having looked at the IEP, there's the case A, case B and case C badgers aren't there?

Yeah.

I think whoever designed this measure of humaneness had an agenda, or certainly if they didn't have an agenda, they've inadvertently come up with some results that would suit opponents of the cull, because out of the nine case C badgers, two were undoubtedly wounded and not retrieved. That's very regrettable and undesirable and I wish it hadn't happened, but the reality is I think that was out of something like 70 or 80 total badgers that were witnessed, and there's an awful lot of data on deer culling and fox culling that would suggest that only two animals to be hit, wounded and lost out of that number is actually pretty low.

Rather it hadn't happened, very undesirable, but in practical field circumstances, whatever species it is that's being shot, there will always be some instances of wounding. It's an unfortunate, highly undesirably, inevitable consequence of shooting animals.

But the other seven case C, the contractor and their buddy and the AHVLA monitor all agreed that there is no evidence that that animal had been hit. Now that in itself asks a few questions, how you can actually miss something at that range, but again, misses do happen. Maybe the animal took a step forward. Maybe there was a twig in the way that wasn't visible that caused the bullet to be slightly deflected. Who knows? Maybe they just pulled the shot. But for whatever reason, and the sort of things you look for, there is an audible bullet strike. It's normally actually quite possible to hear a bullet. It's quite an audible, definite sound when a high-velocity rifle bullet hits an animal.

The animal normally reacts. As you'd imagine, something being hit by a lump of lead flying at 3000 feet per second, you would normally get a reaction. And then there's normally some evidence at the site where that animal was shot. You'd be looking for hair, you'd be looking for blood, you'd be looking for skin, you'd be looking for flesh, and it should have been possible for that animal to be observed in what direction it had gone in after it had been shot or shot at, and you'd be looking for a blood trail or evidence.

And in seven of those nine case C badgers, not one of them had any evidence whatsoever it had been hit. So in any other set of circumstances, the reasonable conclusion would be that it had been missed. The IEP conclusion was that it took more than five minutes to die and therefore it had suffered. Well most of them are probably still wandering around now.

So I think that was a really, really poor conclusion, and in the case B badgers, just because the AHVLA monitor for whatever reason wasn't able to maintain a continuous view, now that could be all sorts of reasons. For example maybe the animal went behind a tuft of grass, or when you shoot something and it collapses, it can sometimes disappear from view. It hasn't gone anywhere, it's perfectly dead, it's just that you can't see it anymore and you have to get near it in order to see it again.

But they were all within 10 metres of where they'd been shot and found stone dead. Yet the IEP concluded they'd all taken more than five minutes to die. Again I would question as to whether that was actually a valid or justifiable set of methodology for assessing humaneness.

There was one case A badger that took more than 60 something seconds to die, and the rest of them all died very quickly, or they took an average of, I can't remember what it was, but there was only one bad outcome in the case A badgers, and as I understand it; that contractor had an issue with his optics which he was unaware of, which can happen, and there but for grace of God go all of us who use rifles with optics.

Sometimes they can get a knock, or sometimes for whatever reason, the point of impact can move slightly, and as I understand it, his point of impact had moved and therefore whilst he was aiming at the right part of the badger, the bullet was hitting the wrong part of the badger, and that guy won't do that again. But the badger was retrieved and it was dispatched humanely in the end.

Again it was very regrettable and the guy was very upset about it, because the last thing he wanted on earth was for something to suffer, but there was and it does happen where optics can sometimes shift their point of impact slightly.

And what about the conclusions on safety then?

Oh just to continue on humaneness, I don't want to bang on about it, but using the kit that I was using and the way that we were using it, I'm really disappointed at the IEP's conclusions on humaneness because as I said earlier on, I shot a significant number of the total number of badgers, and they were shot very humanely, and myself and my buddy took considerable pride in that; that that animals didn't suffer and it was a clean, swift kill.

So onto safety, the IEP concluded that it was safe. Avon and Somerset police didn't raise any concerns, and Gloucestershire said there were some incidents of concern, but overall the IEP conclusion was that it was safe.

I think I would agree with that. I mean certainly all of the contractors went to a training course and were already safe people. So these people all already had a rifle licence. They all were very experienced in the use of firearms. They were already using them for vermin control, deer control, fox control, whatever, so they were all very safe pairs of hands to have rifles in.

And the animal rights protestors, and the wounded badger patrol were guilty of this as were the more extreme elements, they were pretty quick to try and paint a picture of un-safety, because again it suited their agenda, and I know full well that none of our contractors did anything unsafe, but there were accusations of rifles being discharged with protestors present, or being fired in their direction.

No substance behind it whatsoever. No evidence of that; police weren't able to find any evidence of that and quite frankly the only potential concern with regard to safety is if protestors do something

daft. Now one cannot legislate completely for protestors doing
something daft, like concealing themselves somewhere where they
hope a badger might turn up where a contractor's going to be
operating etc.

Contractors will go to very considerable lengths to make sure that
they're operating safely, but I think it's incumbent on the opponents
of culling to realise that they have some responsibilities as well, in
terms of frankly not engaging in unlawful activity and not trying to
contrive circumstances where a contractor could be accused of
practicing unsafely.

**One of the parts of the conclusions was that yes, it can be car-
ried out safely if the guidelines are followed, but they said that
wasn't always the case. So what you're saying is that actually it
was pretty much always the case, and where it seems not to be;
that's as a result of opponents' activities or the way it's been con-
strued or...**

Yeah absolutely. Some of the opponents of the badger cull will do
anything to try and paint contractors, the NFU, farmers, supporters
of the cull in a bad light, and that will include lying and trying to
fabricate or contrive circumstances where either the contractors are
painted in a bad light or they can try and make it appear that the
contractor was doing something they shouldn't have been doing.
They did try an awful lot of devious things to try and achieve those
sorts of outcomes.

I can only speak from personal experience, but the training course
we went on absolutely emphasised the importance of safety, and
when you're a responsible firearms owner, the importance of safety
doesn't really need reminding to you, because that should be at the
forefront of your mind every time that you're using that firearm,
and it is.

All contractors were asked to do risk assessments. We all knew
where the footpaths were, we all knew where safe backstops were
and we all went to considerable lengths to operate safely, and the
conclusions of the IEP were that it was safe and I genuinely believe
it was safe. As somebody who does an awful lot of rifle use both at
day and at night, I'm very confident that I can do so safely, but as I
say, I think it is incumbent upon the anti-cull movement to recognise that some of the things they did and said last time were a
bit daft.

So in terms of, I suppose going slightly beyond safety, some of the anti-cull people were concerned in a way about some of the actions of cull contractors beyond what might be connected with trying to shoot a badger, for example the lobbing of something that goes bang, whether it's a firework or something else, in the direction of protestors, or the exact reverse of what you've mentioned, being followed at speed at night at very close range by a four by four with lights on, this sort of thing.

How do you react to those sorts of stories, because they certainly go round among cull protestors, and obviously it affects people and their view of cull contractors?

Well certainly I didn't have any experience of that and I'm not aware, and certainly on the radio, every night, you could hear instance after instance of cull protestors looking for interactions with contractors. I don't know any contractors that were looking for interactions with the protestors, it's completely pointless, and there were high-speed chases conducted by anti-cull protestors without a doubt, and they were documented and the police had to go and intervene in some of them. So certainly there was a road safety issue there.

And I think it's two fairly polarised positions. I don't think you're going to get many farmers or cull contractors who are going to say "oh well, let's sit down and have a cup of tea and have a chat about how we're going to sort this all out", and likewise I don't see any anti-cull protestors suddenly finding an awful lot of common ground with a cull contractor or farmer, and they are at fairly distant parts of a spectrum of opinion, and it's unfortunately, certainly my experience was the law-breaking and wrongdoing rested squarely with the protestor movement, and they were pretty clever in terms of trying to contrive circumstances where they could cast contractors and farmers in a bad light, and certainly all our experience bears that out as well.

I just want to move onto the government's response to the find-
ings of the IEP report then.   DEFRA said it would introduce
measures to improve the accuracy and performance of field craft
of shooters.   You've kind of mentioned that before, but do you
want to say a bit more about that?

We're waiting to see what that looks like. I think speaking to other
fellow contractors; they're pretty relaxed and comfortable that they
would be able to demonstrate their competence and abilities whi-
chever way the government or agencies want to assess them.

At this point we don't actually know what form that's going to
take. From my own perspective I'm very relaxed about it. I know
full well that I can shoot straight and I know that I can operate in a
professional and humane way, and if there's some form of training
or reassessment that's required in order to prove that, I'm more
than comfortable with it.

Are you also confident that there would be enough marksmen
who would be prepared to say that they're willing to do this, who
are also of an adequate standard in order sufficiently to be able
to cover both cull zones, and perhaps more cull zones in the fu-
ture?

It's a very difficult question to answer. I can only speak for the
cull zone that I'm in, and I can only speak from my own perspective. I think my view is fairly commonly held among the contractor
base. They're all pretty relaxed about it. As I said, we don't actually
know what form it's going to take, and most contractors tend to be
from in or very near to the area they're operating in.

So if there are roll-out areas, I don't imagine, I certainly haven't
imagined myself being asked to go off to ... or to wherever to cull
badgers, because I imagine they will recruit, train and manage
their own contractors from their own local base of pest control
operators, deer stalkers, wildlife managers, whatever, locally.

The other thing DEFRA said it would do was to introduce
measures to make sure that all of the available land area in the
cull zones is adequately targeted by shooters.

Yeah I think there were some flaws frankly in the data gathering
and some flaws in the data analysis. If a contractor has been to a
farm during daylight hours several times, and all of the badger setts

got flooded last winter, and there is absolutely no evidence of any badgers living there, he isn't going to spend a vast amount of time there during the cull when he's got other areas where his efforts will be far better rewarded.

And likewise if a badger sett's on a boundary between two land-holdings, and there's just a natural side which is better to cull them from and you cull them all from that side of the boundary, the farm the other side of the fence looks like you've never been there or done anything there, but the reality is you shot all of their badgers as well, it's just you pulled them onto next door to do so.

So I think there's some, I can understand government's concern to make sure that the effort is evenly distributed and frankly the job's done to a high standard across the whole area, but I think maybe there's a little bit of misinterpretation of some practical realities there, and maybe a bit of data capture that has some room for improvement. I know where the badgers are and I know where they're not. Now I did go to a couple of places just to be on the safe side, and my thoughts were confirmed because I didn't see any badgers there. So you go where the fish are biting.

And they also said they would try and maintain monitoring of humaneness and effectiveness, improve monitoring of shooters' adherence to best practice, and improve cull contractors' compliance with data collection.

As I said earlier on, as a contractor I've no idea what form that's going to take yet, so we've just got to wait and see what government and government agencies and the company come up with before we can have a view.

There were some issues weren't there? I don't know if you've seen, there's a video account of a badger that had been shot in a cage trap that was just kind of slung into the nearest handy bag and slung into the back of a van, and then the cage left with the blood not tidied up and that kind of thing. Now I don't know how much you consider these sorts of approaches to be in response to a problem that is important or not, or whether these are not the right response to a non-problem or something.

I'm not really intimately familiar with the ins and the outs of that set of circumstances, but certainly the training made it abun-

dantly clear what the standards expected in all aspects were and in terms of best practice guidance.

It was very clear in terms of shooting and cage trapping and bio-security, and certainly I had several AHVLA monitoring visits for the humaneness monitoring, and I also had a Natural England visit. There was a selection of trappers that were selected at random to have Natural England monitors come out with them in order to look at contractor compliance with the best practice guidance, and no issues were raised, and I was pretty comfortable with that.

Now if an individual contractor, for whatever reason, for example isn't following the best practice guidance with regard to biosecurity, then I suggest that contractor needs to be reminded of the need to follow best practice guidance with regard to biosecurity. I don't think we all need to be tarred with the same brush as it were.

Just going back, something that came up before then, one of the consequences of the cost sharing as it's already been set up is that the culling is then seen by the police as a private thing, a private enterprise happening on private land, and that it's not then, the culling itself is not then an aspect of government policy. The government policy is to licence the culling, but it's not the government policy to actually be the ones doing culling. That's the cull company and so on.

So coming back, one of the consequences of the cost sharing is that the relationship with the police is different, although I've also had it explained to me that as a result of the Human Rights Act, it's not actually the police's job to enforce government policy anyway, even if it was done directly, but it creates even more distance, if you like, from that possibility. What's your response to that sort of situation?

Well I don't think that was a deliberate move. I think the intentions were honourable in terms of the industry and the government showing that they would be prepared to work together to try and solve an important problem, and the reality is it suits the police quite nicely to be able to sidestep it to a degree, because if this was DEFRA employees doing the culling, as they did in RBCT and other previous culls, then obviously government are that one step closer. The government are the government and the police are the police, and there's nobody in between for them to try and find reasons not to help them.

The reality is it may well not be the job of the police necessarily to facilitate the delivery of culling by a private company per se, but it is the job of the police to intervene and uphold the law, and where you've got persistent and regular instances of intimidation, harassment, property damage, aggravated trespass and things along those lines, then I would suggest the police maybe have strayed too far the wrong side of the line.

And yeah, I know the government were very, very committed to try and make this work, I don't think the government are the slightest bit happy at what we perceive as maybe the ineffective policing of it, but I still don't see it as an event, and whether the police, it's been convenient for their purposes, I don't know, but I don't think that was by design on anybody's part to be honest with you.

And I suppose the other thing that might be going on is that the aim is also to move the cost of this disease problem off the government's books to actually, you know, a shortage of money in almost every region, and this could be one of the things which government doesn't have to pay for anymore and it becomes an entirely private matter that government has licenced, made possible legally, but that's it, and the cost is on the people who are doing it. It's I suppose a sort of privatisation thing I guess. What's your view of that?

Well I think the farming industry were prepared to put their money where their mouth was. They've been asking for the opportunity to cull badgers to try and tackle the disease reservoir in wildlife for a very long time, and I think there's a recognition on the part of the farming industry that the government's budgets are under significant pressure, there's been all sorts of austerity measures. DEFRA's had its budget cut drastically.

There's all sorts of cuts that have been necessary, but at the same time the government are currently under a statutory obligation to compensate farmers for all TB reactors that are culled, and those animals are for all intents and purposes compulsorily purchased by the government and then killed, and the bill for that is costing the government a fortune.

So if you were cynical, yes you could say "well there was an intention to offload the cost onto the industry". I think more realistically, I think there is a recognition of a need to do something about the problem, and by trying to solve the problem you'll hopefully reduce the number of animals the government is compulsorily purchasing and slaughtering, and the industry, which is also suffering at the hands of this disease, is prepared to help with that, including the cost, but I don't see the industry having a lot of appetite for any further movement in that direction until we've got some evidence we've got this one sorted.

I suppose one of the more general criticisms of the culling as a policy is that because of what it is, it's inevitably going to stir opposition from those people who don't like the idea or are in principle opposed or find the way in which the policy has been brought about difficult, and so to fail to take that into account in your policy planning is problematic. Yes the cull might work, but you can't separate the cull from the reaction the cull might get from people who don't like it.

And so what do you conclude? The cull would have worked if only it hadn't had opponents, or the cull doesn't work because it has too much opposition, or the cull does work even though it has opposition.

I think it's fair to say that some contractors would have been able to achieve a greater result in terms of effectiveness if it hadn't have been for persistent activities by opponents of culling, but an awful lot of those activities were illegal.

So my conclusion is that I think everybody must respect the rights of others to hold a different opinion, but not when that means that they're prepared to go out night after night, quite deliberately breaking the law because they don't agree with something, and yes we always knew that there would be some opposition to the cull, but it's also fair to say that we still managed to shoot the best part of 1,000 badgers despite their best efforts and...

Sorry, I guess the comeback would be that it's true, you know, maybe people were doing things that were illegal and if they weren't, they'd have been more successful, but ... there was an issue of a limited number of police, and one argument about a sensible policy is not to try and introduce a controversial policy

that is effectively unpoliceable, and kind of gives people an opportunity to do those things almost with impunity does it not?

I don't think it was unpoliceable. I think an awful lot more could have been achieved by the police with less, and don't forget, the figures that are being bandied around for the cost of the cull, the cost of the cull to the taxpayer would have been pretty much zero had it not been for protestor activities. We mustn't lose sight of the fact that it was farmers who were paying for this. It was farmers that were paying the contractors to do what they were going to do.

I suspect there would have been a small cost to government in terms of AHVLA, Natural England and DEFRA staff that were working behind the scenes in connection with it, but for all intents and purposes, the upfront costs, the cost of blokes going out there and shooting or caging badgers were met by the industry. Any additional costs or resource were only there because of law breaking and activities conducted by opponents of the cull, bearing in mind that it was a pilot, nobody's done a badger cull using cage trapping, and rifle shooting being carried out by a private company before.

So I think it's fair to say that nobody really knew what the level of opposition and the effectiveness of that opposition would be. I think it's fair to say that the cattle industry realised that bovine TB is such an important issue that they were prepared to try and do something about it.

But do you see what I mean though; that the policy of culling takes place in a social context in which there is opposition and it's impossible to wish it away if you see what I mean? It could have been policed more, but it would still have been there or they would have found other strategies to get round it. Do you see what I mean; that actually it's a policy that creates opposition and they both have to be taken into account?

It's very hard to gauge how many direct activists there were operating ... My assessment would be including the wounded badger patrols and all the other more extreme elements, probably between one and two hundred people.

Now we live in a country of 60 odd million, 70 odd million people, and if something's costing the country tens of millions a year, ruining people's lives, families, businesses and resulting in thousands and thousands of cattle being destroyed every year, if a few extremists are able to completely derail that, then I'm not en-tirely sure that's their democratic right quite frankly, and I don't think that should stop us from trying to do something which fun-damentally is the right thing to do, just because one or two hundred people don't like it.

We live in a democracy. There are lots of things I don't like, there have been governments in the past that have done things I don't like, the government now don't always do things that I like, but as a citizen of the United Kingdom I respect the fact that I live in a de-mocracy and if it's the policy of the day, I might not like it, I might vote differently, but I don't go out and break the law and try and prevent it from happening.

Chapter 10

Dialogue

It's time for another team meeting. We need to condense all the interview material I've collected into a list of 30-or-so short statements which cover the main issues and allow us to get a clear idea of what people think about culling badgers and what to do about bovine TB. I say 'people', but I mean 'the 500 people we're planning to recruit to our online discussion forum'. I think we're all aware that the chances of persuading 500, or even 50, people to participate in our artificial forum are slim to nil, but we're putting a brave face on it, trying to think of ways to help 'participants' participate, and hoping for the best. We're down to a not-very-short-list, covering some of the different problems and solutions that have been mentioned. But first, lunch.

After a bit of chat about the way the university is run and how well it motivates its academic staff – along those lines, anyway – my colleagues discuss whether there's any point to our project anymore. The title of the project is called 'Doing TB Differently' – so what are we doing differently? The government has just published a bovine TB control strategy that proposes nuanced set of policies and aims to move away from broad culling to targeted culling, vaccination, biosecurity and a range of new targeted control measures. It's also based on some pretty subtle consultation work which involved, among other things, an online discussion forum and some workshops.

We discuss the situation. The strategy has to survive a general election before it can be taken seriously. Targeted culling would rely on a polymerase chain reaction (PCR) test, which is never going to work.[35] The point of the policy is not so much bovine TB (although the government has to do what the EU says, or it will lose funding), the point is to get the cost of bovine TB off the governments' books and get the farmers to pay for it. Things not going entirely to plan

---

[35] See DEFRA (2010) for a discussion of the limitations.

on that front, but Paterson is prepared to take a lot of public ridicule because success will earn him brownie points inside the party.

All of which means that the project still has a point – it will finish after the election and could give a good account of what issues are contentious, and where different sides might agree, or at least, dis-agree less – although if the Conservatives are still in power after the election it's value would be – hypothetical. Rhetorical. Or some-thing.

Back in the office, I try to clear the rest of the stuff off the agenda before we can get on with choosing our statements. That means bringing up the topic of future funding. I know, I know, I said I wasn't interested in carrying on in academia, but since the new year I've been thinking. There are two thoughts. First, I quite like this job, and maybe it is possible to keep being a university researcher, picking up interesting projects and avoiding the torture of being a tenured academic. Second, the months are ticking past and I'm starting to get worried about what I'm going to do come summer 2015. Three problems come to mind. They're called – in no particu-lar order – mortgage, maintenance, and meals. There's another thing, less of a thought and more of an impression (when will I learn?). I've got the impression that this project is a bit like an audi-tion. We've been funded to collect a load of data and then archive them. No money for analysis or publication, just get the data, do it well and we'll sort the rest out later. Urgent funding.

The professors are having a conversation about grant applica-tions, and how they probably won't put any more in, just for now, having too many projects on the go. Before that has sunk in, I'm bringing up the topic of grant applications. The professors inspect their smartphones. We get over that, somehow, and the professors, who also review funding applications for research councils, start talking about how it's not going to be possible to get any funding to finish this project properly. Any reviewer would think we've already had enough money. It would have to be something else, on a theme, maybe, or a development. A practical application, perhaps. I say ok, maybe the best way of working out what that direction is is to think about some papers to write. I detect a slight uptick in inter-est, and I outline the places where there's something to write about. But then we move on, hacking through the statements, trying to work out what the principles are for including this one over that one. I try to keep the professorial minds on the job. They need to go soon, so better get on with it, then. By about 5, we've got a slightly too-long list that we'll finalise later, and I've got something else. The nod to go to DEFRA's latest consultation event on bovine TB. Biosecurity.

My wife takes the piss. Old men. Post-It Notes. I promise you, you're going to do something with Post-It notes. She should know, after an aborted career as a lobbyist. I try to remind her that I might be old one day but I'm an exception, apparently. As I head off, I'm more concerned about bumping into Angry Voice and saying something derogatory. It has become a real risk as I pull into the car park. In the last few miles, half-listening to the insistent 'voice' of the satnav, I've been thinking about that funding again, I'm thinking about the purpose and effect of the Urgent Funding scheme this project is run on. I'm thinking the purpose is to mop up the issues that should have been funded way back, but weren't because of a lack of funding. And because funds are limited, money is saved by only funding the essential parts of the project. The rest can be done on the personal research time (paid of course) of the tenured academics. That has an effect. You do the hard work, gain first-hand familiarity with the issues, the field – the people. And then you can proceed to another location, thanks, or try doing some analysis and write up in your own personal research time (unpaid). Meanwhile, the tenured academics write it up, publish, gain the plaudits, without having had any meaningful contact with the sources of data or any experience that might challenge the already-formed perspectives they bring to the research. Approaching the entrance of the bland, low-rise brick centre, I am not in a good mood.

He isn't there. There are, though, some blank sheets of paper taped to the walls. I spy some squares of paper, and masking tape. Looks like post-it notes are too expensive, these days. I start to wonder how many degrees the person who cut up the little squares of paper has. Two, maybe? But it's no use, this isn't going to get me anywhere. I try to focus on the things around me. Flipcharts. Voice recorders. Name labels.

Talk. Back when I was doing my second degree a lot of people at the university (College, London) were working on the idea that politics would be better if citizen dialogue could somehow contribute to decisions that had proved, under the current system, to be very controversial. One of the people who was doing research to explore the idea was Professor Jacqui Burgess, and the opportunity to be taught by her was a reason I signed up for the degree. Turned out she was taking a year off, which is how I met Professor Davies.

Deliberative democracy, it was called. Instead of a thin veneer of 'public debate' about an issue, which means a bunch of the usual suspects having their rant about it in the opinion section of the papers, ordinary people would decide by meeting, going through the evidence, discussing it, and trying to come up with a group conclusion. It might not be the only thing that goes into making a decision, but it would mean the final decision on, say, whether to build this new road (as it so often was, in the early 90s) was more deeply founded.

Much of the work was based on the ideas of Jürgen Habermas, a German thinker who disagreed with the likes of Foucault and believed that it was possible to come up with something positive to say about the world: that something is true (Habermas 1987). He thought the way to do it was to get people together to discuss it. Provided the process was fair, the truth was then something on which the group could come to a consensus about. Habermas was shouted down for being naïve: it's simply not possible, some critics said, to get a perfectly fair process – social power will always be there, giving some people an advantage and silencing others. Another problem was more practical. Doing deliberative democracy is long-winded and expensive. Even if you could persuade more people that this wasn't just an unbelievably boring and ultimately unnecessary process, where would they find the time? Work eats time and begets money, so can democracy afford to buy their citizens out of the money factory to the extent that deliberative democracy would make a difference? Some people think it should – they are the ones who think that every citizen should receive an income as of right that they could live on, if they needed or wanted to (for example Lord, Kennet, and Felton 2012). But those are not the sort of people who get into positions of power in the UK. Instead the British elect people who think making money is a good thing and prefer to do democracy on a shoe-string.

But this doesn't mean that policy on bovine TB has been conducted with no deliberation and consultation at all. Up until about 1996 the Badger Panel was a group of representatives of the relevant concerned groups – conservation and farming – who met regularly to discuss policy. The problem was that they could never agree. And then policy culture changed. Evidence-based policy was the zeitgeist. The Conservative Major government struggled with the notion of 'evidence' during the BSE crisis in the mid-1990s, while from 1997 the New Labour government led by Tony Blair tried to embrace evidence-based policy-making as part of it modernization agenda (HM Govt 1999). Professor John Krebs, zoologist and soon-to-be head of the Food Standards Agency was brought in to oversee the definitive end-to-all-arguments experiment that would prove one way or another whether culling badgers was a worthwhile way of reducing bovine TB in cattle. A long decade later, Professor John Bourne, who ran the experiments, and his colleagues, announced their findings (ISG 2007). No it isn't! And then Professor David King cleared his throat (King 2007). Don't you mean 'yes it is'?

One policy trend was never going to be enough. The next was for stakeholder consultations within policy networks (Marsh and Rhodes 1992). Which, once we have all finished staring blankly at Humphrey's smug face, means talking to slightly more interested parties about policy than we might have done in the past – when we only operated in small 'policy communities' made up of people who all, basically, agreed with each other. The policy community was (Smith 1991, Marsh and Smith 2000), and still is – a point I shall get to in a minute – the standard way of working for DEFRA and it's predecessor, MAFF. It's a community of two plus friends: the ministry and the NFU. However, that doesn't mean that new or different groups couldn't gain entry to policy circles. In fact, the British civil service has traditionally been thought of as fairly accommodating of different views (which is not the same as saying that being included had any effect on the policy). It's just that in the case of policy on agriculture, newcomers generally weren't welcome. On other environmental topics, groups such as the RSPB, WWF and Friends of the Earth found that they were invited in after a series of controversies raised public concern and the groups demonstrated that they were 'sensible' (Rootes 1999). So, the Badger Panel had been special in the way that it brought different views into the policy process. But once the government decided to pursue culling – at least as an experiment – opponents were out. They still are. There weren't any opponents of the culls at the workshop on biosecurity I went to, even though many cull opponents are very positive about better biosecurity and have lots of ideas.

Two trends is nothing. Try three. Citizen dialogue. Deliberative democracy arrives in DEFRA. In 2002 the government launched a nation-wide debate about genetically-modified (GM) crops called GM Nation. The aim was to develop a properly informed public view on genetically-modified (GM) crops and foods, driven by the belief that once the public is alleviated of its ignorance and myths about GM, its opposition would decrease (it didn't; GM Science Review Panel 2003). Not to be deterred, a group of government advisors called the Council for Science and Technology wrote to government suggesting that it should include public dialogue in all its policy-making (CST 2005). Citizen dialogue became part of policy-making on badgers and bovine TB in 2005-6 when the then Labour government were consulting about whether culling should be part of their policy response. In 2006 Opinion Leader Research held three 'citizens' panels' with groups of people in different parts of the country, asking them to review the evidence, discuss it and come to a consensus decision:

"When pushed to come to a decision, there is marginal support for a cull in the context of the workshop when participants are requested to come to a consensus decision. However, this is a reluctant decision and is heavily caveated." (DEFRA 2006, p. 7)

With scientists in dispute with each other and the farming community over 'the science', and three 'juries' of ordinary citizens feeling very ambivalent about the idea, Labour, perhaps wisely – politically at least – declined to cull. It seems strange, though, that the people taking part were randomly selected to reflect the demographics of the area, and anyone who might have anything to do with cattle or badgers was specifically excluded. I can see that might help in one way, if you wanted people to take a look at the evidence you've collected in an impartial way; if you want people to respond to it free of any of the entrenched biases that have become such a problem. But on the other hand, it's just glorified opinion-polling, the sort a political party might be interested in to know how popular it's going to be, but that makes no substantive contribution to resolving the problem.

I'm also struck by the way citizen dialogue makes an unobserved exit when it came to the Conservative-led Coalition Government's turn to consult on the idea of culling. It seems that when you start with a conclusion such as 'we are going to cull' it's easier if you don't allow the opposition to turn up in the flesh. Much better if you reduce them to a thoroughly ignorable set of statistics, such as the ones that said that out of 59,540 consultation responses, 61% said 'no to culling' and 'yes to vaccination' (DEFRA 2010, p. 2). Much better to ensure that your opponents are not given an opportunity to sense their strength. It's not as though the new government was ideologically opposed to dialogue, because it turned up again in 2013 when the government wanted to talk about its long-term strategy for bovine TB. Full spectrum bovine chat ensued. Online forum. Citizen dialogue, working with Sciencewise, the new body supporting public dialogue over science and technology policy. Stakeholder workshops – opponents included. Now culling is an accomplished fact, we can talk. It would have been even better if the culling had gone well.

So what the hell are we doing differently? What confuses me is that Steve doesn't think agreement is possible – not just on this issue; he believes that society (he wouldn't say society – not just that, but it's alright for now) is fractured in ways that can't be brought together. He thinks of the world as one made up of differences, so when it comes to any serious issue, he's not expecting people with different views to come to an agreement about what most divides them. At best he's expecting them to say 'we can agree to disagree'. He calls it a state of agonism, a word which still causes me some agony because the dictionaries seem to want to tell me all about animal behaviour or muscles. I think of it as being neither a protagonist (pro-cull, maybe) nor an antagonist (opposed to the cull, getting on farmers' nerves) but realising there are these differences and knowing there is no way to resolve them. A bit like the way Steve views the world, then.

So why bother having any sort of dialogue at all, if no-one's going to agree on anything anyway? It's about another angle on the idea that everything is different – or more correctly, that everything is difference: a geographical angle – and this is where people who try to use Gilles Deleuze's ideas to think are converging (for example, Atkins and Robinson 2013). If everything is different than no one-size-fits-all policy is going to be appropriate at any significantly large scale. The problem with central government is central government: it collects average statistics and comes up with policies that apply them uniformly. Even when it's trying to go softly-softly, such as by distributing leaflets to farmers with advice on how to protect their feed-stores from bovine TB, it makes matters worse because for a lot of farmers the advice is irrelevant, and it can make anything other that killing badgers look futile. But if, *if*, you can get people to move past their battles about culling and start to talk about what else they could do, and maybe trust each other enough to start sharing knowledge – for example, where the badger setts are and which ones seem healthy, or sharing skills such as how to go about vaccinating a badger, or sharing resources by, for example, funnelling money from large conservation funds to help farmers manage biosecurity risks on their farm – if you could do that, then maybe you could get action to reduce bovine TB, less distrust, cynicism and maybe even 'well, actually, we're dealing with bovine TB alright ourselves here and we don't want all the disruption of those culls coming here, thanks. Bit of support money wouldn't hurt though.'

What are we doing? The refrain of a couple of months of team meetings over the summer. The online forum is coming together. In our version, participants will really be able to discuss things, rather than submit one- or two-line comments to some stimulus material offered them by the people running it, as they did during DEFRA's online escapade. Instead we're going to keep our influence on the discussion to a minimum. Set a hare running each day with a new question and see what happens. Does dialogue emerge? How is it different when people are in agreement as opposed to having differing views? Can people find common ground? Could the Internet provide a way to do deliberative democracy on a large scale, but for less money? Could it also help to neutralise those problems to do with social power that have always seemed to get in the way?

Crucially, the lines of responsibility are different. When government consults on policy, everyone tells it what they think government ought to do. But maybe that makes you lazy, because there's no real need to consider what those with a different view are saying. You just have to make sure your voice rings loudly. But what if the people you're talking to can't do anything about the issue either? All they're going to do is read what everyone posted, and write it up – attending as much to the process as to the outcome. It's not futile, exactly; maybe it's inviting participants to take part in a less purposeful way. This is where the Q Methodology comes in. We want to find out what difference it makes to the views of the people taking part in the online discussion forum when they discuss the questions we give them in different groups. One will be entirely made up of cull supporter-types, another of cull-opponent types, and a third will be a mix of the two. We need to understand where our participants are coming from so we can put them in the right group, and we need to assess their views in the same way at the end of the week of discussions to see whether there has been any significant shift. So we need something easy to use, but not so simple that everyone's views are reduced to a single dimension, for culling or against it.

Ugh, statistics is complicated. I've been hunting around for a while now for an example that's going to set me off explaining what's so interesting about Q-methods (like Scott, setting off to conquer the Antarctic), and I've gone wrong several times, retracing my steps with the delete button. And like Scott, someone else has got there first, but as I think it's unfair to make you buy and then read a whole other book just so that you can understand the next paragraphs of this one (not something, generally, that worries most academics) I'm going to try anyway, instead of corpsing in an icy wasteland of blank paper. Here's a little thing I found in an old paper by another long list of researchers beginning with 'Rogers' (Rogers et al. 1998). There's a strong positive correlation between the number of badgers entering a badger social group and the number of badgers leaving it. In other words, badger social groups don't tend to get bigger because of a lot of newcomers joining and they don't tend to get smaller because of a lot of members leaving. What tends to happen, the researchers say, is that some badgers get a habit of leaving their group and then coming back later, keeping 'net migration' for badger social groups at about zero.

Annoyingly, the units of measurement in this comparison of 'in-movements' and 'out-movements' are the same. One movement out of a social group, or into a social group, always means it's one badger moving. A correlation statistic tells you how closely related two sets of figures are, in other words how much one rises when the other rises – a positive correlation – or how much one falls when the other rises – a negative correlation. The correlation statistic is a bit like a percentage but with -1 being the lowest, for a negative corre-lation, and +1 being the highest. The process of calculating a corre-lation statistic enables us to compare units of measurement that are completely different, such as height and weight, without asking nonsense questions like 'am I taller than I am heavy?' (Watts and Stenner 2012, p. 9 – the aforementioned Amundsens). Anyway, Rogers and company ran their data through a correlation calcula-tion. The first thing that would have happened to their numbers is that they would have been transformed into something called z-scores, which deal with any unmatched units of measurement by turning them from absolute measures to relative measures. Relative to what? How? Relative to the average (or 'mean') and using 'standard deviations'.

I think this is going to need a table. Here are some entirely made-up numbers to do with badger movements in and out of social groups over the period of one year.

Table 9.1. In-movements and out-movements of individuals from badger groups. Hypothetical example.

Badger group	In-movements	Out-movements
A	5	4
B	4	6
C	7	5
D	9	8
E	3	3
F	9	10
Total	37	36
Mean	6.17	6
Standard deviation	2.34	2.38

Source: Based on Rogers et al. (1998).

To work out the 'mean' you add up the figures in each column and divide the total by number of figures you added, which is 6 in my wonderfully sophisticated table. So, in the last column, the mean is telling us that, on average, each of the six badger groups experienced 6 out-movements that year, because 6x6=36. But as we can see, the actual data shows that each of the badger groups did not in fact experience 6 out-movements each. The actual numbers vary. The standard deviation is an average of the differences between these actual data and the mean, the average variation or, not very helpfully, 'deviation'. But the calculation has to be a bit more complicated. Some measurements are higher and some are lower. If we subtract the figure for the mean (6) from each of these actual (and yet entirely pretend) measurements, we get three minus numbers, one zero and two positive numbers. If we added these numbers up in this form, the minus numbers would cancel out the positive numbers and the result wouldn't be in the slightest bit helpful. We need to go on a diversion to get rid of the minus numbers. We are going to multiply each of these differences by themselves (this is called 'squaring') – so, to take the first line, -2x-2. When you multiply two negative figures you get a positive number. Great, but in getting rid of the problem presented by the negative numbers but we given ourselves another problem. All our numbers are too big and they are not going to represent a meaningful average difference. This problem though, can be solved as well, once we have gone through the ordinary stages of working out a 'mean' by adding up the 'squared differences' (4+0+1+4+9+16), which comes to 34, and dividing by 6 (the number of groups involved), which equals 5.67, roughly. Finally, we can solve our new problem and reverse the squaring operation. What, when it's multiplied by itself, equals 5.67? No, I don't know either. It's called the square root, and that's the button to press on the calculator. 2.38.

A z-score tells you how many standard deviations from the mean a measurement is. In other words, a z-score is a measurement minus the mean divided by the standard deviation. So, the next table shows the z-scores for our imaginary badger data.

Table 9.2. Z-scores to standardize movements of individuals in and out of groups. Hypothetical example.

Badger group	In-movements	Out-movements
A	-0.5	-0.84
B	-0.93	0
C	0.35	-0.42
D	1.21	0.84
E	-1.35	-1.26
F	1.21	1.68

Source: Based on Rogers et al. (1998)

The differences have been standardised so that, if we were talking about heights and weights, or some other unmatched data, we'd be making a sensible comparison. The point of going through this, though, apart from demystifying a fragment of statistics on the sly, is to give you a feel for it so you're ready for the next bit. Because something quite subtle yet very odd has just happened. In the first table, all the data was about the badger groups. Group A had 5 badgers come in and 4 badgers leave in a year. The measurements relate to what happened to that badger group. But in the second table, the z-scores are not telling us about the badger groups, but the relationship between each individual measurement and all the other measurements in that column. The z-scores relate to what is happening across the badger groups. If the data in these tables are supposed to tell a story (albeit a fictional one), the story in the first table is a horizontal one, we read across the table in rows; the story in the second table is a vertical one – we read in columns. And that has done something very profound to the way we are thinking about the data. In table 1 we think about each group as a whole, but in table 2, each of the groups have been chopped up into two bits: their in-movements bit and their out-movements bit. In so doing, we become able to say something general about the relationship between in-movements and out-movements across the groups as a whole, but we can't say things about what is distinctive of each individual group, even though an untrained eye can very easily see that there are clearly big differences between them, in terms of the amount of 'migration' that occurs.

Many reports you come across in the news, or when you're reading academic papers, that contain a statistical analysis of some data, whether it's about human medicine, psychology, or about non-human things, contains this type of operation. Not Q Methodology. The person who came up with it, William Stephenson, was a student of the statisticians who invented the 'correlation' operation (Stephenson 1953). Stephenson, though, objected to the way z-scores worked when the data involved was about people, because, in effect, the switch from telling horizontal to vertical stories involved chopping people up into little bits and lumping all the same bits together. Here's a pile of human heights. A pile of human weights. Most of all, he objected to chopping up people's views in this way (Watts and Stenner 2012, p. 11).[36] If you've ever been asked

---

[36] For more on Q Methodology see Brown (1980), McKeown and Thomas (1988), and Stainton Rogers (1995).

a question like 'How much do you agree or disagree with the following statements', and given a 'Likert' scale between 1 and 5, like this example, this has happened to you.

Figure 9.1. Example of a Likert scale question.

Strongly disagree				Strongly agree	I don't know enough about this
1	2	3	4	5	
❑	❑	❑	❑	❑	❑

Stephenson thought this was ridiculous, and instead argued that what we should be interested in is people's whole viewpoint across a range of aspects of a given issue. Take, oh, the culling of badgers.

Opinion polls slice people up in the traditional statistical way, and if you want to demonstrate support for or opposition to a currently salient policy, you can pay a polling company to ask a question of a rigorously constructed sample of the UK population that will bias the answer your way. It's expensive, so generally it's only organisations with a political campaign fund, newspapers, and rich individuals who pay for such things, and if they don't like the answer, they don't tell anyone about it. Back in 2013, when the controversy about culling badgers hit a peak, the NFU and the Humane Society International (HSI) both asked the online polling company, You-Gov, to conduct a poll on their chosen question (NFU/YouGov 2013; HSI/YouGov 2013). Before the culls began the NFU asked 'Would you support or oppose the culling of badgers, as part of a range of measures and in specific infected areas, in an attempt to control bovine tuberculosis (TB)?'. The HSI waited until the culls had got going and had experienced a bit of trouble, and then asked 'Regardless of whether or not you supported the badger cull, do you think it has been a success or failure?'. The results were:

Table 9.3. Comparison of opinion polling results.

NFU/YouGov	%	HSI/YouGov	%
Support	29	Success	15
Neither	15	Failure	51
Oppose	34	Don't know	34
Don't know	22		

Source: NFU/YouGov (2013): 'Would you support or oppose the culling of badgers, as part of a range of measures and in specific infected areas, in an attempt to control bovine tuberculosis (TB)?'; HSI/YouGov (2013): 'Regardless of whether or not you supported the badger cull, do you think it has been a success or failure?'

The NFU could say that only a minority of people were against the culls, and the HSI could say that a majority of people thought they had been a failure. YouGov then helpfully sliced up their respondents according to gender, age, social 'grade', and region of the country so we might get a hint of whether there is a correlation between, say, age and view on this question. But Stephenson would have wanted to know which of the people who thought the cull had been a failure had supported the culls as a policy solution, and he would also have wanted to know whether people thought that the failure of the culls outweighed their support for it – in fact, just finding out about two questions would never be enough. Stephenson wanted to know how people's perspective stacked up across 30, 40, or even 60 different questions related to a single topic.

We have a final-ish list of statements. I've put them in the back of the book so you can look at them. No, they're not all brilliant. What does it mean, for example, if someone disagrees with the statement that "Nobody wants to see farms Fort-Knoxed"?. 'I want to see farms Fort-Knoxed', or 'I know some people do, but they're idiots'? In our defence, there aren't many like this one; with the rest it's usually possible to be relatively confident about their interpretation once you take the other statements into account. Do it better next time. If there is a next time, about which there is no certainty, or even much hope. But I'm getting ahead of myself.

June 27th, the opening day of the online discussion forum. We're in the hands of IT experts. Time is stretching, like being on the rack is stretching. As the date has come closer we've looked harder at the website. It's only now we're realising how it ought to be, where the glitches are and what still needs to be sorted out. John, the designer, is still working on them, as well as entering the details of the people taking part. This is weird. This is research, university-based, but right now we're in the hands of a contractor. Then, at four-thirty, we're open. To celebrate, I've arranged to see a game of Twenty20 cricket with a friend. We sit in the kind-of sun and watch, basically, a re-run of my day at work. It looks like our lot are losing, right up until the end, when a middle-order batter wallops a six off the last ball.

The problem with doing your research online is the rate of attrition. I don't mean the gradual degradation of your back and neck muscles as you try to maintain a decent posture in front of a computer for hours on end, although that's a problem as well; I mean the number of people who drop out, give up on taking part because they haven't got time, or lose interest, or experience some glitch they can't be bothered to overcome. The first week of the forum is like that. No-one gets to discuss anything, they're all just given time to complete the first assault of Q-methodology. We worry, all week, about whether we've set too many hurdles, as participants come trickling through. We send daily reminders. John fields problems. The number creeps up to 100. Out of 550 people invited. Out of over 6000 people contacted – again, not by us, but yet another contractor.

In fact, the task we set the market research company was more difficult than that. We said they had to recruit participants from each of three groups: farmers or landowners, 'nature-lovers' (people with membership of or employment at a wildlife, conservation or animal welfare group) and the 'general public', who were randomly selected from across the West of England. When you're doing a Q study, instead of an opinion poll or survey, you're not trying to make a statistically representative sample of the population. Instead, you're trying to ensure that the full range of views relevant to the debate are represented. A statically representative sample is likely, in fact, to chop off the extremes of any set of views held within a population – not in the sense that they are extreme views, but that that very few people hold them: they are outliers. In Q methodology, you're really trying to be inclusive... and strictly speaking the sample is not the people, but the statements. Although you do get some indication from Q about which views are more popular, because more people are lined up with them, the numbers are not, in the end, that important. If, at some level, two or more people appear to share a similar viewpoint, that's significant, as the chances of them doing so are very small. If you then turned that point of view into a survey question and presented it to a statistically representative sample of the population, you could expect a number of people to select 'strongly agree'. It might only be a minority, the sort of minority that pollsters don't mind ignoring, but Q methodologists mind, very much indeed, because right from the beginning they've been concerned for the views of people as whole persons, down to the individual (but no further!).

First each participant answers a few fairly standard questions about themselves. Then they enter the 'Q' section of the site. Our statements appear on the screen in a little box, one by one and at random, and the participants have to drag-and-drop the box into a table with three columns headed 'mostly agree', 'neutral', 'mostly disagree'. This is just housekeeping, but we hope it also helps people get used to the basic process and start to think about their response to each statement. The next stage is the important bit. On the next screen, they're given another table, but this one is different. It looks like an up-side-down Inca temple. It has nine columns, the first and the ninth have two squares in it, the second and the eighth three, and so on: like this.

Figure 9.2. Layout of the grid or array for respondents to sort statements in the current Q Methodology study.

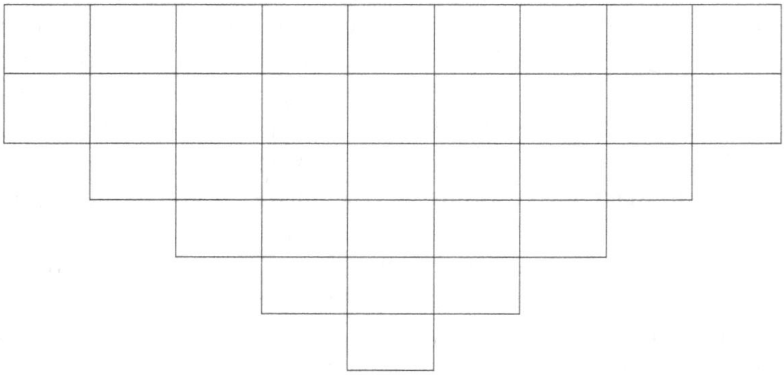

The statements appear one-by-one again, and the participants have to drag-and-drop them onto the grid where they think they best fit. First come the statements they said they mostly agreed with, they find a place on the right, then come the ones they mostly disagreed with, these go on the left. Crucially, the participants are thinking about their response to each statement in relation to the other statements. Do they agree with this one more than that one?

144 people come through the first 'Q' exercise. Enough, just, to carry out our plan for the discussions. They carry on for five days. Ten months later I'm still working on the analysis. The first problem is that despite all the statistical processing, we can't do things we would usually do when analysing the results. We can't use the numbers involved to compare people's responses before and after the discussions, because either they're apples and oranges, or we're looking at the statements individually – going against the design of the whole method. This leads to the second problem – our 'results' are basically interpretations of the data, so we need to agree on what we're going to say. The third problem is the quantity of text that has been typed in by the participants. How on earth do we start to make sense of it? Each problem eats up its own month of time, then I put everything on pause to set up and deal with the discussion workshop, and then the funding runs out. By the end of April 2015 we're got the draft of a paper about the first Q exercise our participants did, giving us an overview of what this collection of almost 150 people from across the West of England think about bovine TB – a sense of the shape of the debate. Is it really polarised or is something else going on? But we're still quibbling with each other about the way to judge the results, slipping back into traditional statistical thinking. What do the numbers mean?

And that's it.

This is what I think we've got. It is, *on the face of it*, a polarised debate. Most farmers, and most conservationists or wildife-supporters, line up exactly how we expect them to, with farmers asserting that badgers are the problem and culling the best way to deal with them, and sceptical of anything else, and the 'nature-lovers' rejecting culling, and uncertain about the evidence related to bovine TB, badgers, and transmission to cows. This is a bit of a problem. Part of the point of taking a Q method approach instead of a standard survey is to bring out a bit more nuance than this. With so many different ways of placing the 34 statements in relation to each other, there was a good chance of showing that the 'two sides' in the debate are more like several. Maybe that would help us start to find ways out of the conflict.

But when I look more closely, it seems as though, yes, there are a couple of things that undermine this simple 'for-and-against' understanding. First, the two most opposing views don't stack up for and against all the statements we asked them about, and there even seems to be some degree of agreement between them on some things. For example, neither position seems to be very enthusiastic about the prospects for biosecurity measures to help. Both are interested in improvements to testing. Neither wants to see whole herds of cattle being culled just because some of them react to the TB test. Both are concerned, albeit to differing extents, about the risks of perturbation. Second, there is a third viewpoint, which accepts that badgers are part of the problem but is more critical of the way these culls are being carried out, without rejecting culling outright. Culling at a smaller scale should be considered alongside a range of other measures. It's not very popular among the participants we've recruited, but numbers aren't the first concern here. A few people sorted their statements similarly.[37] Somehow, they've resisted the temptation to join one or the other of the camps that have been presented to them as 'the debate' for around two years now in the media. Would this view have been shared by more farmers and nature-lovers if the culls had not gone ahead in the way they had? It would be nice to think so, but it would just be speculative – and wishful – thinking.

It's when I'm preparing a summary of these viewpoints for a presentation to a rural research group that I begin to realise there's something else going on. I sketch out the pattern in a table so I can talk through it. It's a relief to be able to say there might be some kind of order to this. But is there really? I'm working with interpretations, words not numbers, and the links I'm making are my links. Does anyone else see it? After the presentation, the research group are polite about our work, and take the table, with rows marked in different colours, well. Someone says that even if we can show that

---

[37] For a more detailed account of this section of the research and the results, see Price, Saunders, Hinchliffe and McDonald (2016).

there's some small departure from a simple polarised situation, that's enough. But they don't talk about it that much. Instead, they start sharing anecdotes of what it's like to work with DEFRA. Embarrassingly, it turns out we have a member of the Independent Scientific Group in the audience, the team that oversaw the RBCT between 1997 and 2006, but instead of turning the discussion into an episode of Mastermind, he cheerfully describes how difficult it was to work with DEFRA, how it seemed like DEFRA was against them the whole time, how DEFRA wouldn't let the scientists meet without a DEFRA minder present. Why couldn't they just let the experts get on with it? Why do they have to try to gerrymander everything?

This was exactly what I was afraid of when I was organising the discussion workshops and someone from DEFRA said they'd come along. Getting a DEFRA bod to join in could be seen as a bit of a scalp, but on the other hand, I never intended to recruit them. I just ended up talking to someone in London because the only relevant person with a connection to the Devon area that the discussion was going to be about had been moved out of Devon up north to deal with an outbreak of avian flu, and was afraid to be caught out being connected with anything that might not exactly be government policy. He refers me to his DEFRA minder instantly, so I ask him if someone from DEFRA, or as he put it 'someone representing the DEFRA network' (whatever that is) could come along. Back comes the same refrain. Couldn't possibly be involved in anything that makes it looks like I'm entertaining alternatives to government policy. Undermines impartiality.

Oh come on. Surely someone with a relevant role in the APHA who is not a complete infant should be able to cope. I try the hard sell, an email full of work-speak. You know what I mean.

...We do appreciate your concerns about impartiality. However, we are slightly concerned that you may not have fully understood the nature of the workshop. Above all, we do not believe that we are asking for anything that would draw a representative from the DEFRA network away from their impartial position in relation to government policy.

The workshop will explore different viewpoints, attempt to identify common ground (if any) between them in terms of shared goals and needs, and open discussion of whether there could feasibly be any local solutions based on those shared priorities. We wouldn't expect a representative from the DEFRA network to engage with anything that draws them beyond national policy, but as any local-ly-based actions that the other participants do agree would neces-sarily take place within the framework of existing national policy, we feel it is important that a spokesperson for this policy is present.

This is why we asking for someone from APHA or DEFRA to represent the viewpoint of DEFRA with regard to current govern-ment policy. Ideally, this would be someone with a relevant respon-sibility or connection with the Devon area, such as the APHA re-gional veterinary lead, but crucially, they should be able to explain the policy, what its goals are, why those goals have been set, and why it is being carried out in the way it is. The whole workshop (which will involve a maximum of 16 people) will take place under the Chatham House rule, and participants will be able to review their contributions before any part of the transcript is finalised.

We feel that this event provides a good opportunity for your team to explain the existing policy to a critical and sympathetic audience in a setting that is safe, and oriented to making the most of the areas where the participants agree, rather than exacerbating con-flicts between them.

I very much hope this explanation persuades you that it is possi-ble for a representative from the DEFRA network to attend...

OK, he says, I'll come. And so will my researcher, as an observer (sorry, I don't remember saying anything about 'bring a friend'). Something about asking for a Devon person and ending up with someone from Whitehall who presumes he can do what the hell he likes with our research design leaves me feeling very grave. Very grave indeed.

I'm supposed to be organising two discussion workshops. Within the team, we're calling them the top-down and the bottom-up workshops. The top-down workshop involves people whose job it is to have something to say about bovine TB, or at least, it's their role. We're looking for people from known farming and wildlife interests, as well as few 'neutrals', people whose primary concern is for the community as a whole, rather than one side or another on cattle and badgers. The bottom-up workshop involves people who live in a defined area within Devon whose lives bring them into contact with the issue of bovine TB in some way. Perhaps they farm there, or volunteer with a conservation charity, or take part in sabbing.

This design is the result of some very long discussions, the sort of conversation where the same person comes up with a different idea every time the subject is discussed. The final design reflects a concern that mixing 'locals' and 'professionals' risks losing something precious: the idiosyncratic ideas of those with a genuine local connection and local knowledge. With the professionals in there too, isn't there a danger that the locals will defer to professionals, sit and listen instead of come up with their own ideas, ideas that would work, perhaps, in their local area, but might not further afield? Ideas that would be smacked down by the properly regulated, but generalised, locally non-specific thinking of professionals who turn to 'research' for answers.

When we propose this design to Diana, the consultant we've asked to run the discussion workshops, she's almost offended. She practises something called 'stakeholder dialogue', a model of facilitating discussions that, she believes, rigorously ensures the equal participation of everyone involved. It's like we're saying we don't believe her methods work. In fact, it's not *like* we're saying that, we are saying that, although not intentionally. She's a professional and in the end will do what we ask, but she challenges us all the way on anything she thinks is doubtful, unclear or needs to be thought through, and this is a big one. I try as best I can to explain the thinking, or what I think is the thinking (because it's not my idea, just my job to explain it), and end up reaching for some academic stuff about the politics of knowledge. Basically, the professionals are likely to be talking a language that is widely given more power in our culture: the language of government. They are likely to discuss bovine TB in numbers, using the results of government monitoring and 'scientific' research, and as the 'locals' are unlikely to feel they can compete with this 'governmental' speak or the 'governmentality' it expresses, we fear they'll be silenced. It's one of the ideas of a historian-philosopher called Michel Foucault, who aimed to point out to us that social phenomena that seem to us as completely natural – that we take for granted – like prisons, or the existence of insanity, or the language of government, are in fact the result of politically charged histories in which alternative ideas and practices were silenced. Gareth Enticott is the academic who has said that 'governmentality' is a problem in the control of bovine TB (Enticott 2001). I don't know whether it helps, but maybe Diana feels like we're coming from a position with a thought-through background to it. This politics of knowledge hits right up against her politics of persons, the idea that she can ensure that everyone participates in an equal fashion. We spend an hour on the phone re-running the arguments around Habermas' theory of communicative action before she agrees to do what the team have decided. In the end it's a waste of time, as we never run both workshops.

After months of trying I recruit, in total, two people to participate in the bottom-up workshop. I've sent out letters and email to lists of farmers, conservationists, and animal rights defenders, and following up with phone calls. I've been round the region putting up posters. I've contacted gatekeepers like the NFU and The Conservation Volunteers. I've posted our call for participants online, and asked other Devon groups to link to it. I'm also looking to recruit a few people with a defined role in the local community, the so-called 'neutrals': ministers, parish councillors. Nothing.

It's not as though I haven't done this before, or as if we're asking far too much – in fact we're going to give participants 50 pounds for their efforts. In mid-December, four weeks before the discussions and before everything stops for the holidays, I call a halt. I'm defibrillating a corpse.

Why? Devon is an important area for dairy farming, and the rate of bovine TB in the herds here is high. There's no doubt the topic is on farmers' minds. Devon is also in line for culling if the policy is expanded in the coming years. The local saboteur groups have been actively supporting the anti-cull work in Somerset and Gloucestershire already, and there's a large and well-supported Wildlife Trust, with plenty of sites and species to engage people's interests – badgers is one of them. Nothing. Maybe people just didn't see, or look at the letters, emails, posters and links. Maybe they weren't looking, everyone's got plenty to be getting on with already without giving up a whole evening of their time to meet and talk to people they don't even like. Or maybe that's the problem. There's too much distrust, too many conclusions drawn about the problem, its solution, and the character of the people on 'the other side'. Maybe even fear.

For a few weeks, I think I might have something – some sabs at the end of an email. Could I persuade one of them to come? First I try to get them to come to the bottom-up workshop, and then, when that dies, to the top-down one. I receive a detailed refusal.

Firstly there is the issue of anonymity, keeping ourselves safe and not compromising our work. We note what you say about Chatham House rules and participating under a pseudonym. Unforuntately [sic] this is unlikely to be enough if someone still needs to be physically present and visible. While sabbing, most of us cover our faces and do what we can to keep our identities from becoming known to fox hunts, cull-involved farmers, etc. This has been shown over many years to be necessary, and we could tell you some horror stories about hunt-affiliated thugs turning up at sabs' workplaces, homes, etc., and making other efforts to intimidate, up to the point of violence.

For this reason none of us would be comfortable sitting around a table with the other parties to this discussion.

Secondly we have to consider what is in this for the badgers. While your project sounds like it will result in something of interest and value to the academic community, we wonder what the non-academic output might be that would further the public debate and political context of the cull in such a way that fewer badgers will be killed. While not wishing to criticise your research or your methodology, we are not sure the case has yet been made that this would be a valuable exercise when seen in this light.

We're afraid, and the risk is too big when we're not even sure you're going to come to the right conclusion.

Maybe I've swallowed too many mainstream prejudices about the relative culpability and aggressiveness of hunt sabs and hunters, but I wasn't expecting that. The fear rolls on though, into our 'top-down' session. For that, I have recruited just the right number of people, 16. One drops out with a flu. And then, on the morning of the session, three more don't turn up. They're all farmers, or connected to farming. Only one of them makes any contact with us. With most of the rest of the participants already here, Diana comes up to me, mobile in hand, buzzing. *X has just texted me to say he's not coming. Concerned about security he says.* She phones him back, but gets nowhere.

12 people in the room, and despite the no-shows, they represent a full range of views on bovine TB, badgers and culling. Or at least, I think they do. There's the DEFRA policy representative, farming and veterinary interests, a neutral-ish landowner and a minister (church, not government). Wildlife and animal welfare groups. An anti-cull sab. I go through a welcome speech, congratulate them on their courage and responsibility for agreeing to take part. Remind them of the arrangements we've made to protect their anonymity.

Diana explains the process and goes through some ground rules. And then we start.

It's only when the participants start opening their mouths that I realised I've misjudged one or two people. I blame myself for one, a 'wildlife' group representative who turns out to be a pro-culling vet. But the other, everyone's surprised. The minister – I thought a natural neutral, concerned for the community etc – is rabidly pro-culling. I start feeling relieved that some of the other farming interests didn't turn up. The 'anti-cull' participants feel the imbalance of numbers as the day wears on. They feel they're on the back foot.

But this is where Diana's method comes in. The key is that every point made by anyone is written down. Nobody's point of view is allowed to undergo the evaluation of the rest of the group before it is recorded. That way, even those in the minority can be confident they have been heard within the process. The only thing is to make sure that everyone is speaking up. Diana and her team use body language, timing and different exercises to ensure even the most timid speak. She starts by asking the participants to write down what they know and what they need to know to move the debate forward. The atmosphere is very concentrated. People are murmuring to each other about the points that are going up, or quietly dictating to one of the 'scribes'. Marker pens squeak over the flip-chart paper that's velcro-ed up in 'walls' around the room. They're asked to record the sources for their knowledge, but I'm struck how vague it is. 'Reports'. 'Websites'. 'Research'. Or nothing at all.

People start querying or rebutting each other's points. Very quietly, people are beginning to work out each other's views. As they do so, a pattern for the rest of the day sets in. These people are not, strictly speaking, having a discussion with each other. They are, and they're not; not directly. Throughout the whole day their attention is oriented to the flipchart paper and the facilitator who is recording their comments and responses, and guiding them through the discussion. This is how outright conflict is averted and Diana is able to steer the participants towards agreements about specific proposals for action.

This is the challenge we've set Diana – to see if she can move these participants towards some kind of agreement, at any level, in one session. If she does, fine. If she doesn't, fine – either way it's data. Understandably, she baulks a bit at this amount of detachment, but laughs it off. Even so, there's a lot of professional pride at stake for her. This is her method, she believes in its power to create agreements, she made it work in the past. It's just she hasn't necessarily been given the country's most divisive rural issue and only one session to do it in.

Through the day, she gradually gets the participants to prioritise the things they want to talk about, and slowly funnels them towards practical matters. She cracks out the post-it notes. She gets them to shortlist four practical actions they are interested in, break them down into small groups and gets them to develop the ideas, to think about how they could be achieved, and then the big question: who was going to do it and when.

And she does it. People put themselves up. Say 'yes, I'll do that'. But a lot of people remain silent at this point. And in the end, there's no time to test support for the ideas across the whole group. But it's there. The hint of a chance of bringing utterly divergent views into some kind of interaction. The ideas are: a local group of different interests to share information and discuss practical actions they could take together; an education initiative; and transparency of data about the disease. People haven't changed their views: they're still going to try to convince each other of their own point of view, just as they had intended when they came to this discussion. They're still going to promote their own propaganda through an education scheme. But, if these ideas worked out it wouldn't matter, because their counterpoint would always be there, and they would no longer be able to escape them into ghettos of individual perspectives and bogeymen for opponents.

The moment is fragile – if something is going to come of this, we'd need to strike now, while these commitments are fresh in people's minds.

But there's no money.

When I speak to some of them later to ask them individually whether they did agree with some of the conclusions from the day, I find that already people are back-sliding on that sense of potential to agree. They agree alright with some of the ideas, things it would be difficult to disagree with, but the answer is always 'yes, but...'. All of them have missed the point. 'I didn't think you'd get anyone to change their minds and I was right'. So what? No-one changed their minds about anything, but you could still discuss practical actions you could take together.

That point is fundamental to mediating conflictual situations (see, for example Forester 1999). Forget the abstract, the hinterlands, the beliefs, the knowledge, the justifications and rationalisations, the positional manoeuvring that people always get into when they're in conflict. It's the pattern I noticed when I was presenting those Q Method results to the rural research group, there was more agreement over the more practical things. Focus on what could be done. Not what you think ought to be done. What you can, in fact, do.

Diplomacy. In the last fifteen years, that pragmatic emphasis on what can be done by nevertheless contending sides has come to be described in social studies of science using the metaphor of international relations. It's not really just a metaphor. For writers and thinkers like Bruno Latour, a "tempest in a teacup" (Latour 2002, p. 21) like the Science Wars is indeed connected with actual wars through the way in which knowledge is organised to develop, or promote, modernity. Writing after, and responding to, the 9/11 attacks, Latour tries to show how the thinking about difference that has influenced him can be used to think about science and knowledge as well as violent conflict. For Latour, it has to do with the way different criteria for what is accepted as valid had been applied, within the project of modernity, to that which we refer to as 'culture' and that which we refer to as 'nature'. In the West, locus of the 'modern', we have 'hypocritically' said that multiculturalism is acceptable, and 'multinaturalism' unthinkable. This is hypocritical because while many different things are allowed to be considered true for cultures, only one set of things are allowed to be true when it comes to nature, or more broadly, reality. This contradiction places non-Western cultures in an invidious position. They can be museum pieces, but they shouldn't try to do anything that follows from the way in which they see the world, such as make factual claims, or try to set up a state. Or, to put it another way, modernity asserts that there is one constitution (nature, reality), within which cultural citizens exist and behave more or less well. This puts the modern West in the position of the police, bringing those who err by, say, making factual statements without a sufficient evidential basis (but perhaps, on the basis of a tradition, morality or religion) or threatening to commit genocide or developing weapons of mass destruction, into line. The problem is, Latour writes, that modernity:

"was never an accurate account of the strange ways in which the West became entangled with every nation and every living and non-living entity on Earth. How to reconcile, for instance, the war cry for emancipation, progress and detachment from any archaic constraint with the progressive imbroglios of humans and nonhu-

mans at an ever-expanding scale that characterizes the West?"
(Latour 2002, p.19).

In other words, as the West has attempted to make itself modern
by transcending nature with ever more technology and development, we have, in reality, become ever more grandly and deeply
involved in multiple cultures and the processes of nature itself, right
across the globe with the economy, up to the top of the atmosphere
with its emissions, and right down to DNA and the CERN particle
accelerator. Latour is saying that if there have been plenty of reasons for suggesting that reality and modernity are not the same
thing up until recently, 9/11 surely tells us that what modernists
think is real is not shared by those cultures that were supposed to
be behaving themselves so we could look at, appreciate and help to
support them through tourism. Cultures are revolting. Latour is
suggesting that it's time to admit that our opponents are not people
who are wrong and need to be brought back into line, either
through the exercise of intellectual discipline or through international military policing actions, but enemies, with whom we must,
ultimately, negotiate.

"Diplomats know that there exists no superior referee, no arbiter
able to declare that the other party is simply irrational and should
be disciplined. If a solution is to be found, it is there, among them,
with them here and now and nowhere else. Whereas rationalists
would not know how to assemble peace talks, as they will not give
seats to those they call "archaic" and "irrational," diplomats might
know how to organize a parley among declared enemies who ...
may become allies after the peace negotiations have ended." (Latour
2002, p. 38-9)

Only once you recognise your enemies as such, and not simply as
'wrong', can you move towards 'peace'.

When he's not trying to be too clever, Latour can be very convincing. I'm particularly struck by the way the terms that frame what
he's saying, war and peace, seem to mirror the terms being used
back in the positivist dispute in German sociology, revolution and
reform, and the way this idea of 'multinaturalism' echoes Houdebine's efforts to recognise that there might just be people, ways of
seeing the world and of being in it that are just, positively, different.
These thoughts make a huge difference to the way one would approach intellectual or violent conflict. But I'm confused. On the one
hand, I'm confused that Latour seems to be making so much out of

a binary opposite, war and peace, even though he has spent his whole career working against thinking in this way, focusing on the opposition of nature and culture. On the other hand, I'm worried that his idea of diplomacy gives an implicit nod to violence: because diplomacy happens only once the balance of forces has been worked out, only once fighting is at a stalemate. It would be ok, perhaps, if we were any good at getting round a table to negotiate before we were calling each other rude names, or fighting a war, or before anyone gets shot in a field in Somerset, or suffers post-traumatic stress disorder from the night a bunch of black-masked figures rocked your car while you were still in it, threatening to turn it over. But then, maybe I'm the one forcing violence and non-violence into too-clean opposites, when, in real life, they depend on each other for meaning. My head is spinning.

*

In the last few months I've started reading poetry again, as an antidote to the desertification of academic writing. I quickly discover two kinds: poetry I can follow, and poetry I can follow not at all. Reading introductions and prefaces, scanning websites, trying to work out what's wrong with my brain, it turns out that not being able to understand it is sort of the point. The beginning of the point. The point being, roughly at least, that language and meaning are the problem because they're constructed around the mistake that 'I' really exists and that language non-problematically transfers intended meaning from sender to recipient. Even when meaning does manage the bumpy journey between two self-deluded 'I's, it's doing so on the back of norms that are maintained on the back of acts of control.

All this is, again, roughly, an extension of the ideas of Nietzsche, Deleuze, and Derrida into literature, and as I've found a lot of what I've read about them interesting (if difficult), I think, maybe, I ought to be interested in these poems, too. I get a couple of anthologies from the university library. I lose them in the waiting room in Exeter Saint David's on my way home, but find them stuffed behind my laptop in my rucksack an hour and a half later after a fruitless conversation with a man in lost property. I find the poems -

boring, at best. At other times I'm just annoyed and frustrated. I suppose this is a compliment – this is supposed to happen. The more I think about these poems and this experience, I can see how what is going on is consistent with the idea of thinking beyond the human – with the sort of questioning of what is and what values are (or could be) that I've been learning about, and I can see that these ludic poems make me think at the edge of, and beyond, thought that is possible, and that is a good thing, and that the challenge is to overcome boredom; but still something is missing, there's a dryness to these poems and they're making me think there's also a dryness to these ideas about truth and values, becoming and folding that leaves me thirsty for something else.

I find it first in the philosophy section, but I find it best in the words of another poet, Seamus Heaney. It's not a poem, though, but a story about Northern Ireland.

"- a minibus full of workers being driven home one January evening in 1976 was held up by armed men and the occupants of the van ordered at gunpoint to line up at the side of the road. Then one of the masked executioners said to them, 'Any Catholics among you, step out here.' As it happened, this particular group, with one exception, were all Protestants, so the presumption must have been that the masked men were Protestant paramilitaries about to carry out a tit-for-tat sectarian killing of the Catholic as the odd man out, the one who would have been presumed to be in sympathy with the IRA and all its actions. It was a terrible moment for him, caught between dread and witness, but he did make a motion to step forward. Then, the story goes ... he felt the hand of the Protestant worker next to him take his hand and squeeze it in a signal that said no, don't move, we'll not betray you -" (Heaney 1995, no page).

I'll let you work out what Heaney was preparing his audience for with a phrase like 'the presumption must have been' as he spoke in Stockholm, where he had gone to accept his Nobel prize. Heaney went on to say why he thought this story matters.

"The birth of the future we desire is surely in the contraction which that terrified Catholic felt on the roadside when another hand gripped his hand -" (Heaney 1995, no page).

What do you make of that squeeze of the hand? Is it just a form of practical agreement, 'we can do this together', albeit of the most intense and courageous kind, or is it something more fundamental? - Not just an overcoming of difference, but the formation of a new shared value. Our lives.

What I'm wondering is whether it's really enough to be satisfied with practical agreement. To leave people's values and beliefs out of it. To leave the people out of it. Isn't it, somehow, pessimistic? Why should we assume that we have to let people off the hook and let them go home still believing they're right, still fundamentally denying the reality of another's incommensurable position? Do we really, to get them to agree on anything more that further platforms for extended argument, have to threaten them with a gun?

The philosopher I discover is Iris Murdoch. Before she was a novelist she was also a precocious moral philosopher. She was critical of some of those who followed Nietzsche in rejecting morality, known as existentialists, for their concentration on the vertiginous moment of reality-making that they burdened themselves with – if there are no values but my values, I have to come up with some and re-affirm them with my every act. That's hard work. Cue bouts of personal crisis, dressing in black and chain-smoking in a Paris café (Gilles Deleuze's solution: drop the static, solid sense of 'I'). Instead, Murdoch argued that identifying the real and moral character of a person or anything else could only come after a long and sustained process of attending to it, allowing our understanding of the people and things around us to develop according to the perceptions afforded by generous observation. Loving attention, she called it (Murdoch 1970). Moral goodness comes with clear perception.

It's probably not a good idea to compare the ideas of Deleuze and Murdoch too directly and simplistically (and at my level, it would only really be simplistic), but there are a few other reasons why I'm drawn to Murdoch's work. She seems to deal with things much more efficiently. I'm not just talking about the modest 100 pages or so of thinking in which she argues her core ideas, compared to the over 800 in which Deleuze and his colleague Félix Guatarri expand upon theirs. The difference in length is just a consequence of their different approaches. Deleuze and Guatarri decided that they needed to reinterpret reality around a new set of concepts that got us away from the common sense identities that we are unhelpfully attached to. Murdoch makes this approach look like hubris. Instead she seeks to defend and carve out a space in philosophy for what she sees as the process through which the world becomes reinterpreted. If moral struggle is what that process is, Murdoch offers loving attention as the ideal way of conducting it. I nearly called that process 'moral philosophy' then, but my sense of what moral philosophy is has been conditioned by the sort of work Murdoch criticises, that conducts a sort of dry apportioning of moral value or desserts based on external categories and actions. The moral struggle Murdoch is talking about, though, despite being so private that there may be no surface sign of its happening, seems so much closer to life as felt, and as a result not just less 'dry' as a way of thinking but also more sustainable – more like a way of thinking it's worth living with.

In her workshops, Diana draws on a lot of psychological and social psychological thinking that is startling in the way it makes our behaviour look predictable. Personality, that objective quality that is studied in psychology, is something different from our will. Personality is made up of what can be publically observed, our actions or behaviour, and it allows psychologists to predict how we might react in certain situations. This behavioural approach leaves the human will somehow isolated within the person, only to emerge in rare moments of crisis. What is interesting is that Murdoch links behaviouralism and existentialism as ways of thinking that leave the will dangling in this way, forcing its way into the course of life only rarely, causing angst. But Murdoch thinks that this angst is less to do with the vertiginous experience of making oneself out of nothing, and more like fright at discovering that one's behavioural tendencies, when examined, bear little relation to how one thinks one ought to act. Deleuze and Guatarri deal with 'will' by talking about 'desiring machines', which seem to me to make more of an equation of will and need. As a result, they seem to place humans – or at least the systems that humans are a product of – on a par with other processes of life (although 'desire' levels up as well as down). Murdoch deals with 'will' by getting away from the isolated, spasmodic, somewhat macho notion of existential intention by talking about 'attention': "Will continually influences belief ... and is ideally able to influence it through a sustained attention to reality" (1970, p. 40). What we have is perhaps not great moments when we exert our pure will on existence, but a fairly weak but constant opportunity to steer our life and above all, our understanding of it, to be not just more accurate, but ideally, more just, loving. That shift from existential decision-making to constant attention makes quite a big difference when it comes to our relationship with knowledge. Murdoch writes:

"Moral concepts do not move about within a hard world set up by science and logic. They set up, for different purposes, a different world" (1970, p. 28).

I think maybe this is why the people who took part in the discussion forum didn't arrive at the sense of 'agonism' as Steve hoped. They were still antagonists who had, despite themselves, talked about a few things that could be done together. Maybe that's ungenerous. They were partially – minimally – agonists, who accepted it would be better to work together, but were still trying to deny or delete the different views of other people. We've all got used to the idea that knowledge comes first, then we decide, and this pattern was also built into the structure of the discussion forum, with the participants being asked early on 'what do we know?' and 'what do we need to know?'. We all now seem to presume that the world is set up by science, so that being right also makes us morally good and our antagonists evil. Murdoch again:

"It is significant that the idea of goodness (and of virtue) has been largely superseded in Western moral philosophy by the idea of rightness, supported perhaps by some conception of sincerity" *(1970, p. 53).*

For Murdoch, our big problem is the self, which gets in the way of a clear perception of reality, a reality made up of, amongst other things, other private selves. Only by attending to reality can we come to know it better, and the more we know reality, the less present is our own self. To persist in that attention, to let go of our comfortable selves, we need to care enough about the things we attend to. We need loving attention. Loving attention speaks immediately to something you can do; it requires nothing more and nothing less than your attention. Like the Protestant who had looked beyond the denomination of his colleague's religion enough to see an individual life like his own. Just the thought of it puts the emphasis on practical agreement in its place: pessimistic, minimal, primitive. But for now, it's the best our dried-out, impersonal, professional, governmental culture can be persuaded to achieve.

Conclusion:
Community, science, policy

September 2015. Culling has begun again in Somerset, Gloucestershire, and now Dorset. The badger project has been over for three months, though we're still working on the first academic journal article to come out of it. We're also still working on a way to get to the next stage, an 'impact' project where we invite the relevant stakeholders from across Devon and try to agree a method and an agenda for working together, just as the participants in Diana's workshop suggested. We've been told that if we can get the partners, we'll get the money. I've been hawking our proposal around all summer, but only in the last few weeks has anything started happening. Basically, our best chance is for the two biggest voices for conservation and farming in the county to join or support the plan from the beginning. I've got a meeting with them.

Alexis de Tocqueville had one big concern about democracy, a problem that could come out in one of two ways: either as majority tyranny, or mild despotism. In a democracy in which the majority believe their will is expressed through their democratic institutions, there runs a risk that anyone who doesn't fit in is silenced, pushed out or crushed by the insensitivity of institutions confident in the naïve view than democratic might is always right. But there is also a risk that, far from being a genuine reflection of the majority will, democracy can become a sort of administrative process. People opt for a peaceful, private life rather than the challenges of political engagement: they choose independence rather than freedom and let the state make its decisions without paying too much attention to what people think, doing what it thinks is best, for whom being an open question. In practice, it would form a relatively small policy community. To both versions of the problem de Tocqueville had the same response: free association of ordinary people – organisation, representing minority concerns to the majoritarian state, opening up democracy in a lazy electorate and a closed administration. As I leave the meeting, I'm thinking about Alexis de Tocqueville.

One thing I've learnt is that the APHA (that branch of the DEFRA 'network' with responsibility for bovine TB) is setting up local policy groups to discuss further policy measures to bring down the disease. Some policies might get taken up nationally, some might be implemented locally. It's going to include farmers, vets, maybe a moderate conservation-bod. Who we want to work with, not who is actually involved in the debate. Because, I was told, we're not really interested in people who don't have any practical interest on the ground.

At the start of this, I said I was setting out to see if there was some way through the conflict over badger culling without picking sides, that reduces conflict and incidence of the disease. There is and there isn't. Environmental conflict mediation, stakeholder dialogue, is a pretty well-developed, though small, field of work and the people who work there are good and report success. But the work is slow and expensive, so the people who are going to pay for it have to care, or be made to care enough to cough up and commit time. And it looks, two years on, like those behind the culling, boosted by a new majority Conservative government, don't seem too worried about any difference of opinion that might get expressed on the ground in Somerset, Gloucestershire, or Dorset. Dorset is a conservative county anyway, and the resistance in Somerset and Gloucestershire came from across the country as much as it did locally. Into a third season of culling, that kind of commitment is hard to sustain, and the job is getting easier (there aren't so many badgers). There might be a few hard-cases still around, but the campaign has run its course – that's what social movements are like anyway, they keep moving, if they continue to exist at all. We can treat culling as a fact. Let's move on.

July 2016. The government, under a new Prime Minister, are considering applications from six new areas for more culls this summer, on top of the three ongoing culls in Somerset, Gloucestershire and Dorset (*Farmers Weekly 2016*). And, somewhat out of the blue, a publisher has finally taken an interest in what I've been writing, so it's time, after months of something completely different (still a researcher, though) to refresh my connection with the topic, pick up the thread of my thought, and tidy up the manuscript. There's a timely public talk being given by an Exeter mammal scientist about the science of bovine TB, and it seems like a good moment to get my head back into the issue.

As the room fills up I recognise a few faces from the various stages of the research project. There's been plenty going on in UK politics recently, and there will be for plenty of time to come, what with the EU referendum, and the result. Badger politics has scarcely disturbed the editors of the national press and broadcasting. It's no longer new, and things have settled down into a steady pattern – the yearly announcement of the next culls, and the yearly quibbling over the results of the last. The same groups in support, the same ones in opposition. My guess is that the cull's opponents are now struggling to achieve the numbers of on-the-ground participants that made them such a phenomenon in the beginning, and at any rate, they have never been close to forcing an accommodation that could be seen as a step forward in political practice in this area at least. The question seems to be what else might keep a check on the easy slide towards a mild, consensual (consensual, that is, among the in-crowd) despotism? De Tocqueville's answer is 'pure science', by which he means not what we think of as science now, but more broadly, more abstractly, the pursuit of truth. When no-one else is practising much freedom in a democracy, intellectuals must think it.

If there's something that bothers me slightly about Iris Murdoch's thinking, it's that she writes in opposition to 'science' (in the narrower sense) while at the same time arguing that 'truth' can only be accessed through reducing the influence on perception of ourselves. What bothers me is the thought that this is exactly what 'science' is supposed to achieve: a rigorous methodological consistency that makes observation free of the distortions of ego. It's not that element of science that Murdoch has a problem with, it's the insistence of science on allowing only that which is publically observable to count. The inner life doesn't count because it isn't publically observable. The problem for Iris Murdoch is that 'science' could, conceivably, get better at making what was hitherto private moral struggle an observable process by, perhaps, using brain imagery to show the brain activity that takes place (although wouldn't making the private public in this way change the nature of the struggle itself?). The problem for 'science' is that it is always already contingent on the sort of inner processes that it purports to deny. Many scientists are indeed enthusiastic about – nay, *love* – their subjects, and this is rarely more evident than with those who study animals.

Fiona Mathews (Associate Professor) clearly loves her subject. She is keen on badgers, cattle, farming, and science. As she summarises the relevant scientific work on badgers and bovine TB so far, she sometimes cues us up to believe she's going to tell us what she thinks about, say the RBCT. And she does – but what she thinks is pure, egoless, science. The problem, she says, with the RBCT, is that there was not enough replication. In other words, there weren't enough cases of each kind to deliver sufficiently robust conclusions. She goes on to summarise her own work, in which she and a colleague have been looking at the ecological factors on farms that might affect the incidence of bovine TB in cattle. She has found that farms with smaller herds that are more distant from another herd, contained in areas with more and wider hedgerows, are associated with a lower incidence of bovine TB, and that farms with larger herds, more maize and deciduous woodland are associated with a higher incidence of bovine TB.

And then the questions. There are a few from farmers and naturalists, knowledgeable, interested, concerned, and Fiona deals with them engagingly. And then come the questions from the more committed types, some of whom I've met. Dissatisfied, contrary, hectoring. Why didn't you - ? You're underestimating -

And, on a personal level at least, I feel sorry for her. Two people start arguing with each other through their questions – well, lectures – to her and I just catch a flicker of bewilderment at what is going on. This is, borderline, a hijacking. But not only that: the basis of the points being made is so obviously partial and scanty that Fiona's response, still somehow engaging in some positive part of each contribution, is heroic. But this though, far from being yet another example of 'radio phone-in' syndrome, represents for me the continuing problem with 'science', or at least, the way it's done. Believing that 'science' makes knowledge implies a process of angst-ridden, existential decision-making in which we have to bring our beliefs and actions into line with the new reality. 'When the facts change, my mind changes' is easier said than done. In reality, it's not done at all, because facts, knowledge, are not separate from minds and will. What science produces is, among other things, utterance, to which people attend, more or less and in differing ways. The knowledge is being made now, in this room, in silence for the most part, as what Fiona says is given some kind of attention. Fiona's intentions are clearly good, she carries out her role brilliantly, and it's not her fault that she's been raised, professionally and intellectually, through an institution of science whose screaming naïvety is portrayed as a virtue. The paradox, and the worrying thing, is when 'science' is mobilized by its senior representatives or fellow philosophical travellers, or anyone finding themselves in a political dispute, to make a power-play, suggesting that political decision-making ought to be led, or informed *in the first instance*, by scientific evidence, contributing to precisely the circumstances in which political stalemate occurs, namely the false belief in the separation of knowledge and will.

*

Another paper comes out and receives some media coverage. It reports research that tracked badgers and cattle and shows that badgers tend to steer clear of cows (Woodroffe et al. 2016). But other similar papers with contradictory results have not received the same level of attention (see Böhm, Hutchings and White 2009). The new paper suggests that badgers are unlikely to transmit bTB to cattle through direct contact, but badger faeces, their latrines, might still be a problem. The implications for management, suggest the authors (at least one of whom is a declared critic of the culls), is much more emphasis on biosecurity (the practices so thoroughly criticised by farmers as useless) as well as more focus on what happens to cattle slurry when a herd tests positive with bovine TB. DE-FRA is funding more research, and says a lot of restrictions are already in place. Cull opponents say this means the culls should be discontinued, and they're carrying on. The obvious distress of the people caught up in this contention leaches through the reporting of it (*Guardian* 2016).

I'm caught by a tension between the sense that I've somehow committed to declaring at some point what policy I think should be implemented and by my immediate reservations about doing so. I would rather the culls were not happening, which is saying no more than many of those who support the culls have said, but my reason for that preference is that the whole process is adding to the sum of human suffering, not reducing it; an odd, sidestepping reason, but one that seems accurate enough. Culling animals when it is not clear to all who might care that there really is no other option is not humane for the humans that are forced, or feel forced, to be involved. Doing something they would much rather not be doing, a refrain I've heard so often throughout this project, is about as close to withdrawing consent as you can get without actually doing it; for some it's about reducing a sense of personal responsibility, shifting it onto a determining situation, a fact, albeit an awful one. But to declare, positively, what I think ought to be done has its own immediate drawbacks. Firstly, the reality is that culling is happening, and looks set to continue. Secondly, doing so would run up against precisely the sort of process of diplomacy that I do think could end in more humane outcomes. Diplomacy, stakeholder dialogue, can't work if each participant starts out with one, inflexible, policy position (or it can, eventually, but a huge amount of time is wasted trying to shift people off their fixed position) (Fisher and Ury 1987). And the reality is, yes, some kind of stakeholder process is taking place, but you only get to take part if you're not going to challenge any key planks of the policy, including culling. A more open process is not an option, for reasons ranging from control of the policy to fear of violence.

Protest is also happening – or at least, a campaign of opposition, and for democracy it seems healthy that it does, or, less abstractly, that there are people bearing witness to what is happening, preventing there from being some too-easy consensus established around the policies. But the zeitgeist for protest has moved on, such that even the activists who are good at making agenda-setting interventions would probably receive only a little media attention now. The presence of committed campaigners keeps the opportunity for something to happen that changes things open – some criminality or safety-breach witnessed, for example, or the consistent failure to meet expected outcomes. But the focus for many people minded to protest about issues like this is, and always has been, elsewhere; in the last years, it has been on fracking. Protest is unlikely to force any enemies to come to a more inclusive table for negotiation that fully reflects the concerns that claim a stake in the problem. More scientific research is being done which could, incrementally, trim policy towards more effective disease management and eradication practices. What else is there to be done? What contribution could 'sociology' make, from the place we – us, here, now – are at, with little to effect, but writing and reading?

Other than to think differently, and prior to that, attend differently? Social research is a way of carefully looking, of attending to other people, what they say and do, how they act collectively, the consequences of their actions, individual or collective, intended or unintended. Interviews such as those that I have recorded extensively here are a challenge to the easy assumptions that are the usual fuel for judgements within controversial contexts, fed by the microscopic quotes and soundbites found in media coverage. With more details set down we can carefully scrutinise people's selectivity with information and the way they divide up the world around them so that their world seems the only possible world to them. We can also begin to understand the commitments people have to that view, the lifetimes of work invested in running a business, building an ethic, or exploring an aesthetic. Confronting ourselves with these records, we are presented, then, with both the weakness of these views and the strength that comes with them. Opinion, delivered to us in public opinion surveys, give us only a big half-picture, a sum total of the weak part of the views people hold. Q Methodology tries to involve both the weak view and the strong person that comes with it in making a biggish canvas and a slightly different kind of picture on it, one that again challenges us to get beyond the simplistic for-and-against assumptions on a much larger scale than by conducting interviews alone. It also provides a map of the opportunities available for a more inclusively negotiated conflict, pointing out a path from the passive recording of views to more active attempts at positively influencing the field. But so tight are the politics around bovine TB, so angry the conflict, and so hard and expensive the work that needs to be done, that our team – any academic team – struggle to offer more than a small model for what could be done. The approach we have explored, the practical application of some kind of 'diplomatic' process to a contentious area of policy, calls for courageous shifts in thinking and practice among people such as DEFRA civil servants, ministers, and industry representatives. Beyond an academic setting where careful, systematic and fair-minded attention is a professional necessity that attracts those to whom it appeals, what sort of thing might support anyone in making a change to their thinking and practice that is more constructive than the status quo, more humane, or simply, good?

    This is where I think much social thinking stumbles. The inner life construed as simply a matter of thought and feeling, represented through some kind of language, its meaning taken with more or less confidence and difficulty, does not quite touch on all of experience that matters. At least one very awkward thing is left – the will, intention. The strong, heroic, but ultimately detached will leads either nowhere at all, angst-ridden, or towards tough, interests-based 'diplomatic' negotiations. The weak, patient, connected will, with little power but its constant best attention offers some slight steer. But it remains private, difficult to talk about, at odds with the assumptions of most social thought. And maybe this is where it's possible to make more use and more sense of the idea of the uncanny, or as Freud put it, 'that class of the Terrifying which leads back to something long known to us, once very familiar' (Freud 1919, p. 123-4). A feeling about something as frightening, awful, evil, bad (or perhaps in our contemporary way of thinking, *wrong, incorrect, unscientific*). If in our thinking we establish these kinds of boundaries between ourselves and other people, if we establish a boundary aesthetic, is there not a danger that we come to make too much of the early sense of dread/elation/disgust/anger/contempt that we experience as we consider or approach them, those different in values and opinion from us, that we come to believe that our feelings justify the way we see things, make things seem more real that way, because we felt them? As a result, do we, as we engage in a social conflict over a policy like the culling of badgers, fight over the truth of our experience, a truth entirely dependent on our selection of information, our patterns of thinking, and the extent of our unquestioned commitment to them? Of course it is true, that experience of those others happened, but that is all.

Attention that comes with a commitment to be just, whether academic research or personal attentiveness to others, is no simple process, no simple progression in which more attention brings more rewards of fair and accurate assessment of the way things in people are. It's awkward, difficult, uncomfortable, because what we think is corroborated by our feelings in a way that leads us back to what we presume to be true of other people (that they are bad/wrong) rather than the more straightforward truth that they are like us (familiar), and different. Here then, at last, is a 'policy' that I can offer to anyone who is or wants to become involved, in the form of a question. Is what you are planning to do going to help those on all sides of the argument feel more comfortable, both in their engagement in the issue and their contemplation of their differences? For the sake of our 'humaneness' we owe that care to each other; and yet, for now, we cannot pay.

List of Acronyms

ABC	Acknowledge, bridge, comment
AHVLA	Animal Health and Veterinary Laboratories Agency, merged with the Bee Inspectorate, the Plants Health and Seeds Inspectorate, the Plant Variety and Seeds Group and the GM Inspectorate to form the ALPHA in 2014.
APHA	Animal and Plant Health Agency
BBC	British Broadcasting Corporation
BCG	Bacillus Calmette-Guérin
BCMS	British Cattle Movements Service
CST	Council for Science and Technology
DEFRA	Department for Environment, Food and Rural Affairs, UK
DIVA	Differentiate infected from vaccinated animals
DNA	Deoxyribonucleic acid
DOC	Department of Conservation, New Zealand
EFSA	European Food Safety Authority
ETUI	European Trade Union Institute
EU	European Union
FOI	Freedom of Information
GABS	Gloucestershire Against Badger Shooting
GM	Genetically modified
GPS	Global positioning system
HSA	Hunt Saboteurs Association
HSI	Humane Society International
IEP	Independent Expert Panel

ISG	Independent Scientific Group on Cattle TB
NETCU	National Extremist Tactical Cordination Unit
NFU	National Farmers Union
PCR	Polymerase chain reaction
PGCHE	Postgraduate Certificate in Higher Education
RBCT	Randomised Badger Culling Trial
SHAC	Stop Huntingdon Animal Cruelty
VLA	Veterinary Laboratories Agency, merged with Animal Health to form the AHVLA in 2011
VNTR	Variable nucleotide tandem repeating
WBP	Wounded Badger Patrol
WTF	Work it out for yourself

List of References

AHVLA (2014a) *Monitoring the efficacy of badger population reduction by controlled shooting during the first six weeks of the pilots. Report to DEFRA.* Animal Health and Veterinary Laboratories. Available at: https://www.gov.uk/government/uploads/system/uploads/attachment_data/file/300383/ahvla-efficacy-report.pdf [accessed 26 Aug 2016].

AHVLA (2014b) *The efficacy of badger population reduction by controlled shooting and cage trapping, and the change in badger activity following culling from 27/08/2013 to 28/11/2013. Report to DEFRA.* February 6th. Animal Health and Veterinary Laboratories. Available at: https://www.gov.uk/government/uploads/system/uploads/attachment_data/file/300385/ahvla-extension-efficacy.pdf [accessed 26 Aug 2016].

AHVLA (2014c*) Monitoring the humaneness of badger population reduction by controlled shooting. Report to the Independent Expert Panel and Defra.* November 26th. Available at: https://www.gov.uk/ government/uploads/system/uploads/attachment_data/file/300388/humaneness-report.pdf [accessed 26 Aug 2016].

Atkins, P.J., and Robinson, P.A. (2013). "Coalition culls and zoonotic ontologies." *Environment and Planning A. 45(6),* pp. 1372-1386.

Avon and Somerset Constabulary (2014) *Investigation report: complaint against police.* HC/CO/82/14. Available at: http://badger-killers.co.uk/wp-content/uploads/Taskers-investigation-report-edit2.pdf [accessed 27 Aug 2016].

Baker, C. (2015). *Bovine TB statistics: Great Britain.* House of Commons Library Briefing Paper, 6081, 13th May. Available at: http://www.parliament.uk/briefing-papers/SN06081.pdf [accessed 26 Aug 2016].

Bartle, J. (2000). "Political awareness, opinion constraint and the stability of ideological positions." *Political Studies* 48(3), pp. 467-484.

BBC (2006). *Four jailed in grave-theft case.* May 11th. Available at: http://news.bbc.co.uk/1/hi/england/staffordshire/4762481.stm [accessed 26 Aug 2016].

BBC (2014). *Interview with Owen Paterson,* Secretary of State of Environment, Food and Rural Affairs. [Radio 4 PM programme], April 3rd.

Ball, S.J. (1994). "Political interviews and the politics of interviewing." in Walford, G. (ed.) *Researching the Powerful in Education.* London: Routledge.

Berg, B.L., and Lune, H. (2014). *Qualitative Research Methods for the Social Sciences.* 8th ed. Harlow: Pearson.

Biernacki, P. and Waldorf, D. (1981). "Snowball sampling: Problems and techniques of chain referral sampling." *Sociological Methods & Research,* 10(2), pp.141-163.

Böhm, M., Hutchings, M.R. and White, P.C.L. (2009). "Contact networks in a wildlife-livestock host community: identifying high-risk individuals in the transmission of bovine TB among badgers and cattle." *PLoS One* 4(4), pp.e5016.

Bovine TB Blog (2005). Anything you can do...... Available at: http://bovinetb.blogspot.co.uk/2005/04/anything-you-can-do.html [accessed 26 Aug 2016].

Bovine TB Blog (2006). Spoligotypes. Available at: http://bovinetb.blogspot.co.uk/2006/11/spoligotypes.html [accessed 26 Aug 2016].

Brown S.R. (1980). *Political Subjectivity: Applications of Q Methodology in Political Science.* New Haven, CT: Yale University Press.

Buddle, B.M. and Young, L.J. (2000). Immunobiology of mycobacterial infections in marsupials. *Developmental & Comparative Immunology,* 24(5), pp.517-529.

Chambers, M.A., Rogers, F., Delahay, R.J., Lesellier, S., Ashford, R., Dalley, D., Gowtage, S., Davé, D., Palmer, S., Brewer, J. and Crawshaw, T. (2011). "Bacillus Calmette-Guérin vaccination reduces the severity and progression of tuberculosis in badgers." *Proceedings of the Royal Society of London B: Biological Sciences, 278(1713), pp.1913-1920.*

Clegg, F. (1982). *Simple Statistics: A course book for the social sciences.* Cambridge: Cambridge University Press.

Colquhoun, D. (2014). *Publish and perish at Imperial College London: the death of Stefan Grimm.* DC's Improbable Science. Available at: http://www.dcscience.net/2014/12/01/publish-and-perish-at-imperial-college-london-the-death-of-stefan-grimm/ [accessed 26 Aug 2016]

Coole, Diana, and Samantha Frost, eds. (2010) New materialisms. Durham, NC: Duke University Press Books.

Corner, L. A. L., Murphy, D. and Gormley, E. (2011). "Mycobacterium bovis infection in the Eurasian badger (Meles meles): the disease, pathogenesis, epidemiology and control." *Journal of Comparative Pathology* 144(1), pp.1-24.

Countryfile (2015). *Deer culling in Britain: facts and statistics.* Available at: http://www.countryfile.com/explore-countryside/ wildlife/deer-culling-britain-facts-and-statistics [accessed 26 Aug 2016].

Cronon, W., ed. (1996). *Uncommon Ground: Rethinking the human place in nature.* New York: WW Norton & Company.

CST (2005). *Policy through dialogue: informing policies based on science and technology.* Council for Science and Technology. Available at: http://webarchive.nationalarchives.gov.uk/ 20060217000323/http://www.dti.gov.uk/cst/reports/files/policy-through-dialogue/report.pdf [accessed 26 Aug 2016].

DEFRA (2005). *Most common breeds of cattle in GB (NUTS 1 areas) on 01 April 2005.* Department for Environment, Food & Rural Affairs. Available at: https://web.archive.org/web/20060214133105/ http://www.defra.gov.uk/animalh/diseases/vetsurveillance/repor ts/pdf/cattle-gb010405.pdf [accessed 26 Aug 2016].

DEFRA (2007). Dairy *Cattle Lameness - Practical Solutions To A Persistent Problem.* Department for Environment, Food & Rural Affairs. Available at: http://adlib.everysite.co.uk/resources/000/ 250/222/cow_lameness.pdf [accessed 26 Aug 2016].

DEFRA (2010). *Bovine TB and the use of PCR: summary of 12 July meeting.* Department for Environment, Food & Rural Affairs. Available at: http://www.warmwell.com/pcr-meeting100712.pdf [accessed 26 Aug 2016].

DEFRA (2011*). Agricultural Statistics and Climate Change.* 2nd Ed. Department for Environment, Food & Rural Affairs. Available at: http://webarchive.nationalarchives.gov.uk/20130305023126/http: /www.defra.gov.uk/statistics/files/defra-stats-foodfarm-enviro-climate-climatechange-120203.pdf [accessed 26 Aug 2016].

DEFRA (2013a). *Request for information: EU Directive stating explicit requirement for a badger cull or documentary evidence of pressure from the EU of Brussels to bring bovine tuberculosis under control.* 15th July. Available at: https://www.gov.uk/government/ uploads/system/uploads/attachment_data/file/239596/5618.pdf [accessed 26 Aug 2016].

DEFRA (2013b). *The 'edge area' strategy: Rollout of new TB control measures.* Department for Environment, Food & Rural Affairs. Available at: https://www.gov.uk/government/uploads/system/ uploads/attachment_data/file/251470/pb14040-tb-info-note.pdf [accessed 26 Aug 2016].

DEFRA (2014a). *The Strategy for achieving Officially Bovine Tuberculosis Free status for England.* Department for Environment, Food & Rural Affairs. Available at: https://www.gov.uk/ government/uploads/system/uploads/attachment_data/file/300447/pb 14088-bovine-tb-strategy-140328.pdf [accessed 26 Aug 2016].

DEFRA (2014b) *Defra response Pilot Badger Culls in Somerset and Gloucestershire: Report by the Independent Expert Panel.* Department for Environment, Food & Rural Affairs. Available at: https://www.gov.uk/government/uploads/system/ uploads/attachment_data/file/300424/pb14158-defra-response-independent-expert-panel.pdf [accessed 26 Aug 2016].

DEFRA (2015). *Farming Statistics - Livestock Populations at 1 December 2014, United Kingdom.* 19th March. Department for Environment, Food & Rural Affairs. Available at: https://www.gov.uk/ government/uploads/system/uploads/attachment_data/file/414334/structure-dec2014-uk-19mar15.pdf [accessed 26 Aug 2016].

DEFRA (2016a). *Agriculture in the United Kingdom 2015.* Department for Environment, Food & Rural Affairs. Available at: https://www.gov.uk/government/uploads/system/uploads/attachment_data/file/535996/AUK-2015-07jul16.pdf [accessed 26 Aug 2016].

DEFRA (2016b). *UK Dairy Industry Statistics.* Department for Environment, Food & Rural Affairs. Available at: http://researchbriefings.files.parliament.uk/documents/SN02721/SN02721.pdf [accessed 26 Aug 2016].

DEFRA (2016c). *Background and methodology to the National Statistics on the Incidence of Tuberculosis (TB) in Cattle in Great Britain.* Department for Environment, Food & Rural Affairs. Available at:

https://www.gov.uk/government/uploads/system/ uploads/ attachment_data/file/537057/bovinetb-annex-13jul16.pdf

[accessed 26 Aug 2016].

DEFRA (2016d). *TB in cattle in Great Britain - headline statistics dataset.* Department for Environment, Food & Rural Affairs. Available at: https://www.gov.uk/government/uploads/system/ uploads/attachment_data/file/529316/bovinetb-headline-15jun16.ods [accessed 26 Aug 2016].

DOC (2016). *Possums.* Department of Conservation, New Zealand. Available at:

http://www.doc.govt.nz/nature/pests-and-threats/ animal-pests/animal-pests-a-z/possums/ [accessed 26 Aug 2016].

Deleuze, G., and Guattari, F. (1988). *A Thousand Plateaus: Capitalism and schizophrenia.* London: Bloomsbury Publishing.

DePaulo, B.M. and Bell, K.L. (1990). "Rapport is not so soft anymore." *Psychological Inquiry,* 1(4), pp.305-308.

Enticott, G. (2001). "Calculating nature: the case of badgers, bovine tuberculosis and cattle "*Journal of Rural Studies* 17, pp. 149-164.

Enticott, G., Franklin, A. and Van Winden, S. (2012). "Biosecurity and food security: spatial strategies for combating bovine tuberculosis in the UK." *The Geographical Journal,* 178(4), pp.327-337.

EFSA (2014). "The European Union Summary Report on Trends and Sources of Zoonoses, Zoonotic Agents and Food-borne Outbreaks in 2012." *European Food Safety Authority Journal* 12 (2): 3547.

Available at: http://www.efsa.europa.eu/sites/default/files/ scientific_output/files/main_documents/3547.pdf [accessed 26 Aug 2016].

ETUI (2016). *Strikes in Europe.* European Trade Union Institute. Available at: http://www.etui.org/content/download/ 23998/199748/ file/interactivemapstrikes_20160729.pdf [accessed 26 Aug 2016].

Farmers Guardian (2007). Are cattle really the cause of bovine TB spreading across the country? Available at:http://www.farmersguardian.com/are-cattle-really-the-cause-of-bovine-tb-spreading-across-the-country?/10145.article [accessed 26 Aug 2016].

Farmers Guardian (2015). NFU Scotland warns of dangers of reqilding Britain. July 17th. Available at: https://www.fginsight.com/ news/ nfu-scotland-warns-of-dangers-of-rewilding-britain-4858 [accessed 26 Aug 2016].

Farmers Weekly (2003). Rethink health strategies. February 28th 2003.

Farmers Weekly (2016). Livestock Event 2016: More badger culls planned this summer, says Defra minister. July 7th. Available at: https://www.fwi.co.uk/news/more-badger-culls-planned-this-summer-says-defra-minister.htm [accessed 26 Aug 2016].

Financial Times (2012). China's ever greater expectations. November 8th. Available at: http://www.ft.com/cms/s/2/1fb9441a-2998-11e2-a5ca-00144feabdc0.html#axzz2BWwfaNDn [accessed 26 Aug 2016].

Fisher, R., and Ury, W. (1987). *Getting to Yes.* New York: Simon & Schuster.

Forester J. (1999). "Dealing with deep value differences", in Susskind L.E., McKearnan S., Thomas-Lamar, J. (eds*) The Consensus Building Handbook,* London: Sage, pp. 463-93.

Foucault, M., (1979). *On Governmentality.* I & C, Vol. 6, pp. 5-22.

Freud, S. (1919). *On Creativity and the Unconscious.* Translated by Alix Strachey, New York: Harper & Row.

Fuller, D. (1999). "Part of the action, or 'going native'? Learning to cope with the 'politics of integration'." *Area* 31(3), pp. 221-227.

Gallagher, J., and Clifton-Hadley, R. S. (2000). "Tuberculosis in badgers; a review of the disease and its significance for other animals." *Research in Veterinary Science* 69(3), pp.203-217.

Galletta, A. (2013). *Mastering the Semi-structured Interview and Beyond: From research design to analysis and publication.* New York: NYU Press.

Gandy, M. (1999). "The Paris sewers and the rationalization of urban space." *Transactions of the Institute of British Geographers* 24(1), pp.23-44.

Giddens, A. (1984). *The Constitution of Society: Outline of the theory of structuration.* Berkeley: Univ of California Press.

Gitlin, T. (2000). Afterword, in Mills, C. Wright. *The Sociological Imagination.* Oxford: Oxford University Press, 2000. p. 233.

GM Science Review Panel (2003). *GM Science Review First Report: An open review of the science relevant to GM crops and food based on the interests and concerns of the public.* Available at: http://image.guardian.co.uk/sys-files/Guardian/documents/2003/07/21/gmsci-report1-full.pdf [accessed 26 Aug 2016].

Godfray, H.C.J., Donnelly, C.A., Kao, R.R., Macdonald, D.W., McDonald, R.A., Petrokofsky, G., Wood, J.L., Woodroffe, R., Young, D.B. and McLean, A.R. (2013). "A restatement of the natural science evidence base relevant to the control of bovine tuberculosis in Great Britain." *Proceedings of the Royal Society of London B: Biological Sciences* 280.1768: 20131634.

Goffman, E. (1974). *Frame Analysis: An essay on the organization of experience.* Cambridge, MA: Harvard University Press.

Goudy, W.J. and Potter, H.R. (1975). "Interview rapport: Demise of a concept." *The Public Opinion Quarterly,* 39(4), pp.529-543.

Griffin, J.M., Williams, D.H., Kelly, G.E., Clegg, T.A., O'boyle, I., Collins, J.D. and More, S.J. (2005). "The impact of badger removal on the control of tuberculosis in cattle herds in Ireland. Preventive veterinary medicine." 67(4), pp.237-266.

The Guardian (2005). Why animal activists forced widow, 67, to give up her fight. January 22nd. Available at: https://www.theguardian.com/uk/2005/jan/22/animalwelfare.sciencenews [accessed 26 Aug 2016].

The Guardian (2013). Badger cull in Somerset on the trail of the marksmen. Available at: https://www.youtube.com/watch?v=5q9gA0Ih1tY [accessed 26 Aug 2016].

The Guardian (2014). Badger cull company used Somerset's constabulary 'as private police force'. May 25th. Available at: https://www.theguardian.com/environment/2014/may/25/badger-cull-company-avon-somerset-police [accessed 26 Aug 2016].

The Guardian (2016). Bovine TB not passed on through direct contact with badgers, research shows. August 5th. Available at: https://www.theguardian.com/environment/2016/aug/05/bovine-tb-not-passed-on-through-direct-contact-with-badgers-research-shows [accessed 26 Aug 2016].

Habermas, J. (1987). *The Theory of Communicative Action.* Vol. II. Trans. McCarthy, T. Boston: Beacon Press.

Hammett, D., and Sporton, D. (2012). "Paying for interviews? Negotiating ethics, power and expectation." *Area* 44(4), pp.496-502.

Harvey, W.S. (2011). "Strategies for conducting elite interviews." *Qualitative Research* 11(4), pp.431-441.

HM Govt (1999). Modernising Government. Presented to Parliament by the Prime Minister and the Minister for the Cabinet Office by Command of Her Majesty, March 1999. Available at: https://www.wbginvestmentclimate.org/uploads/modgov.pdf [accessed 26 Aug 2016].

Heaney, S. (1995) *Nobel Lecture: Crediting Poetry.* December 7th. Available at: http://www.nobelprize.org/nobel_prizes/ literature/laureates/1995/heaney-lecture.html [accessed 26 Aug 2016].

Hinchliffe, S. (2007). *Geographies of Nature: Societies, environments, ecologies.* London: Sage.

HSI/YouGov (2013). *YouGov / HSI Survey Results.* Available at: https://d25d2506sfb94s.cloudfront.net/cumulus_uploads/docum ent/d2fr6coba8/YG-Archive-HSI-results-151013-badger-cull.pdf [accessed 26 Aug 2016].

Independent (2014). Kelly Brook's ex-Gladiator boyfriend David McIntosh 'crashed van full of dead badgers during controversial cull'. Thursday 113th March. Available at: http://www.independent.co.uk/ news/people/news/kelly-brooks-ex-gladiator-boyfriend-david-mcintosh-crashed-van-full-of-dead-badgers-during-9188925.html [accessed 27 Aug 2016].

Independent (2015). France increases its wolf cull after disputed attack on 16-year-old boy. Monday 8th June. http://www.independent.co.uk/news/world/europe/france-increases-its-wolf-cull-after-disputed-attack-on-16-year-old-boy-10306100.html [accessed 26 Aug 2016].

IEP (2014). *Pilot Badger Culls in Somerset and Gloucestershire.* Independent Expert Panel report presented to the Secretary of State for Environment, Food and Rural Affairs The Rt Hon Owen Paterson MP, March 2014. https://www.gov.uk/government/uploads/ system/uploads/attachment_data/file/300382/independent-expert-panel-report.pdf [accessed 26 Aug 2016].

ISG (2007). Bovine TB: *The Scientific Evidence. A Science Base for a Sustainable Policy to Control TB in Cattle. An Epidemiological Investigation into Bovine Tuberculosis. Final Report of the Independent Scientific Group on Cattle* TB. Presented to the Secretary of State for Environment, Food & Rural Affairs The Rt Hon David Miliband MP, June 2007. Available at: http://archive.defra.gov.uk/ foodfarm/ farmanimal/diseases/atoz/tb/isg/ report/final_report.pdf [accessed 26 Aug 2016].

King, D. (2007). *Bovine Tuberculosis In Cattle And Badgers: A Report By The Chief Scientific Adviser, Sir David King.* Presented to the Secretary of State for Environment, Food & Rural Affairs The Rt Hon David Miliband MP, July 2007. Available at: http://www.bovinetb.info/docs/RBCT_david_%20king_report.pdf [accessed 26 Aug 2016].

Kuhn, T.S. (1962). The Structure of Scientific Revolutions. Chicago, IL: University of Chicago Press.

Latour, B. (2002). *War of the Worlds,* Prickly Paradigm Press.

Latour, B. (2004). "Why has critique run out of steam? From matters of fact to matters of concern." *Critical Inquiry* 30.2: 225-248.

Longhurst, R. (2010). "Semi-structured interviews and focus groups." In Clifford, N., French, S. and Valentine, G. (eds.) *Key Methods in Geography*, 2nd edition. London: Sage pp.103-115.

Lord, C., Kennet, M., and Felton, J., eds. (2012). *Citizens' Income and Green Economics.* Reading: Green Economics Institute.

Máirtín, D.Ó., Williams, D.H., Griffin, J.M., Dolan, L.A. and Eves, J.A. (1998). "The effect of a badger removal programme on the incidence of tuberculosis in an Irish cattle population." *Preventive Veterinary Medicine*, 34(1), pp.47-56.

Mansfield, H.C. (2010). *Tocqueville: A very short introduction.* Oxford: Oxford University Press.

Marsh, D. and Rhodes, R.A.W. (1992). *Policy Networks in British government.* Oxford: Clarendon Press.

Marsh, D. and Smith, M. (2000). "Understanding policy networks: towards a dialectical approach." *Political Studies* 48(1), pp.4-21.

Massey, D. (2005). *For Space.* London: Sage.

May, T. (2005). *Gilles Deleuze: an introduction.* Cambridge: Cambridge University Press.

McAdam, D., McCarthy, J.D. and Zald, M.N., eds. (1996). *Comparative Perspectives on Social Movements.* Cambridge: Cambridge University Press.

McKeown, B.F. and Thomas, D. (1988). *Q Methodology: Quantitative Applications in the Social Sciences.* London: Sage.

Melucci, A. (1996). *Challenging codes: Collective action in the information age.* Cambridge: Cambridge University Press.

Monbiot, G. (2013). *Feral: searching for enchantment on the frontiers of rewilding.* Harmondsworth: Penguin.

Mouzelis, N. (2003). *Sociological Theory, What Went Wrong?: Diagnosis and remedies.* London: Routledge.

Murdoch, I. (1970). *The Sovereignty of Good.* London: Routledge.

NFU (2016*). NFU response: CPRE's New Model Farming paper.* Available at: http://www.nfuonline.com/news/latest-news/nfu-response-cpres-new-model-farming-paper/ [accessed 26 Aug 2016].

NFU/YouGov (2013). *YouGov/NFU Survey Results.* Available at: https://d25d2506sfb94s.cloudfront.net/cumulus_uploads/docum ent/xfmldpkgmt/YG-Archive-NFU-results-100513-badger-cull.pdf [accessed 26 Aug 2016].

Pepper, D. (1996). *Modern Environmentalism: An introduction.* London: Routledge.

Plows, A., Wall, D. and Doherty, B. (2004). "Covert repertoires: Eco-tage in the UK 1." *Social Movement Studies* 3(2), pp.199-219.

Price, S., Saunders, C., Hinchliffe, S., McDonald, R. (2016). 'From contradiction to contrast in a countryside conflict: Using Q Methodology to reveal a diplomatic space for doing TB differently', paper in revision for submission to *Environment and Planning A.*

Rogers, L.M., Delahay, R., Cheeseman, C.L., Langton, S., Smith, G.C. and Clifton-Hadley, R.S. (1998). "Movement of badgers (Meles meles) in a high–density population: individual, population and disease effects." *Proceedings of the Royal Society of London B: Biological Sciences,* 265(1403), pp.1269-1276.

Rootes, C.A. (1997). "Environmental movements and Green parties in western and eastern Europe" in Redclift, M. & Woodgate, G. (eds) *International Handbook of Environmental Sociology,* Cheltenham and Northampton MA: Edward Elgar, pp.319-48.

Rootes, C.A. (1999). "The transformation of environmental activism: activists, organizations and policy-making", *Innovation* 12(2): 155-173.

Rootes, C.A. and Miller, A. (2000). "The British environmental movement: organisational field and network of organisations'. Paper prepared for the workshop *Environmental Organisations in Comparative Perspective,* ECPR Joint Sessions, Copenhagen, April 14 – 19.

Sabatier, P.A. and Jenkins-Smith, H.C. (1993). *Policy change and learning: An advocacy coalition approach.* Boulder, Co: Westview Press.

Smith, M.J. (1991). "From policy community to issue network: Salmonella in eggs and the new politics of food." *Public Administration,* 69(2), pp.235-255.

Smith, N.H., Gordon, S.V., de la Rua-Domenech, R., Clifton-Hadley, R.S. and Hewinson, R.G. (2006). "Bottlenecks and broomsticks: the molecular evolution of Mycobacterium bovis." *Nature Reviews Microbiology,* 4(9), pp.670-681.

Smith, N. and Hilscher, R. (2006). mbovis.org. Available at: http://www.mbovis.org/spoligodatabase/GBmetadata/maps/maps%20england%20and%20wales.htm [accessed 26 Aug 2016].

Snow, D.A., and Benford, R.D. (1988). "Ideology, frame resonance, and participant mobilization." *International Social Movement Research* 1(1), pp.197-217.

Sokal, A.D. (1996a). "Transgressing the boundaries: Toward a transformative hermeneutics of quantum gravity." *Social Text* 46/47, pp. 217-252.

Sokal, A.D. (1996b). "A physicist experiments with cultural studies." *Lingua Franca* 6(4), pp.62-64.

Stainton Rogers, R. (1995). "Q methodology." In Smith, J.A., Harré, R. and Van Langenhove, L. (eds.). *Rethinking Methods in Psychology*. London: Sage.

Stengers, I. (2005). "Introductory notes on an ecology of practice" *Cultural Studies Review* 11, pp.183-96.

Stephenson, W. (1953) *The Study of Behaviour: Q Technique and its Methodology*. Chicago: University of Chicago Press.

de Tocqueville, A. (1862). *Democracy in America*. Vol. 1. 2nd ed. Translated by Henry Reeve. London: Longman, Green, Longman & Roberts.

Team Badger (2013). *Petition*. Available at: http://teambadger.org/petition.html [accessed 22 Jun 2015].

The Times (2013). UK under pressure from EU to cull badgers. May 22nd. Available at: http://www.thetimes.co.uk/tto/ environment/article3771202.ece [accessed 26 Aug 2016].

Tilly, C. (1999). "From interactions to outcomes in social movements", in Giugni, M., McAdam, D. and Tilly, C. eds *How Social Movements Matter*. Minneapolis: UMP.

Van der Tuin, I. and Dolphijn, R. (2010). The transversality of new materialism. Women: a cultural review, 21(2), pp.153-171.

Vogel, S. (2011). *Germany: Industrial relations profile*. European Foundation for the Improvement of Living and Working Conditions. Available at: http://www.eurofound.europa.eu/sites/ default/files/ef_files/eiro/country/germany.pdf [accessed 26 Aug 2016].

Watts S., and Stenner P. (2012). *Doing Q Methodological Research: Theory, method and interpretation*. London: Sage.

Whitaker D.A., Macrae, A. I. and Burrough, E. (2004). "Disposal and disease rates in British dairy herds between April 1998 and March 2002." *Veterinary Record* 155, pp.43-47

Widder, N. (2012). *Political Theory After Deleuze*. Bloomsbury Publishing.

Wilson, A. (2012). *United Kingdom: Industrial relations profile.* European Foundation for the Improvement of Living and Working Conditions. Available at: http://www.eurofound.europa.eu/sites/default/files/ef_files/eiro/country/united.kingdom.pdf [accessed 26 Aug 2016].

Wood, M. (2003). *Making Sense of Statistics: A non-mathematical approach.* Basingstoke: Palgrave Macmillan.

Woodroffe R., Donnelly C.A., Ham C., Jackson S.Y.B., Moyes K., Chapman K., Stratton N.G., Cartwright S.J. (2016) "Badgers prefer cattle pasture but avoid cattle: implications for bovine tuberculosis control." *Ecology Letters,* online in advance of print. http://dx.doi.org/10.1111/ele.12654 [accessed 26 Aug 2016].

Woodroffe, R., Donnelly, C.A., Johnston, W.T., Bourne, F.J., Cheeseman, C.L., Clifton-Hadley, R.S., Cox, D.R., Gettinby, G., Hewinson, R.G., Le Fevre, A.M. and McInerney, J.P., (2005). Spatial association of Mycobacterium bovis infection in cattle and badgers Meles meles. *Journal of Applied Ecology,* 42(5), pp.852-862.

List of Statements for
Q Methodology analysis

No.	Statements
1	You can ignore the cost of the cull because without the protestors, it would be a very cheap policy
2	We've allowed the badger population to build up to such enormously high levels
3	Culling isn't sustainable because you have to keep on culling badgers forever, it's going to be expensive
4	We need a better TB test regime which means that they are picking up the majority of the cattle that need be removed from the herd
5	If you've got a rumbling TB problem in your herd in the last 20 years, you need to get rid of the whole of your herd and start again
6	Farmers in or near cull zones should expect to suffer from diseased badgers spreading out across the countryside
7	Relax the regulations so that it is easier for those who are trained to control badgers in their area
8	The incidence of TB in badgers is relatively low
9	Why do we worry about TB so much, there's far bigger welfare issues for cattle
10	It has not been proven that badgers are giving TB to cows

11	Biosecurity[38] measures are limited, you can reduce risk but you will never, ever stop it
12	TB in the badger population is driven very much by cattle
13	We cull rats, we cull pigeons, there's no big deal about culling badgers
14	If it's feasible to trap badgers in a cage and shoot them then surely it's feasible to trap them in a cage and vaccinate them
15	Investigate gassing of setts, which has to be the most humane way of dealing with animals
16	We are seeing a steady spread of TB across the country from wildlife transmission
17	Reduce the badger population from Cheshire to Hampshire and vaccinate everything that remained in that area
18	The entire concept of the badger cull is a total mess
19	We need more collaboration between the different groups to solve the dispute about badger-culling
20	Nobody wants to see farms Fort Knoxed
21	I don't think we have the right to cull wildlife to the extent planned in the culls
22	How do you separate grazing cattle from badgers? It can't be done
23	It is logistically very challenging to try to catch badgers and inject them with vaccine

---

[38] In this context, 'biosecurity measures' are understood as actions, other than culling or vaccination, taken to limit contact between cattle and wildlife, or that limit the exposure of cattle to bTB spread by wildlife.

24	Trap badgers, test them to see if they've got TB, if they have then kill them. I could live with that
25	The cattle vaccine could be offered to farms who would then undertake not to sell their cattle for export
26	The trouble is at the moment the badger is the most protected animal on the planet
27	Until you get rid of the wildlife reservoir, you're never going to get on top of TB
28	Find a way of testing the level of severity of TB in any one badger sett or population and cull those worst areas
29	We should be pursuing badger vaccination. It's cheaper than shooting them, when it's done on a voluntary basis
30	A lot of the disease that arises, like TB, is probably due to the way we're farming and the intensity of it
31	Culling is just an out-dated way of trying deal with disease
32	Increase the number of cattle inspectors and introduce random inspections on farms
33	The badger vaccine is seen as a magic bullet by a lot of people, but they don't understand the science behind it
34	Badgers control their own population, so the theory of a badger population explosion doesn't really stand up

Index

www.ingramcontent.com/pod-product-compliance
Lightning Source LLC
Chambersburg PA
CBHW072059040426
42334CB00041B/1460